Successful Southern Gardening

Sandra F. Ladendorf

Successful Southern
Gardening
A Practical Guide for
Year-round Beauty

The University of North Carolina Press
Chapel Hill and London

To Ray

© 1989 Sandra F. Ladendorf
All rights reserved
Manufactured in Japan

The paper in this book meets the guidelines for permanence
and durability of the Committee on Production Guidelines
for Book Longevity of the Council on Library Resources.

93 92 91 90 89   5 4 3 2 1

Library of Congress Cataloging-in-Publication Data

Ladendorf, Sandra F.
    [Southern gardening]
    Successful Southern gardening: a practical guide for year-round beauty /
by Sandra F. Ladendorf.
        p.   cm.
    Includes index.
    ISBN 0-8078-1831-3 (alk. paper)
    ISBN 0-8078-4241-9 (pbk.: alk. paper)
    1. Gardening—Southern States.   I. Title.
SB453.2.S66L33   1989   635.9′51′75—dc19   88-20634
                                                        CIP

page ii: Kochia and marigolds, annuals that glow in the morning sunlight

page vi: *Phlox* 'Millstream Daphne' is a clear-colored phlox selection of Linc Foster

page x: Water adds music, movement, and interest to any garden

All photographs are by the author unless otherwise indicated.

Contents

Acknowledgments

Gardening is a cumulative activity. My addiction to plants and gardening probably began when I picked some pansies and pulled weeds in my parents' garden as a small child. Today, my mother marvels at my involvement in the world of plants. As she recalls, it was almost more trouble than it was worth to get me to pull those weeds. However, as I watched my mother and father enjoy their Maine garden on summer evenings, admiring the roses, dead-heading the petunias, dusting for aphids, or feeding their plants with a manure "tea," I absorbed their love of flowering plants and took gardening for granted as one of life's normal activities.

If I start to list the many people who have taught me something about gardening over the years, it would almost make a book in itself. Credit for getting me started years ago must go to Betty Magnusson, who patiently kept giving me beautiful African violets, which I killed by overwatering until one day when one of those violets began to thrive. Success with African violets led to indoor light gardening, gesneriads, tomato and marigold production, then other annuals, perennials, trees, and shrubs—the world of plants.

I also often bless the late George Lee, who taught me how to take my first azalea cutting, how to plant erythroniums, how to divide *Iris cristata*—how to develop a woodland garden of thinned, tall, deciduous trees, an understory of native dogwoods, and paths rich with daffodils, azaleas, trilliums, epimediums, rhododendrons, and hundreds of wildlings.

Here in the South, I have learned about southern gardening from so many people that I hesitate to mention some in the fear that I will omit other equally important gardeners. I appreciate all of the know-how both amateurs and professionals have shared so freely.

We are fortunate to live in Chapel Hill, where the North Carolina Botanical Garden flourishes. Everyone on the staff has been repeatedly helpful, and I learned a lot while working as a volunteer in the propagating group there.

In my first days in North Carolina, Ken Moore, assistant director of the garden, said, "You must meet Bill Hunt and Elizabeth Lawrence, both experienced southern gardeners and garden writers." Bill continues to be a willing resource, and I'm grateful for the visits I spent with Elizabeth in her Charlotte garden.

Friends in the Chapel Hill Garden Club have been generous with plants and information. I call Betty Wilson for information about small bulbs, hellebores, and all sorts of matters horticultural.

North Carolina State University also continues to be a wonderful resource. If I have any problem, I call Mrs. Elizabeth Shue, secretary of the Horticulture Department, and she points me in the right direction, whether I am looking for an interview on lawns or cucumbers or need an answer to an esoteric question about tree-staking or pathogen control. I have three pages of names in my phone book of NCSU people who have been informative and helpful.

J. C. Raulston is one expert at State whom I call repeatedly. He is a walking encyclopedia of horticultural information and shares it generously. Through his university teaching, his innovative arboretum, and his extensive lecturing throughout the South, he has inspired hundreds of gardeners.

The agricultural extension agents in our area, Toby Bost (Durham County), Irv Evans (Wake County), and Jim Monroe (Orange County), have fielded many questions cheerfully.

I regularly tap the expertise of friends in the Garden Writers Association of America. George Elbert has been very helpful with legal matters; Ted Marston, Nona Wolfram-Koivula, Peggy Crooks, Elvin McDonald, Peter Tonge, Susan Bruno, Derek Fell, Fred Galle, Maggie Oster, and Drayton Hastie are just a few of the many other members who have responded to a number of phone calls from me. All the members of that professional group are wonderfully supportive of one another. I bless Maggie Bayliss, who gave me the final shove when I was deciding whether or not to plunge into this demanding project.

A number of local friends have become regular sources of information for me. I frequently call Bob Welshmer about azalea culture, and his wife Jane is generous with her knowledge about ferns and native plant gardening. Bob Solberg answers all my hosta questions. Bob Hardison and Charles Hubbard have shared their many years of vegetable gardening experience with me and my newspaper readers, and Lee Calhoun is an excellent resource on fruits, particularly old apples.

Within one mile of our home, I can visit a dear neighbor, Edith Kaylor, who has been gardening on her acres for more than thirty years (she keeps excellent notebooks and is a fount of local experience); Dr. Stanley Bennett, who has a large arboretum where he has raised most of his trees from seed; John Cheesborough and his wife Elise Olsen, a daffodil specialist, who are developing an extensive and fascinating garden; Cliff Parks, who is hybridizing for cold-hardy camellias, and his wife Kai-Mei, who is operating a rare woody plant nursery; and Phil Nelson, who enjoys experimenting with new vegetable varieties and shares his thoughtful opinions with me each year.

Dorothy Bonitz generates enthusiasm for gardening in general and herbs in particular. Jimmy Massey, head of the herbarium at the University of North Carolina, answers my taxonomic questions and freely shares his knowledge and enthusiasm about day lilies. Librarian Bill Burk at the UNC Botany Department library kindly digs out horticultural minutia for me.

Many nurserymen, people in public and private gardens, members of a number of plant societies, particularly the American Rock Garden Society, and innumerable gardening friends and acquaintances have all contributed to this book in one way or another, and I appreciate them all.

Very special thanks must go to a group of superb gardeners who were generous with their time, helpful suggestions, and expertise, as they each reviewed a chapter:

Tony Avent, landscape supervisor, N.C. State Fair Grounds
Toby Bost, agricultural extension agent, Durham County
Art Bruneau, turf specialist, North Carolina State University
Jim Darden, teacher, writer, nurseryman
August A. De Hertogh, head of the Department of Horticulture, North Carolina State University
Fred Garrett, director of the landscape gardening program at Sandhills Community College
Nancy Goodwin, cyclamen specialist, owner of Montrose Nursery
Pamela Harper, garden writer and photographer
Paul Jones, curator at Sarah P. Duke Gardens
Rex McDonald, nurseryman
Adrienne Mellon, marketing communications director, Goldsmith Seed Company
Ken Moore, assistant director of the North Carolina Botanical Garden
Harry Phillips, garden writer, former curator, North Carolina Botanical Garden
Judd Ringer, founder of Ringer Corp.
Gene Strowd, expert rosarian, lecturer, judge

Last but never least, I'm grateful for the low-key, cheerful patience of my editor, David Perry, and for the continual support and encouragement he has provided.

1

Introduction

"This has been a very unusual season" was a phrase I heard repeatedly during our first years here in North Carolina. The fall was unusually wet; the winter was unusually dry; spring came early or late; summer was extraordinarily dry, or wet, or cool. I did recognize that indeed our first snowstorm was unusual, because the University of North Carolina closed for the first time since the Civil War. Being paralyzed by 3 or 4 inches of snow amazed and amused me, since we had just arrived from East Lansing, Michigan, where school children routinely trudged off to school after a 12- or 18-inch fresh snowfall.

After several years of living in this beautiful corner of the United States and gardening intensively here, I have learned that if there is one constant in zones 7 and 8, it is the variability of the climate. We gardeners here learn to deal with extreme heat, drought, humid hot nights, freezing cold, spotty rainfall, the lack of protective snow cover in winter, and swift, wide swings in temperature, particularly during the winter months. Gardeners who move here from northern climes, where there was a forced winter hiatus from gardening, have to learn that they can transplant and garden on many pleasant winter days. We also *must* water during the winter here if we have a dry period.

We learn to garden to a different beat. Rather than rushing to get bulbs in the ground before it freezes, in the South we must wait for our ground to cool off; we should not plant bulbs before the middle of November. Trees and shrubs are generally planted in the springtime farther north. Here, the nursery industry is trying to educate us all to plant our woody materials in the fall, so that they will get well established before the summer heat. While it is possible to put containerized plants in the ground any time of year, it is inadvisable to plant nursery material as summer approaches. The later one plants, the more tender care one must give those plantings *all* summer.

Many tender bulbs, like dahlias and amaryllis, are hardy here and can be left in the ground to perennialize. Gardening in the South is different, it's exciting, and it's fun.

It's easy to be a springtime gardener in the South. Just plant some daffodils and azaleas beneath the native dogwoods, use our native phloxes as a ground cover, then stand back and enjoy the vibrant splashes of color. Developing a beautiful garden for twelve months of the year is much more of a challenge, but it is quite possible.

Since I have played the "whither-thou-goest" role for my peripatetic husband as his work has moved us around the country, we have grown lilacs and asters in Connecticut, raphiolepsis, calochortus, and ceonothus in California, and hardy rhododendrons and sweet peas in Michigan. Now we are luxuriating in the beauty of azaleas, lycoris, crinums, and numerous southeastern native plants here in this home in Chapel Hill, North Carolina. If a gardener cannot plan, develop, and enjoy a fifty-year-old garden, then it is wonderful to have gardened east, west, north, and now south in our vast country.

I've learned that some plants, like sedums, hostas, trilliums, and day lilies, are ubiquitous. They grow and thrive everywhere. Others, like the beautiful *Cornus canadensis*, which carpets New England woods but seldom survives here in our hot, humid summers, are more narrow and specific in their needs.

Rhododendrons that thrive in the cooler mountain areas of North Carolina are marginal plants in the Piedmont—beautiful, but marginal. At the other end of the range, the fragrant and lovely southern gardenias are also marginal here, frequently killed to the ground during our more severe winters.

Here, I have learned, the enthusiastic and determined gardener can have a twelve-month garden. We can harvest lettuce and carrots in January and enjoy the cheerful blooms of *Cyclamen hederifolium, Viola corsica,* and the witch hazels during midwinter. The farther south the gardener lives, the more varied the winter garden can be.

In the scramble to become a competent southern gardener, I have made a number of mistakes, and I can tell a few joyful success stories. I have learned so much about southern gardening from the wonderful books of Elizabeth Lawrence, from neighbors and friends who are experienced southern gardeners, from the many interviews I have done for my newspaper column in Raleigh's *News and Observer,* from frequent visits to interesting public and private gardens wherever my travels take me around the South, and from practical experience digging, planting, propagating, pruning, and doing all the other garden tasks in our yard.

The material in this book is drawn from all of these experiences. It is not a "complete" book about any part of gardening. Rather, it is designed to whet your appetite, bring you basic information and occasional tidbits about the most sophisticated methods of today, and then suggest the best references and point you in the right direction, so that you can research and learn more about the parts of gardening that fascinate you.

I never want to see the words "complete" or "everything about" in the title of a book of mine. No book is ever complete. Just in the time lag between finishing the manuscript and holding the published book in hand, new plants have been introduced and improved techniques for propagating or growing have been developed. Certainly no general gardening book can begin to tell it all. I have briefly mentioned subjects to which entire books have been devoted, like Vertrees's *Japanese Maples*, Galle's *Azaleas*, Nightingale's *Cyclamen*, or Welch's *Manual of Dwarf Conifers*.

I intend never to say "this is the only way" or "this is the right way" to do any part of gardening. The minute one makes such an absolute statement, surely up will pop some other gardener producing perfectly satisfactory results by doing things in quite a different manner. There are usually a number of ways to accomplish any task. Recommendations flatly stated are for the novice gardener. (We all need a few guidelines when beginning a new venture.) Where you may discover "rules" throughout the book, they are either recommendations based on the most current research, or they are intended to suggest the best way for a beginner to start. The one message I would like to convey to all readers is that gardening is fun, great fun. Throughout the year, we are well rewarded for our labors.

Gardening is also a wonderfully soothing avocation. Horticultural therapy came into existence for a very good reason. Working with plants *is* good therapy, not only for the aged, ill, or imprisoned, but for every sane and busy worker in this frenetic world of ours. There is a relaxing, tranquilizing magic about having our hands in the earth, pulling a few weeds, cutting some clematis or roses for enjoyment in the house, or growing a few seedlings under lights. I became aware of how beneficial my addiction to plants was during the early years of marriage, when I was raising four small children. Once in a while, I would be ready to blow my top. I learned that if I went down to the basement and worked with the African violets, gesneriads, and orchids in my indoor light garden for half an hour, I could return to my active family, calm, serene, refreshed and ready once again to cope.

Life changes; patterns vary. Those small children are now adults, and my husband and I have changed our living style accordingly. Now, we often spend an hour or so working in the garden together after he gets home from the office. We both need to stretch our muscles and do something physical after our sedentary hours at our respective desks. Gardening is definitely a joint project at our house. I may refer to my garden occasionally, but it is definitely *our* garden. While I do all of the propagating and much of the low pruning, transplanting, weeding, and feeding, my husband maintains the lawn, handles the chemicals and does all of the heavy work in the garden. We both find great joy in gardening.

Even the days we don't labor in the garden, we walk the trails together, appreciate whatever has come into bloom that day, note a newly fallen branch that needs to be removed, or admire a spectacular mushroom and enjoy that unwinding time together. Gardening is a wonderful, rewarding, and enjoyable activity for all of us, for people of all ages. A 1981 visit to Wisley, the Royal Horticultural Garden in England, underlined that point nicely. Wisley presented a series of small display gardens designed for families of different ages. The first was predominantly a play yard, intended for a family with small children and a limited budget. The next was a more costly garden with sophisticated landscaping for a slightly older, more affluent family. The third was a collector's garden, for the keen gardener who wants one of everything. And the last display was a garden created entirely of high, raised beds, designed so that the gardener could plant, weed, and harvest from a wheelchair.

Designing our gardens to fit our needs and interests is where we all should begin. I get a number of letters from readers asking me to tell them what to plant in a garden. Rather than answers, I come up with questions:

How avid a gardener are you? Are you interested in working on a high-maintenance garden or do you want one demanding a minimum of care? Perhaps you want some of both—an attractive, low-maintenance landscape for the front of the house and an intensive rock garden or rose garden in the backyard?

What are your color preferences? Do you want a soothing, all-white garden like Vita Sackville-West's famous one at Sissinghurst, or are you looking for a wild riot of color? Personally, I hate mauve and try to avoid any tinge of mauve in our garden. Mauve may be your first choice as a pleasing color for blossoms. We all differ, thank heavens. Wouldn't life be boring if we all gardened in precisely the same way?

What are your plant preferences? I have a particular weakness for the primrose family. Perhaps you hate primroses but delight in hostas or azaleas. We all develop plant favorites and garden discards. As you grow a number of plants yourself, and particularly whenever you visit other gardens, pay attention to your visceral responses. When you see a 'Peace' rose, do you immediately think, "That is the most beautiful flower in the world. I've got to grow it," or do you react with, "too showy, blatant—not at all what I want in my garden"?

Elizabeth Lawrence always visited other gardens with her notebook in hand, observing her reactions to new plants and noting interesting gardening techniques and uses of old favorites. We would probably all benefit from that sort of gardening notebook.

What is the style of your home and garden? Do you want a formal bed edged with dwarf boxwood or is yours a contemporary house demanding informal treatment? Do you entertain frequently or seldom? Is the sound of water in your garden important to you? Do you want to attract birds?

What is your garden budget—extravagant, moderate, or minimal? Do you intend to employ professionals, either to design or to maintain your garden, or are you a do-it-yourselfer?

In this book, I refer frequently to our county agents and the Agricultural Extension Service. At present, the county agents are superb sources for local solutions to local problems. Due to the recent Gramm-Rudman-Hollings Act, the extension service has felt severe budget cuts, and the entire design and concept of extension service is being reexamined. The services offered to homeowners may change considerably during the next decade or two.

The coming years in horticulture are going to be exciting ones, I think. Amateur and professional plant breeders are continually working to bring us new and better plants. Another group of plantsmen are working just as avidly to collect and save old varieties of trees, shrubs, roses, perennials, fruits, and nuts. With the opening of the borders to China, plant collectors are again able to visit that horticulturally rich country. Cautious exchanges are taking place between Chinese and American botanists. Desirable plants, both old and new, will become more widely available.

Unfortunately, some undesirable plants will also be promoted in the garden marketplace, because they are fast growing and cheap to produce. As in all purchases, caveat emptor. Be aware that if you read an advertisement that makes preposterous claims for a magically climbing strawberry vine or a desirable tree that grows 30 feet in a year, those claims are just that, preposterous. Ignore all advertisements that fail to identify any plant by its botanical name.

All too often, plants are sold that are labeled incorrectly. Many times, it is an honest mistake. Most of our nurserymen are honorable people, working hard to produce a quality product. Occasionally, mislabeling is a deliberate fraud. I clearly remember one Michigan nurseryman cynically telling me that when he ran out of 'White Cascade' petunias, he would put 'White Cascade' labels in any white petunia, "because that's the variety the customers ask for."

It is important, I think, for us all to be willing to pay for well-grown, quality plants, which are not necessarily the biggest ones. Often it is better to seek out a plant variety that will stay dwarf and compact, like the desirable dwarf conifers. Along the same line, it takes more time and effort and therefore is more expensive to produce herbaceous perennials vegetatively than to raise them from seed, but vegetative propagation is the only way to obtain the true cultivars. We have seen some poor stokesias, coreopsis, and other plants marketed under desirable cultivar names.

The mailorder nurseries listed are ones I have dealt with and found reliable. Only a small percentage of the hundreds of American nurseries are listed, of course, and you may have superb local growers in your town or region. I only turn to mail order if I cannot find the plants I am looking for in a local nursery. You may be pleasantly surprised at sources you find locally. In just the last few years, five small specialist nurseries that are offering cyclamen, ferns, dwarf conifers, rare woody plants, and nursery-propagated southeastern native plants have opened in this area, and each nurseryman is doing an outstanding job in his or her own way. They are contributing a great deal to the local gardening community. I have enjoyed growing their plants and also interviewing and writing about these specialists.

Every writing project involves a number of choices. Since garden writers must choose an authority for plant names, I have used *Hortus Third* as a reference for nomenclature throughout this book. In several instances, either the plant mentioned was not included in *Hortus Third* or I overrode that authority after consulting with a specialist on a subject.

Rather than using the awkward "he or she," plural forms or writing around the problem each time I wanted to mention one gardener, I have chosen to use "he" as a universal. I am a woman gardener. I know that a large percentage of gardeners are women. No antifeminist statement is intended. It just seems simpler to use "he," a pronoun that Webster's unabridged *Third New International Dictionary* says is "that one whose sex is unknown or immaterial" in its second definition of the word.

Lists of plant societies and recommended nurseries, as well as a suggested reading list, are included at the back of the book. The addresses of all societies and nurseries mentioned in the text can be found there. No information becomes more quickly dated than addresses of plant societies and nurseries, but the information is as valid as my editor and I can make it at the time of publication.

All temperatures are in Fahrenheit; all measurements are in feet and inches.

I think garden writing should be accurate, opinionated, and entertaining. I see it as having two basic functions: to generate and stimulate enthusiasm for the hobby of gardening and to educate. In the following pages, I hope I manage to do a little of both.

2

Soils

Scoop up a handful of your garden soil. Does it sift through your fingers like sand? Are you holding a hard clump of clay that will not mold unless you hit it with a hammer? Or is your soil a wonderful loam that holds its form when lightly squeezed, but falls apart when given more pressure?

Soil is the thin layer of the earth's surface that is made up of mineral and organic matter and is able to support plant life. The formation of soil began with the weathering and erosion of the earth's original rock crust. The action of water, wind, and temperature gradually peeled and flaked the surface into finer and finer particles. This physical disintegration has been accompanied by a chemical process that reduces rocks to their elemental minerals and provides important micronutrients.

Soils and soil content can vary considerably, even in very short distances, depending on how the soils were originally deposited and later modified or farmed. Here on our Piedmont hill, we have a most unpleasant type of red clay. In the part of our lot that is a deciduous woodland, where oak, hickory, and tulip tree leaves have been falling and decaying for years, several inches of soft, rich duff cover the clay. Just a mile away, one neighbor has a wide, lovely strip of loam running through his predominantly clay acreage. Some of the gardeners in town are dealing with a fast-draining substance locally called Chapel Hill gravel. An hour's drive south of here, gardeners are struggling to grow plants in almost straight sand and yet, just 25 miles west, in Hillsborough, there are acres and acres of rich, fertile farmland.

Many housing developments are built on former tobacco or cotton farmland here in the South, and that land has been sadly depleted. For decades here, and throughout much of the country, farmers took the land for granted. They sowed and they reaped, but they didn't replenish the soil. Only in a few relatively small pockets of farmland, like Amish country, were the farmers skilled in enriching the soil as they used it.

There are two ways to look at our soil. We can see and feel its physical character, its texture. Through chemical analysis, we also can learn about the nutrients in our soil. As gardeners, we want to provide our plants with soil in which they will thrive. Some plants are flexible and will grow almost anywhere. Others demand specific conditions, like poor soil, a bog, alkaline or acid soil, summer baking, or dry winter shelter.

Before we discuss ways to improve your garden soil, let's take a look at the various components of soil, earth—the ground we walk on. The texture of soil is determined by mineral particles of various sizes. Sand or fine gravel provides the largest mineral particles. Because these particles are large, they help to separate the other particles and allow spaces in the soil, spaces for air and water. A reasonable amount of sand in your soil provides good drainage and aeration. While adequate drainage is highly desirable, a soil that is predominantly sand, such as that in our coastal regions, is too porous and drains too quickly. It acts as a weak anchor for the roots of plants growing there, and it needs considerable amending to be a satisfactory garden soil.

Many parts of the South have clay soil. Clay is comprised of minute particles that fit tightly together and have reduced spaces for air circulation. If you have ever looked at a southern farmer's field after its initial plowing, when 6- to 12-inch clots of red clay have been turned over, you know how tightly compact clay soil can be. It, too, can be improved by amending.

Medium-sized particles are called silt.

Lucky gardeners begin with a rich loam, defined in Webster's as a friable, crumbly soil that contains 7 to 27 percent clay, 28 to 50 percent silt, and less than 52 percent sand, a soil that drains well but has adequate humus to hold water and nutrients long enough so that they are available to the plants.

Sand, clay, silt, and humus are the four major physical components of soil, components that may be combined in literally hundreds of different ways to form soil structure. If you are buying land for a nursery business, a truck garden farm, or your home and hobby garden, you will be interested in the quality of the soil. One way to learn about the general character of the soil in any given area is to obtain a copy of the county soil map, available without charge from the United States Department of Agriculture, Soil Conservation Service. Many, but not all, of our counties have been mapped. Your county office of the Soil Conservation Service can give you more information about your particular county and provide the map, if available.

But let's assume that you have already purchased your land and are about to landscape the house, start a flower garden, plant a lawn, and perhaps raise some vegetables.

If you are going to build a new home, arrange with your contractor for him to remove the topsoil from the site, place it to one side and return it to the graded area around the house after construction is complete. In many developments, the contractors simply scrape up the topsoil from the building site and sell it, leaving the new homeowner with the construction debris, discarded cans, and lime rubble buried in the less desirable subsoil. Perhaps you have already contended with that sea of muddy clay at a new home, before the lawn was established and the gardens developed.

In both the house and the yard, there are trade-offs between purchasing a new home or an older, established house. With a new house under construction, you can follow the progress of the building and supervise the grading of the property. But other than the minimal landscaping provided by the builder, you are left to develop the yard yourself. Starting from scratch is a lot of work, but it does allow you to design and plant the grounds just as you desire. If you buy an older home, you will have an established yard. Depending on the interests and gardening activities of the previous owners, the yard may be magnificent or dreadful. Yours will be a job of renovation, replacement, and renewal for both the house and the yard.

I have seen existing homes where the land was graded so that water would pour into the garage in a heavy rain. On other properties, the lawn areas were left with low spots that did not drain well and were soggy. Here at our home, during the rainy season, water would run off the hill to rest against the foundations of the house. The land had been graded incorrectly so that there was a continual, gentle slope toward the house. We have corrected that condition by laboriously installing drainage pipe all along the front perimeter of the house, with runoff channeled down the hill away from the house. We also built a garden that slopes away from the building. It is best to correct grading problems at the time of construction, when heavy equipment is on the site and there are no established plantings to protect. It is so much easier to do it right in the beginning than to try to correct a drainage problem later.

But, let's assume you have your home, new or old, and you want to establish a lawn and garden. The details of lawn development and maintenance will be covered later, in the chapter on lawns, so in these pages, let's discuss gardens, soils for your gardens, and your various options.

You may want to develop attractive landscaping around the house, create a rose garden or a perennial bed in a sunny spot, have a vegetable garden with a few rows of annuals for cutting in another sunny location behind the house, and perhaps plan a shade garden beneath some tall trees. Whatever the native soil on your property, whether you want to improve a predominantly sand or clay soil or to maintain a rich loam, you will want to amend it annually with organic material. You can add composted manures, plow under crop residue, or add organic materials like peat, peat moss, leaf mold, compost, bark, sawdust, or grass clippings. Because of our climate, organic materials break down more quickly in the South than in cooler parts of the country. We need to keep replenishing the material for the beneficial microbes to work on. These organic materials improve the soil in two ways. They add a desirable quality to the physical properties of the soil and, as they break down, they release nutrients to the soil and create a habitat in which plants can thrive.

The very serious gardener double-digs his beds for his roses, perennials, or vegetables. This method of soil preparation entails a lot of work, but it results in a very well-prepared garden. To double-dig, you begin at one end of the bed and remove a strip of the soil 2–3 feet wide and 12 inches deep. Carry that soil to the far end of the garden bed and pile it there. Return to your hole in the ground and then use a fork to break up the soil at the bottom of the hole. Try to loosen it for another 8–12 inches. Add a generous layer of organic matter, perhaps a combination of composted manure and sawdust or composted leaves, and fork it thoroughly into that bottom layer. If it is to be a flower bed, some gardeners also add superphosphate at this time. When the soil ingredients in the bottom layer are well mixed, begin your second strip by tossing the soil from its top 12 inches onto the soil you have just amended in the first strip. Add more compost or other organic material and thoroughly mix it into that layer of soil. You continue to work your way slowly and patiently down the length of the bed, digging and amending two layers of the soil, so that when you have finished, the entire bed will have been improved to a depth of 18–24 inches. At the end of the bed, you will use the stockpiled soil from the first strip to fill in the last hole.

Double-digging is extremely effective, but, as you can tell from the description, it is a lot of work, particularly if one is dealing with chunks of heavy clay. The construction of raised beds is initially more expensive but far easier than reworking difficult clay, so many southern gardeners choose this option. It is easier to provide good drainage in a raised bed than in a heavy clay soil, and if there is one word you will read repeatedly in this book, it is drainage, drainage, drainage. Whether you want to raise vegetables, roses, bulbs, daphnes, or ericaceous plants like rhododendrons and azaleas, the key to success is adequate drainage.

How you build a raised bed, which materials you use, depends on the location. A raised bed should be aesthetically pleasing. Its design should be in keeping with its location. Too often, I have seen an awkward rectangle of railroad ties filled with marigolds and petunias and sitting in the middle of the lawn, unrelated to the building and unappealing to the eye.

A charming, small, brick courtyard enhances a one-story brick home

If the beds are for landscaping on the front of the house, the construction must be compatible with the house. A formal brick house calls for equally formal raised bed construction. A casual, contemporary home of glass and wood will be most attractive with compatibly asymmetrical beds formed of railroad ties or treated wood. Low rock walls may be appropriate in your situation. In the vegetable garden, you may simply build raised mounds of soil or edge the raised beds with simple boards or unattractive but functional concrete blocks.

Constructing raised beds can be a do-it-yourself project for the handy and patient gardener who enjoys that sort of a project. It takes time, a talent for design, and a lot of work. Beautiful brickwork and perfect stonework are crafts that take professional masons a long time to master. I have seen some beautiful walls and walks crafted by amateurs, but many of us prefer to hire someone else to do this work. If you do employ a landscaper for this construction, a word of caution. Anyone can toss a spade, a fork, and a mower in a pickup truck and call himself a landscaper. In most parts of the country, these workers are unregulated. If I called ten companies listed in the phone book or advertised in our newspaper, I might reach some young people who are graduates of our finest programs in landscape gardening, and some others who are high school dropouts with no knowledge of plants, gardening, or landscaping skills. Ask your friends and neighbors for recommendations. Find out who did garden construction work you admire. When you have several recommendations of people who do quality work, ask those landscapers to come to your home, review your plans with you, and give you a detailed cost estimate of your project.

If you recognize that you have no design skills and do not want to research or work on this project yourself, spend more money and hire a competent landscape designer who will develop a plan that pleases you, hire the manual labor, buy the supplies, and supervise the installation.

But let's assume that you want to build your garden beds yourself. The garden is attractively designed. You have the boards, bricks, or other materials in place. The next step is to fill the bed. Before you add material to the site, it would be helpful to break up the soil at ground level with a fork and mix in some organic material. Loosening the soil under the bed will allow roots to penetrate below the depth of the bed.

Then fill the bed. In an ideal situation, you would order a load of quality topsoil. In our area, today there is no such product on the market. Perhaps gardeners in Iowa, where I heard one farmer say his topsoil was 40–50 feet deep, can still purchase excellent topsoil. But when I bought what was sold as topsoil here, the truckload was essentially sand. Most local professional landscapers here use a mixture of bark, sand, and horse manure to fill their beds, and you will probably have to do something similar. Check around among your gardening friends, and you can locate the same sources from whom the professionals purchase their mix. Buy directly and eliminate the middleman.

Mound the soil mix high in the new bed, for any recently shoveled material will settle. Preferably, wait and let it be rained upon and settle before planting.

Be aware that if you bring in local topsoil (or its equivalent) or manure, you will probably also be bringing in some weed seeds. It may take two or three years to eliminate them from your new garden. Regular and frequent attention to weeds the first season will alleviate this problem considerably.

In a totally informal woodland garden setting, one gentleman who retired here chose to ignore the local soil completely. He wanted to raise azaleas, and since these plants are shallow rooted, he developed an extremely successful azalea garden by spreading several truckloads of bark over his entire sloping woodland garden. The bark is approximately 6 inches deep, the azaleas thrive, and the only strain on his back is shoveling additional bark as needed. This garden does drain very quickly and needs regular watering during our hot dry periods, even on the established plantings.

His is an unusual specialty. Most of us want the serenity of some lawn near the house, some attractive landscaping at the front of the house, and then perhaps flower beds and a vegetable garden. No matter what you want to grow on your land, the sensible first step is to take a soil sample and have it analyzed. Kits are on the market for do-it-yourself soil analysis, but most experts seem to agree that they are so inaccurate that it is better to send your sample to your state testing service or to a qualified professional laboratory.

Some states offer free soil testing to their residents. Others do it for a minimal charge. Check with your county agent. Since many parts of the South are agricultural, the recommendations are frequently worded for farmers, but it's easy to translate the laboratory recommendations to the home situation where the gardener wants to know how much lime to apply to his lawn or vegetable garden.

Depending on your gardening plans for the season, you may want to take one or more samples. First, let's assume that you plan to establish a new lawn in the front yard or want to renovate an old one. Take a bucket, a spade, and a spoon or trowel to that area. In at least ten different spots around that yard, plunge the spade into the ground, pull it back so that soil is exposed, and with the trowel or spoon, scrape down the exposed soil for several inches and dump the soil you collect into the bucket. Continue taking these small samples all over the area to be improved. Stir all the samples together and then, from this well-mixed soil, take out the small amount you need for the laboratory. When you send the sample to the lab, mention your proposed use of the land and ask for specific fertilizer and lime recommendations for a lawn. Make a separate soil sampling for each project—another lawn at the back of the house, perennial beds, rose garden, azalea plantings, or vegetable garden.

If you will be planting in an established garden, you may find that a soil test will indicate an excess of some chemicals. For example, one rosarian here has found that some toxicity has built up in his old beds. He now has his soil tested twice a year and follows the recommendations. In 1987, he was using only nitrogen because of his soil conditions. None of us can tell which nutrients our garden needs or precisely what the pH is by looking at the soil. Don't guess, test!

Most gardeners seem to be more confused about fertilizing than any other single aspect of gardening. Some of us never even had high school chemistry. NPK, boron, and magnesium are mysteries. However, the most nonscientific of us can understand enough about fertilizers to use them intelligently. *Read the label!*

I suspect that many of us, whether gardening, assembling a Christmas toy, or repairing the car, tend to charge right in and do it without looking at directions. Make an exception when using garden chemicals. Not only read the label, but follow the directions.

Every complete fertilizer label will have three numbers on it, clearly stated. Those numbers may be 5-10-5, 20-10-5, 12-12-12, or one of many other combinations. The first number always represents the nitrogen content; the second, the phosphate; and the third, the potash. NPK.

The label will also provide use recommendations. Just as we need a balanced diet of protein, fats, carbohydrates, and so on, our plants must have a diet balanced for their needs—hence the many different labels. (It is also possible to buy each fertilizer component separately.)

The three numbers on the label are expressed in percentages. For example, in 100 pounds of 10-6-4, 10 percent, or 10 pounds, of the material is nitrogen, 6 pounds, phosphate, and 4 pounds, potash. The remaining 80 percent is an inert carrier material.

Nitrogen is vital to our plants, because it promotes the vegetative growth, the leaves and the stems. If you know that nitrogen stimulates leafy growth, you can understand why all lawn fertilizers are high in that first number on the label. Fertilizer recommendations are generally given per 1000 square feet. For example, instructions for a spring lawn fertilization might read "2 pounds of nitrogen per 1000 square feet." If you are using 10-6-4, a typical lawn formula, you would need to apply 20 pounds of 10-6-4 over that area. If you are not sure just how large 1000 square feet is, be simplistic about it. Go out and measure a patch of lawn that is 10 feet by 10 feet, which will give you 100 square feet. When you can easily visualize 100 square feet, it is simple to work with that mental image and study your yard to see just how many square feet of lawn or garden you have. (The perfectionist can measure every square inch.)

Phosphate and phosphoric acid are forms of phosphorus, the second chemical element on your fertilizer label. Phosphorus provides several benefits to our plants, like building strong cell walls, but its primary function is promoting flowers, fruits, and seeds. If you ever find that your garden needs a boost of phosphorus, the dry, granulated superphosphate is quickly available to the plants. In the days when bone meal was produced by physically grinding up bones, it used to be a beneficial material, supplying phosphorus to the plants very slowly. Most gardeners stirred it into the soil beneath bulb plantings. However, today's methods of bone meal production leave so little nutrient value that researchers working with bulbs at North Carolina State University no longer recommend this product.

The third number on the fertilizer label is potash, which helps the general vigor of your plants and promotes healthy root systems.

The other elements that our plants use are calcium, magnesium, and sulphur, plus boron, chlorine, copper, iron, manganese, molybdenum, and zinc, the seven trace elements. Generally, in the areas of clay and clay loam soils throughout much of the South, we don't need to be concerned about the tiny amounts of these elements plants need unless the pH is over 7. These micronutrients do tend to become deficient in regions with sandy soils.

What is pH? The scientific definition says that it is the logarithm of the reciprocal of hydrogen ion activity. To the dirt gardener, it is a measure of the acidity or alkalinity of the soil. Soil pH is measured on a scale from 0 to 14. Seven is neutral, numbers higher than 7 are alkaline; the lower numbers indicate acidity. It is helpful for gardeners to remember that each increment means a tenfold increase. If your soil moves from a pH of 6.5 to 5.5, it is ten times more acid. If, heaven forbid, it should go to 4.5, it would then be 100 times more acid than the 6.5 soil. Your soil test will tell you the pH of the area tested, and the laboratory performing the test will also give you recommendations for adding lime to raise the pH (moderate the acidity) or for adding sulphur to lower the pH (increase the acidity).

In the garden, just as indoors with house plants, it is important to look at the entire picture. One of the most common questions from newspaper readers is "How often should I water my house plants?" It sounds like a simple question waiting for a simple answer, but I can offer no formula in response to that question. Instead, I want to know which house plants— cacti, orchids, or African violets? Is the house warm or cool, dry or humid? Do the plants receive sunlight or not? Is the potting medium heavy or free draining? Are the plants growing in plastic or clay pots? Is the pot too large or too small? Are we talking about 2-inch pots or 12-inch ones? All these and other factors influence just how often an indoor gardener should water house plants.

Outdoors, matters are even more complex because we have less control over the various factors that are all interrelated. Heat may speed up the release of fertilizer elements. Rainfall may leach desirable chemicals out of the soil. Too much phosphorus may induce an iron deficiency. Too much calcium may cause a trace element deficiency. And so on.

Fortunately, most of us are unlikely to encounter any serious problems if we have our soil tested and follow directions about fertilizer use. Most complete fertilizers also have minute amounts of some trace elements in them. Just as you check your garden plants for insect infestations, look at them regularly for signs of nutritional problems. For example, browned edges are a sign of fertilizer burn.

One problem I have encountered several times is iron deficiency. This is indicated when a plant has leaves with green veins and a yellowing of the areas between the veins. This foliar yellowing, or chlorosis, is easy to treat with chelated iron, available at your garden center. "Chelated" is the key word. The iron has been treated so that it will be available to the plants. Your soil may actually have enough iron in it, but it is in a form that is unavailable to the plants, and so they develop that chlorotic, yellowing foliage which, if untreated, may continue to worsen and eventually kill the plant.

In addition to the dry fertilizers we may choose to use on our gardens or lawn, we can also buy slow-release fertilizers, like Mag-Amp and Osmocote, that are available in various formulations and are good for different periods of time. These products are more expensive, but there may be certain situations—for example, if you have a nursery area to support your hobby and are propagating azaleas or other shrubs there—where using pellets that will release nutrients over a period of four months will save you a lot of time and be worth the expense.

For bulb growers, a 9-9-6 Holland Bulb Booster has been developed, based on research at North Carolina State University. This fertilizer incorporates some slow-release material so that gardeners can feed the bulbs just once a year, rather than the two times recommended if you use an ordinary, balanced fertilizer.

In recent years, we have seen some bio-organic fertilizers introduced to the market. These products contain natural ingredients high in protein and carbohydrates, blended with desirable bacteria and enzymes. During the 1980s, a series of turf tests at Michigan State University has produced some intriguing and promising results. By adding both beneficial bacteria and the slow-release, organic fertilizer, a healthy balance was restored to depleted or overfertilized lawns that were suffering from thatch and other lawn problems. With the quality of the soil improved, many of the disease problems disappeared. Interestingly enough, in a series of tests run at other locations throughout the country, it has been found that these products are particularly effective in the South.

Water-soluble fertilizers also have their place in our catalog of gardening items. These products dissolve in water and can be applied with watering cans or hose attachments. They are useful as starter solutions for newly planted material, they allow foliar feeding of shrubbery, and they provide another convenient way to feed plants in a nursery area. I find that I use the water-soluble plant foods on house plants, in my nursery, and for other containerized plants. In the woodland garden, I throw around the dry granules of triple 12 with considerable abandon. There is such competition from the tree roots that it would be hard to burn my hostas, azaleas, epimediums, primroses, and other compatible plants. I do try to avoid getting any of the granules in the crowns of my plants, and I don't fertilize during our dry, 97-degree days. We can, however, feed later in the season here in the South. If you once raised roses or azaleas in Michigan or Connecticut, you probably gave your plants their last fertilizer in mid-August. Since our winters are shorter and frost comes later, we can feed a month or so later too. We want to stop just early enough in the fall that we are not pushing soft, new growth that will be zapped by the first hard freeze.

In some situations, cover crops—sometimes called green manures—work wonders on improving the soil. They are useful in an area you will plow, like a large vegetable garden or a proposed vast new lawn, when you have months to grow annual rye, buckwheat, alfalfa, clover, or one of the other cover crops. We have a neighbor who plants half of his huge vegetable garden each year in one of the legumes that will add nitrogen to his soil. He then plows that crop under in the spring and plants his vegetables on that half of the area while again growing a cover crop on the other half. Another gardener, a man who works with soil research professionally, recommends fall sheet-composting, with layers of leaves and vegetative matter tilled into the ground, as the easiest way to replenish the soil.

Whatever method we choose, we need to keep replenishing the soil with organic material each year. I've mentioned compost a number of times. Compost is simply vegetative matter that has been broken down through desirable biological action. Every garden should have a discreet compost pile or two in a corner of the yard. You can buy composting bins, build attractive wooden forms, enclose areas with chicken wire, or simply pile up your vegetative kitchen refuse, leaves, grass clippings, and manure.

Wherever we have lived and gardened, my husband and I have also deliberately made compost piles. We use the crumbly, dark brown end product as a soil conditioner, as a mulch, and also as one component of potting soil. Compost will improve the tilth of either clay or sandy soils, and it's free, if you don't count your labor as a cost.

The organic materials in a compost heap will break down without any help from us. Due to our heat and humidity, the process of decomposition is much quicker here in the South than in northern gardens. You know that if there is a pile of branches in the woods, you can just leave it alone and in a few years, they will have disintegrated into a wonderfully rich-looking, crumbly soil amendment. In our woods we have found several treasure troves of natural compost created from brush piles made years ago by people clearing our land.

Fallen leaves decompose, without any help from the gardener. Making compost can be as simple as piling vegetative refuse in a shady, unobtrusive corner of the yard and letting it decay. With no care or attention, it takes about a year to produce usable compost. However, the more effort you put into it, the more quickly you can create compost. One expert said he produced compost in just twelve days by turning the pile with great frequency. I suspect most gardeners fall somewhere in the middle. We are willing to help the process along but not about to make a daily project out of it.

A bin of some sort is useful. Experts seem to agree that a cubic yard is the minimum size for an effective compost pile, so design your space to be no less than three feet by three feet. The best-looking and most-useful compost bin we have had was a wooden one in California. It was a very long bin, divided into three sections. One section held finished compost, ready to be added to the garden. The second bin held compost in progress, and the third was the collecting bin where we threw the current supply of grass clippings, leaves, and other vegetative matter. Air holes were drilled in the sides of these bins, and the front sections were removable for easy shoveling.

For those gardeners with small yards, there are several commercial units on the market that are fairly small and unobtrusive. Typically, a bin or other open-bottomed container is placed on bare ground, unless you are composting in an area of heavy tree roots. There, it is best to place a piece of plastic under your bin, to prevent roots from entering the pile. Unfortunately, it will also slow up composting, because earthworms and other organisms cannot enter the pile. Earthworms circulating through your compost are desirable; tree roots are not.

It is even possible to make a small amount of compost by throwing leaves and kitchen refuse in a large plastic bag, adding some water and fertilizer, punching a few holes in the bag so that air can enter, and placing the bag in the sun. If you turn the bag over every day, you should have compost in a matter of weeks.

Most gardeners need a full-sized compost pile. Build your compost pile like a club sandwich—a layer of well-rotted manure, for example, and then a thick layer of your garden refuse, some fertilizer or an activator, and then another layer of leaves and trimmings. Add a little lime unless you intend to use the compost on rhododendrons, azaleas, and other acid-loving plants. When your pile is 3-feet high or more, cover it with a light layer of soil or plastic or burlap. Heat will be generated by the decomposition process, and you want to hold that heat in the pile.

Turn the pile frequently. A pitchfork is ideal. Moisten the compost as needed. Several experts say that the material in the pile should feel like a wrung-out sponge. If flinging damp material with a pitchfork is too hard for you, try a Compostool. It's a relatively new gadget on the market that you poke into the pile. As you pull it out, paddles open and mix some of the material.

The finer the materials, the more quickly they will break down, so if you have a shredder, put it to good use when building your compost pile. Remember that finely shredded materials need to be turned with great frequency to provide the necessary amount of oxygen to the pile. Also, do not include rose trimmings (thorns) or evergreen pieces like ivy, fir, or yew. They are very slow to decompose. One of the relatively recent innovations in composting is the introduction of biological activators, like Compost Plus, Grass Clipping Compost Booster, and Brown Leaf Compost Booster. According to tests run at California State Polytechnic University, Pomona, these additives speed up the decaying action and help the gardener to produce compost faster.

Whether you do it the slow and easy way or actively hurry compost production along, do make composting as normal a part of your gardening activities as pulling a weed or watering the lawn. You'll reap the rewards as you use the compost in your vegetable garden, potting soil, and flower beds.

I mentioned using compost as mulch. Mulching, covering the soil with a layer of some material, is desirable throughout the country but it's a very important technique for southern gardeners. A mulch placed over well-watered ground helps keep the soil moist, protects the plants from heat and drought, keeps weeds down, and prevents mud splashes on plants and buildings. In display gardens, we want an attractive mulch. Which organic material you use depends on your locale. Here in the Piedmont, our standard, least-expensive mulch is either pine needles or bark. In other places, gardeners may use cocoa hulls, peat moss, sawdust, ground corncobs, buckwheat hulls—whatever is available and reasonably priced. In a garden area that is not on show, like the vegetable or cutting gardens, many gardeners use newspapers as mulch. I have even seen strips of discarded carpet used as a practical mulch in a research test garden. Organic mulches offer the advantage of decomposition. The sawdust or compost you put on top of the garden one year can be worked into the soil the following year. If fresh sawdust or bark is used, the gardener has to add some extra nitrogen to replace that which is used in the decomposition of the mulch.

The best mulches are airy materials. I'm not fond of peat moss, because it tends to crust. If you use this or other organic mulches that will compact and crust, break the surface with a rake occasionally. And when you put any organic mulch near a tree or shrub, pull it a couple of inches away from the trunk. How much to apply depends on the material you choose. A rule of thumb is that the lighter and airier the material, the more of it you can use. Where you might put a couple of inches of bark around a newly planted Japanese maple tree, you might pile up several inches of loose pine straw.

In certain places, inorganic mulches, like stones or plastic, serve well. These mulches have to be removed before the garden can be reworked. I use a fine gravel mulch on the scree garden. I also have used black plastic in the vegetable garden, where it was a great help in minimizing the weed problem. Mulch for looks. Mulch to minimize work. Mulch for the health of your plants.

As you garden, always keep in mind that a healthy soil, replenished annually with compost or perhaps tilled-in, organic mulch, with numerous earthworms and healthy bacteria busily at work, will reward you with more beautiful flowers, healthier lawns, and delicious vegetables.

3

Trees

I've come late to an appreciation of trees. For many years, they were simply the background to the shrubs that provided the backdrop for the flowering annuals and perennials I loved to grow. Now I treasure them for themselves, for their form, size, foliage, texture, color, fruit and/or flower. I raise some species from seed and some cultivars from cuttings, and I seek out good forms of our native dogwoods and redbuds in nurseries. I appreciate the tall, 80-foot canopy provided our acres by the mature oak, hickory, and tulip trees—and we enjoy a fire in the fireplace every winter evening from our own logs. We thin the tall trees so that the woodland trails will get enough light for azaleas, hostas, primroses, epimediums, and all the other shade-loving plants we are growing there. And here and there we have enough space and light to plant additional trees of particular beauty.

While we began with a wooded lot, as do many southern gardeners, others start in what was formerly a bare farm field. Those gardeners can be very selective and only plant choice trees. Or perhaps your lot is somewhere in between. You have a few tall deciduous or pine trees and considerable open space. If you are building and have native trees on the lot that you want to preserve, make sure that the ground around them is not disturbed by the bulldozers. Many buyers write a clause into the purchase agreement with a penalty to be paid should any specified trees be killed or injured. Don't allow additional dirt to be piled around the trunks of trees you want to save.

Give considerably more thought to which trees you select than to which shrubs or perennials to plant. The trees will be with you longer, and they are a major investment. While most of us plant small trees and wait for mature growth, sometimes it is wise to spend the money to bring in a sizeable tree—for example, a shade tree for the southeast corner of a home on one of those bare acres. With today's equipment, like the Big John 88, nurserymen can successfully move trees that are up to 40 feet tall.

Primroses, daffodils, hellebores, and ferns add to the beauty of an azalea trail

Ken Miller, a young landscape architect from St. Louis, gave a thought-provoking talk to a meeting of garden writers not too long ago. "Doctors can bury mistakes; architects can only plant trees," he quipped. Then he went on to talk about the architectural qualities of trees. In his practice, he chooses some trees for their strong vertical line. He uses others as a focal point in a garden, and occasionally he creates a "room" effect underneath the canopy of a treasured, large, old tree. A hammock stretched out in such a cool shady oasis looks very inviting.

"When I design a garden, the first thing I think about is where to put the saucer magnolia, the serviceberry, or the ornamental crabapple," he said. "Trees can serve as fantastic objects in a garden." Like any good floral arranger or landscape architect, Miller is constantly aware of all of the elements of design. He consciously blends lines, forms, patterns, textures, colors, and space to create a harmonious and interesting garden.

"Noteworthy texture plants find their way into the best gardens," he said. Two examples he mentioned were *Ajuga pyramidalis* cv. 'Metallica Crispa' and cut-leaf Japanese maples.

The springtime exuberance of an ornamental crabapple tree

Ajuga pyramidalis 'Metallica Crispa' (photograph by Pamela Harper)

He also considers scale and proportion, balance, rhythm, dominance, and contrast when working in a garden. Contrast in any garden is very important, and it can be provided in many ways, including using vivid or subtle colors and playing with the various hues of green. Miller finds dark greens most valuable in garden designs. "The contrast between light and dark increases the energy level," he said.

"It is easy to make attractive garden designs with large drifts of the same plants," Miller said. "The difficult challenge is to design an attractive collector's garden." As an example of a successful collector's garden, he showed photographs of the rockery near the Climatron at the Missouri Botanical Garden. In this garden, the repetition of rounded mounds ties the garden together and gives it a pleasing unity.

Vertical quality is also important. It is provided to the rockery by small shrubs and dwarf evergreens. I'm sure you have visited flat gardens where no plant or object was more than 2 feet tall. Boring! Trees are our most common tool when we want a strong vertical. Nothing soars up to the sky more dramatically than a narrow, columnar cypress.

"Competing objects are distressing to me," Miller said. He emphasized the importance of having both primary and secondary objects. Several trees of the same type and size compete with one another.

His recommendations reminded me of Harland Hand's garden in California, where Hand skillfully uses strong verticals in strategic placements throughout his hillside garden. Some are tall poles; others, handsome evergreens. In another garden, a tall sculpture might carry the visitor's eyes upward, but most often, the vertical element in a garden is supplied by the trees.

"I don't want to design a 'pretty' garden—might as well put in rows of petunias," Miller said, as he showed photographs of a number of uneventful and boring gardens. "'Cute' is even more distressing." Then, as he whizzed through several slides of gardens that ranged from interesting to spectacular, "Why can't we say 'nice,' 'inviting,' or even 'awesome'?"

It is really difficult to plan an awesome garden, but I think nice and inviting gardens are well within the reach of all of us. And, like Ken Miller, let's begin with the trees.

If you start with a wooded lot, as we did, then yours is a matter of management, selection, and elimination. If you want a vegetable garden or a home orchard, then you will clear a large piece of ground in order to provide at least six hours of sunlight to your fruits and vegetables. You can do it slowly and painfully yourself, or you can spend the money to have someone with heavy equipment come in and quickly clear the land. Think twice before you practice false economy. We all do it, at times. One friend had his

The exfoliating bark of a choice maple, *Acer griseum* from China, adds a rich texture to a garden. This tree thrives in the South.

The skeletal forms of deciduous trees in winter are as important to the garden as their leafy summertime umbrellas

Harland Hand creates strong verticals in his garden with thrusting trees, poles, and weathered posts

field cleared but decided the additional cost to remove all felled trees, tree roots, and debris was too high. He has regretted it ever since, as he has lived with the unsightly mounds at the edges of his field.

For a shade garden, you need to selectively thin the tall trees. Whether your high canopy is of pine or deciduous trees, look up and be sure that the openings between the trees are generous, so that the garden at ground level will receive a good deal of flickering light as the sun moves across the tree-tops during the day. Be sure to check deciduous trees in full foliage, and remember that all of the trees will continue to grow. Thinning mature trees for a garden below is one instance where more is better. It is so much easier to fell trees on undeveloped land than to try to take them down later without breaking a rhododendron branch or smashing a planting of azaleas.

Above all, let me urge you to avail yourself of the services of a professional tree man for the felling of any but the most modest of trees. While my husband and I are usually enthusiastic do-it-yourselfers, trimming or removing 80-foot trees is a job for experts. This fact was brought home to me in two ways. In Michigan, we were welcome visitors in one garden where the host greeted us in a wheelchair. He had been trying to do his own tree work and had taken a bad fall, breaking both legs and keeping him from his job for six months. He saved no money on that tree work.

Later, at our present home, we employed a young tree man to remove three trees. Because of the locations and conditions of the trees, he cut down each one in a different manner, with precision, artistry, and skill.

Management of your trees, like management of your lawn, shrubs, roses, or petunias, means looking at them routinely. Catch infestations early and treat, if possible, or remove the infested tree so that the problem does not spread to its neighbors. Look up to see major branches that have partially split from a tree, and check after severe storms to see if the top has been knocked out of one of the tall trees, and have these dead parts removed before they fall to injure people, house, or garden. Learn how to prune low trees yourself.

If you are beginning with a large, bare lot, John Simonds, in his book *Landscape Architecture*, has some practical suggestions. He says, "Choose as the dominant theme tree a type that is indigenous, moderately fast-growing, and able to thrive with little care. These are planted in groups, swaths and groves to provide the 'grand arboreal framework' and overall site organization."

Particularly here in the South, I think his recommendation about using native trees that will need little care is sound advice. The exotics, or non-native trees, that are commonly grown in a region usually come from another part of the world with similar climatic conditions. Dr. Clifford Parks of the University of North Carolina studied the woody plants commonly cultivated in central North Carolina and found that most of our exotics came from southeast Asia, with a few from the drier Mediterranean region. They are the most compatible.

It's hard to ignore pine trees if you live in the South. They are such an inherent part of our native landscape. Approaching a number of southern airports, one flies over a billowy carpet of native pine forests. Many of the new neighborhoods in our fast-growing area have been carved out of pine groves.

Pines can be terrible pests. Many roadsides in the South are lined with volunteer pine seedlings. Roadside crews have to clear them every few years. On our property, we lop off the volunteers wherever we do not want them. Pines make things easier on the gardener in one way—they do not stump sprout. You do not have to use a stump killer after you cut off the young tree, as you do with deciduous material.

The native pines are also a nuisance at pollination time each year. In early spring, the cars in the driveway, the furniture on the screen porch, and all the windowsills are dusted with a golden powder. For me, the pollen is just an annoyance, but for one neighbor who is allergic to it, pine pollen is a real health problem.

Nonetheless, pines are a beautiful and important part of our landscape. If yours is one of those large, empty lots, you may want to plant a grove of native pine trees. In any yard, you may want to select a specimen pine for your landscaping. Some pines are handsome plants.

The eastern white pine (*Pinus strobus*) is useful both in reforestation and as an ornamental specimen. It carries soft, flexible needles in groups of five. It gives a pleasingly fluffy look to the landscape. The cones of a white pine are long and narrow. While the species has a maximum height of 120 to 200 feet (depending on which expert I consult), there are dwarf forms of these pines as well as many other evergreens. *Pinus strobus nana* will remain at about 6 feet in height, and there are a number of other forms on the market. *Pinus strobus pendula* (the weeping white pine) makes an intriguing specimen plant.

The tallest southern pine is our loblolly pine (*Pinus taeda*). In *Know it and Grow it*, Carl Whitcomb describes it as not very ornamental but extremely useful as an overstory tree to provide light shade for azaleas and other shade garden plants. Whitcomb's book, by the way, is a very useful reference book for southern landscaping plants. It provides brief information about zone, size, form, texture, leaves, stem, flowers, fruit, color, propagation, culture, and pests.

My favorite of the native pines is the longleaf pine (*Pinus palustris*). It is a handsome tree with needles varying between 9 and 18 inches in length. While it is an important timber tree, I personally value it for flower arranging. All pine branches are useful in winter arrangements, but the longleaf adds something special. Flower arrangers should plant some longleaf pines on their land or at least locate a good source nearby.

In your local nurseries, you may also find the slash pine (*P. elliottii*) and the Virginia pine (*P. virginiana*), other natives that are useful for mass plantings. A number of nurseries also carry the Japanese black pine (*F. Thunbergiana*). While it will grow well throughout zones 7 and 8, readers near the coast might really pay attention to this pine. It is native to the seacoast of Japan and thrives under coastal conditions.

Like other pines mentioned, the Japanese black pine adapts to a number of different soil conditions, and it is a vigorous grower. If you like an oriental look in your garden, this pine tolerates open pruning readily and can be shaped into a most attractive Japanese specimen.

Another oriental native, *P. Bungeana*, is planted for the beauty of its bark. It is called the lace-bark pine because the bark on a mature tree flakes off and the trunk displays patches of gray-green, gray, and white.

Harder to locate, but available from specialist nurseries are more exotic pines. *Pinus Griffithii zebrina* is flourishing in the Coker Arboretum in Chapel Hill. Its long, drooping needles with subtle stripings make it a smashing specimen tree. This is one of the most beautiful and elegant pines. Native to the Himalayas, *P. Griffithii* (syn. *Wallichiana*) is valued as a timber tree in China and Nepal. Here, like a number of other pines, plant it for its beauty.

The list of other desirable and decorative evergreens is extensive. The cedars, like *Cedrus atlantica* (the Atlas cedar), *C. deodora* (the deodar cedar), and *C. libani* (cedar of Lebanon), make handsome specimen trees in a large lawn. They are potentially tall trees that grow slowly and perform well throughout our region. In youth, they have a narrow pyramidal form which tends to become more open and spreading at maturity. Flower arrangers like to find a mature *C. deodora* in order to collect its decorative, roselike cones, which add such a handsome touch to Christmas wreaths and swags. There are a number of attractive forms of these cedars on the market.

Dr. Stanley Bennett, a neighbor who has developed his own arboretum, introduced me to the handsome Chinese fir (*Cunninghamia lanceolata*). It is another pyramidal evergreen with attractive, small cones that are held on the tree after the seeds fall to the ground. Whitcomb recommends this tree as a fine substitute for the Colorado blue spruce in the South.

Cryptomerias are close relatives of the cunninghamias and are equally beautiful and underutilized. *Cryptomeria japonica* is one of those tall, narrow trees to consider for its strong vertical accent in the landscape. These trees are very popular in Japan but not as widely used in this country. They thrive in our part of the United States.

In addition to all the varieties of evergreens mentioned, there are junipers and firs and spruces that will serve us well in our landscapes. The list of good conifers is extensive. One plant that deserves special mention is the fast-growing Leyland Cypress (*Cupressocyparis leylandii*). It is a tree of narrow pyramidal form, relatively drought resistant, tough, and reliable. I've seen it used effectively in hedges, and it also can be used as an individual specimen tree. It was found in England as a natural hybrid of two American species, *Chamaecyparis nootkatensis* and *Cupressus macrocarpa* (the Monterey cypress). The two species are never found growing together in nature, but in a garden setting, they crossed and produced this fine offspring.

One companion planting in the Duke Gardens that charms me is that of the two fossil trees, the deciduous dawn redwood (*Metasequoia glyptostroboides*) and the deciduous *Ginkgo biloba* growing side by side. These trees are called fossil trees because they were found in fossil records long before it was realized that the living plants still existed. The metasequoias are fast-growing conifers that were discovered in China only about forty years ago, but today they are available in many of our local nurseries. The one at Duke has a particularly beautiful surface root mass at its base.

The list of deciduous, broad-leafed trees that are lovely, hardy, and desir-

The golden sparkle of *Ginkgo biloba* foliage in autumn

able for our zones is quite extensive. When possible, I always like to select a plant that offers more than one virtue. For example, the ginkgos are not only shapely, pleasing trees throughout the year, but they give us a spectacular burst of yellow fall color. Then, unlike most of the deciduous trees that shed over a long period of time, the ginkgos drop all of their leaves at once—interesting.

But the ginkgos come from China. Let's begin with our native deciduous trees that we should consider for our landscapes. There is a long list of both maples and oaks that are native, beautiful, and desirable. The willow oak (*Quercus phellos*) is one of my favorites. Its fine, willowlike foliage is graceful. The tree form is pyramidal in youth, and later it spreads out into a large shade tree. Whitcomb notes that it transplants better than many oaks, and judging from the speed with which our white oaks' seedlings shot down deep taproots this spring, I can understand why oaks generally would not transplant well. It is probably desirable to buy containerized, relatively small trees and let them put their roots deep into the soil. White oaks (*Quercus alba*), red oaks (*Quercus falcata*), laurel oaks (*Quercus laurifolia*), and a number of other oaks are all desirable, tall shade trees.

We all love the bright fall foliage of red maples (*Acer rubrum*). There are hardy types of this species from New England to Texas. I grew up with two large red maples as street trees on our city lot in Bangor, Maine. Here, each fall I admire a row of tall and glorious red maples near a country farmhouse on our road. The sugar maple (*Acer saccharum*) is another colorful, large, native shade tree for our part of the country as well as New England. These and other native maples are large, vigorous, and relatively shallow rooted. Don't make the mistake the builder of our home in Michigan made. He planted a charming, 10-foot maple in a relatively small hole in a concrete patio. By the time we bought the house, the concrete was cracked and the tree was already out of scale for its location. Do not plant any large trees in cramped locations, and don't use maples if you want to plant a shade garden beneath the trees. Maples produce dense shade, in season, and the shallow roots offer too much competition for plantings.

An Asian gem, or rather, a whole group of gems, is the Japanese maple (*Acer palmatum*). 'Bloodgood' is the red-leafed variety most widely available, but there are numerous beautiful cultivars in a wide range of sizes. Charming bonsai plantings can be created with Japanese maples. These trees are lovely in large containers on a terrace or patio, and they are ideal small specimen trees for any garden. 'Dissectum' has exquisite, finely cut foliage. A friend just gave me 'Butterfly,' which has beautifully variegated foliage.

It would be easy to develop a passion for Japanese maples. If this group

The exotic flower of our native tulip tree

of plants interests you, be sure to obtain *Japanese Maples*, by J. D. Vertrees. This book will introduce you to more Japanese maple cultivars than you ever dreamed existed. The trick, of course, is to locate them. I am happy to find the most common ones available at many large nurseries today. There also are a number of specialist nurseries that offer some of the more unusual forms.

In addition to the oaks that are native on our property, we also have high hickories and tulip trees (*Liriodendron tulipifera*). The only hickory I might deliberately plant is the shagbark hickory (*Carya ovata*), for its spectacular bark. Tulip trees have exotic, tuliplike, fragrant, yellow flowers, marked with vivid orange blotches. The only problem is that the trees shoot 70 to 80 feet up in the air, and the only flowers we see, usually, are the few the squirrels trim off and drop at our feet. I do wish some scientist would manipulate some genes and produce a dwarf tulip tree.

Tulip trees number among those unique plants that are native only to the southeastern United States and Asia—one species here and one species in

China. In recent years, Clifford Parks has crossed the two species and produced flowers that are larger and more beautiful than either species. I hope these trees gradually get introduced to our nursery trade.

One shade tree I would never plant is the mimosa (*Albizia Julibrissin*). I prefer to admire this southern tree in someone else's yard. When the silky puffs of pink flowers adorn the lacy foliage, the trees are quite handsome. However, they seed themselves around the yard so generously that we are still removing innumerable seedlings six years after we cut down the two mimosas here.

If you want a birch tree, the river birch (*Betula nigra*) with its peeling tan bark is an attractive tree. The cultivar *B.n.* 'Heritage' has lighter bark and is resistant to borers. It thrives in the summer heat of zones 7 and 8 if given enough water, as you might guess from its common name.

Catalpa bignonoides is a southern native that makes a large, rather coarse, flowering tree for large areas. The white flowers are beautiful but messy if the tree is grown over sidewalks or driveways. It is a lovely tree to put at a distance, to enjoy as part of a grand vista.

Another native tree that produces messy refuse is the sweet gum (*Liquidambar Styraciflua*). The round seed pods are a nuisance in some circumstances but are fine collectibles for arrangers who use them in winter wreaths. It is a handsome tree, columnar when young; oval in maturity. I have always treasured it for its fall color.

Zelkova serrata (the Japanese zelkova) should be much more widely planted in southern landscapes. It is handsome and undemanding. It makes a fine shade tree. Other than being susceptible to an occasional attack by Japanese beetles, it is pest-free.

We can also grow black gums, winged elms, ashes, hackberries, honey locusts, and a host of other shade trees in this part of the country.

Then there are magnolias. What is more southern than a large *Magnolia grandiflora*, covered in big, creamy flowers, with its skirts sweeping the ground? This evergreen tree is glorious year-round. The flowers are lovely, the seed pods are decorative, and the leathery leaves are always handsome—wonderful for Christmas decorations. I only wish we had a large enough site to offer one of these magnificent trees. I'll just enjoy the beautiful, aged ones in town and on the Duke campus.

Magnolia is a large genus of flowering trees, containing both evergreen and deciduous varieties. Some, like *M. fraseri*, are rare and seldom seen. Others are commonly available. *Magnolia stellata* is widely planted. While it is a handsome tree in flower, it often loses some of its buds to frost in zone 7. Frustrating. Why not plant *M. x Soulangiana* (the saucer magnolia) here and enjoy its more reliable flowers? There are a number of cultivars of both of these deciduous varieties on the market. Dr. Bennett has just given us a *M. virginiana*, and we are looking forward to its fragrant, white flowers.

There is a host of small, flowering, understory trees that work well when growing beneath thinned stands of tall oaks and hickories. Certainly the dogwoods that sprinkle the woods with their white sparkle create their own magic each April. Our native dogwood is *Cornus florida*, which has an extensive natural habitat from Florida to Maine. If you choose to grow only this species, you have a long list of cultivars to choose from. Probably the two most commonly available are 'Cloud Nine', a floriferous white form with much larger flowers than the species, and 'Cherokee Chief', a deep pink. *Cornus florida* also comes in variegated foliage and in double, dwarf, and weeping forms. I try to add different cultivars as I can locate sources. Although I treasure dogwoods, I pull out native seedlings regularly. I was reluctant at first, but I soon realized that for every dogwood I wanted to attain its potential, I had to remove approximately ten other seedlings around it. They are delightful weeds in our woods. (While I would urge gardeners to buy cultivars for their improved qualities, should you want to transplant some native dogwood seedlings, remember that smaller is better. These trees do not willingly take to transplanting, and a small one is much more likely to survive.)

We all should plant *C. kousa* (the oriental dogwood). It produces its showy, pointed bracts a month later than *C. florida*, and they stay on the small tree a long time, thus greatly extending the dogwood season. They are slow to establish, so planting one is for the patient gardener. We were delighted to discover one coming into flower the second spring we were in this house, thanks to an earlier gardener who had planted it at the edge of the woods. *Cornus kousa* also has very decorative, strawberry-sized, red fruit in late summer.

Donald Wyman, in *Trees for American Gardens*, is particularly enthusiastic about *C. controversa* (the giant dogwood). He says it makes an excellent specimen because of its picturesque habit—wide spreading, with horizontal branches. It is an Asian native that adapts nicely in our part of this country.

Redbuds (*Cercis canadensis*) too are native here on the property. They line stretches of our country road. A couple of the years we have lived here, the redbuds and the dogwoods have bloomed together, and that is a magnificent sight. While the redbuds are rather spindly and insignificant in the woods, if you clear around them and give them a little more light, they make attractive specimens. The white form (*C.c* 'Alba') that I saw blooming in full sun at the Missouri Botanical Garden was floriferous and shapely. I

A choice, white form of our native redbud tree

have a seedling of the Greek species, *C. Siliquastrum*, growing in my nursery. I hope it continues to thrive, because the flowers of that species are larger and more pink than our native.

We have several buckeyes that will perform well in our zones. My favorite is the red buckeye (*Aesculus pavia*), which makes a nice, small, compact understory tree with showy spikes of red flowers in late spring.

Two lovely small natives with white flowers are the fringe tree (*Chionanthus virginicus*), which I treasure for its floral display and its powerful fragrance, and the sourwood (*Oxydendrum arboreum*). The latter is both beautiful for its sprays of small white flowers that hang down like graceful fingers and valuable as a source of nectar for what many beekeepers prize as the best honey.

I do see a number of golden raintrees (*Koelreuteria paniculata*) blooming in home gardens. Both the early summer flowers and the seed pods are decorative. You may have noticed an "escaped" princess tree (*Paulownia tomentosa*) on a roadside in your county. This oriental tree is striking when planted in a large landscape setting, because it produces its large panicles of blue-purple flowers in the spring before the rather coarse foliage appears.

The fringe tree is attractive both winter and summer and bears lacy white flowers with a delicious perfume each spring

There is a long list of *malus* species and cultivars that are available. The flowering crabs are an important part of our bountiful springtime gardens. When you shop for these small trees, look for disease-resistant varieties. One local nurseryman is particularly enthusiastic about 'Callaway' because it not only puts on a lovely springtime display of white flowers, but provides a generous crop of large fruits in the late summer.

Ornamental pears, too, are planted throughout our area—overplanted, in the case of the *Pyrus calleryana* selection (the Bradford pear) which is often planted as a street tree. Designers don't seem to recognize that those cute little trees that are so attractive when they are 10 feet tall will grow into huge specimens, 40 feet or more. If someone says to me that he wants a small, flowering tree for a patio area—how about a Bradford pear?—I take him to my neighbor's yard where two immense and handsome specimens dominate a large field. If you want a large, decorative pear, look for 'Aristocrat' or 'Red Spire', cultivars with improved branch and foliage characteristics. Also, Wayside is offering a dwarf form of the ornamental pear, *P.c.* 'Faurriei', described as staying under 25 feet in height.

And of course we mustn't forget the traditional southern plant, the crape myrtle. Some are shrubs, others are grown as single or multiple trunk small trees. I value ours for its winter form and the beautiful, smooth, mottled bark almost as much as for its summer flowers.

Many more lovely, flowering trees abound that can enhance our southern landscapes. The problem with the more unusual trees is finding one to buy. I have been happy to see more and more of these trees in local nurseries. *Franklinia alatamaha* blooms in the summer, when few other trees flower. *Stewartia malacodendron* is a rare and lovely small tree with white flowers. For the most southern part of our area, in zone 8, gordonias are handsome small trees with large, white flowers. Laburnums, with their lovely hanging racemes of yellow flowers, are not planted enough in the South, nor is the silverbell tree (*Halesia carolina*). *Prunus mume*, from Japan, produces a lovely, airy pink or white snow of flowers in midwinter, when it is most welcome. Some years, Dr. Bennett's trees, which he raised from seed of plums he bought on the sidewalk in Tokyo, begin their show at Christmas time. Even more choice and longer blooming is its relative, *Prunus subhirtella* 'Autumnalis'. It blooms in one neighbor's yard from November until March, here in zone 7. It also does beautifully in zone 8. It is at the top of my "want" list, just now.

And don't forget our native holly (*Ilex opaca*). While I discuss a number of hollies in the following chapter on shrubs, this particular holly can be trained into a most attractive small tree. Some fine, selected cultivars are on the market. For a generous display of berries on *I.o.* 'Merry Christmas' or 'Bountiful', remember that you must plant both male and female trees.

If you are looking for rare and unusual trees, along with many of the desirable, common varieties, and are willing to start small, there are two interesting sources. Order the Forestfarm catalog, which offers an extensive selection of rooted cuttings or seedlings. Friends who have ordered from this firm recommend it highly. If you really want to begin at the beginning and raise your trees from seed, order the list from Maver Nursery. They offer an amazing list of seed from around the world. Dr. Bennett says that the Chiltern Seed Company offers the most extensive and interesting list.

He likes to raise trees from seed to increase genetic diversity. If we propagate plant material from cuttings or tissue culture, we get exactly the same plant, genetically. If we raise a batch of seed from one pinecone, many different characteristics will show up in the seedlings. Some will be markedly inferior and should be discarded, but other seedlings in the batch may have improved characteristics. For example, Dr. Bennett has two sibling sequoia seedling trees in his yard, and one is clearly more cold resistant and hardier than the other.

If you are not interested in propagation but you want a large number of common evergreen or deciduous trees, check with your county agent. Policy varies from state to state and even from county to county, but in many counties, seedling trees are offered to the citizens of those counties either very inexpensively or without charge.

Whichever trees you select, unless you have a professional tree man move in large specimens, you will be planting the trees yourself. Most books recommend the $5.00 hole for the fifty-cent plant. Amend the soil with compost, peat moss, old sawdust, or other organic materials and plant the tree. J. C. Raulston's approach to tree planting at the North Carolina State University arboretum is interesting. He does not amend the native clay at all. He plants the tree, waters well, and mulches. The tree then makes it or it doesn't. Most of his trees do thrive there. A number of large specimen trees were donated to the arboretum and were moved successfully with a Big John spade.

What I would suggest is to dig a generous hole and then wash out the growing medium from your containerized plants and stir that into the existing soil. Today, most growers are using a very light peat and perlite mix for all of their plants. If you take the plant directly from the container and pop it into a hole dug in clay or sand, the roots will stay in the loose mix and not establish well in their new home.

If the tree has been overlong in the container and the roots are coiled around the outside of the root ball, uncoil them or take a sharp knife and cut the sides of the root ball. Spread out the roots in the hole, fill with amended soil, then water the tree and mulch it. Keep the new tree well watered the first year, even if it is one of the most drought-resistant plants. All plants need regular watering to get established.

To stake or not to stake is a matter of some disagreement among the experts. The most current thinking suggests we should not stake newly planted small trees unless they are in a particularly vulnerable location, such as a windswept area near the coast. If you do stake a small tree, do it carefully so that the tree is not injured. One method is to take short sections of an old hose and put them over the staking wires where the wire loops around the tree. Use three wires and make a sturdy, three-cornered support for the tree. Even better, follow the suggestion of one of our local nurserymen and use burlap strips, not wire, to tie the young tree into position. The burlap will decay in about a year, by which time the tree should be well established. This way, there is no chance of injuring a tree with staking supports that should have been removed but were forgotten.

Pruning should be an annual affair, beginning with that small tree you plant. Prune at planting time to remove crisscrossing branches and any dead material. Evergreen trees and shrubs should be pruned during the winter. However, Ted Kipping, expert tree surgeon from San Francisco, suggested that we should prune all of our deciduous trees in full leaf, rather than at the conventional time in late winter, and his arguments make good sense to me.

By waiting until the tree is covered with foliage, we can see the level of growth, tell which branches are dead—not always possible with a dormant branch—and see how dense the foliage is. Ted's methods began to develop as he noticed that winter after winter he was pruning suckers out of the same trees. He was trying to open the trees for good air circulation and to provide light for photosynthesis. "Any leaf that is not receiving light is not functioning," says Ted.

There's got to be a better way, he thought, so he did some research and found that tree men in England and France had discovered the same thing: summer pruning of deciduous material is better.

When Kipping begins to work on a tree, he applies what he calls the rule of the four Ds, removing all dead, damaged, diseased, or deranged branches. By deranged he means those branches that are criss-crossing or shooting straight up, creating any framework that departs from the normal, open pattern of healthy growth.

By pruning in leaf, we can see precisely the expanded proportions of the tree or shrub. We can see exactly which branches are getting shaded out. We can clearly see which branches are alive, which are ill, and which are damaged. We can also see the posture of the tree or shrub when bearing the full weight of the foliage. In case you forget how much leaves weigh, try to rake for an hour or two. Leaves have a lot of wet weight.

After dealing with the four Ds and then thinning for air circulation and the best use of available light, Kipping suggests judicious tipping of branches to encourage flower and/or fruit production for the next year, like pinching back your chrysanthemums. Unlike winter-pruned deciduous trees, which put out a lot of additional wood, woody plants stay pruned after summer pruning unless they receive a heavy dose of nitrogen. Kipping does prune all evergreen trees and shrubs during the winter months.

Kipping also emphasizes that it is important to maintain the rhythm of the spacing and detailing when pruning a tree "Aesthetically it will work—and it also works for the health of the tree," he says. I saw his poetry in action when I visited a yard in San Francisco where he had artfully pruned some large, magnificent Monterey Cypress trees, opening them so that the view beyond could also be enjoyed. He urges us all to look at individual

The rhythm and form of artfully pruned trees (photograph by
Ted Kipping)

trees—to appreciate their natural forms and rhythms, to admire on coastal
cliffs or mountainsides the windswept trees pruned and shaped by nature,
and to study Japanese gardens with trees pruned to understated elegance.

Most experts, including Kipping, today are recommending that we homeowners not paint tree wounds as was the custom in the past.

As I have learned more about trees from Ted Kipping, Dr. Bennett, J. C.
Raulston, Fred Garrett, Paul Jones, and other experts on woody plants, I
have come to an appreciation of the beauty and richness of diversity in the
many trees we can grow here, and I have also come to understand that we
homeowners need to manage our trees as actively as we do other parts of
our gardens.

As a postscript, let me add that if you should lose several sizable trees due
to lightning, a tornado, or other sudden disaster, photograph the tree damage, hire a tree appraiser, and file a deduction with your tax forms. You may
be surprised at how valuable your trees were. Of course, since the tax rules
change yearly, this advice may be invalid five years from now. At least inquire. Your dead trees may be worth a considerable tax savings.

4

Shrubs

We all use shrubs in so many ways that it is difficult to begin to list them all. For example, at Christmas time, I like to "deck the house" with a winter bouquet of variegated holly trimmed with red berries, displayed in my grandmother's cut-glass pitcher. Later, the tumbling fountains of golden forsythia shout "Springtime!" to me. It's a joy to work in the garden during the spring days when viburnums perfume the yard or to brush by the January branches of the witch hazels and enjoy both their winter flowers and their fragrance. I like the architecture of *Tsuga canadensis var. prostrata* 'Cole's Prostrate' drifting over a rock, the precise, conical shape of the Alberta spruce, and the oriental character nandina provides in foliage, flower, and berry.

Vertical junipers spike above the globular forms of azaleas, boxwood, or hollies beside the front doors of many homes. In addition to that type of decorative landscaping, in our first home on a tiny city lot, my husband and I established privacy from the street with a tall privet hedge. Perhaps you separate your property from your neighbor's with a hedge of Lawson cypress. Hedges can be created out of many different shrubs and used for many different purposes. A mixed hedge or shrubbery of deciduous, flowering shrubs can produce a wonderful effect at the far end of a spacious lot.

Some shrubs are cherished for their flowers, others for their berries. Some are evergreen; others, deciduous. Shrubs come with large or fine foliage, variegated or plain foliage—leaves that are shiny, dull, puckered, leathery, lacy, smooth, or prickly. The variety is almost infinite. We have a rich choice when we select shrubs for our garden.

Azaleas and camellias are such important southern shrubs that they merit their own chapter, so I won't mention them here. But in addition to these ubiquitous evergreens, we have a number of other valuable and attractive evergreen shrubs to incorporate into our landscaping.

Tsuga canadensis 'Cole's Prostrate'

Hollies have to head the list. Evergreen hollies are wonderfully versatile plants. They can be grown as single specimens, in grouped plantings, or as hedges. They can be allowed to grow naturally, can be pruned severely, or can even be espaliered into precise geometric shapes. The late Clancy Lewis of Michigan State University, who was one of the country's leading dendrologists, said, "The hollies can probably do more to revitalize the landscape than almost any other group of plants." This statement has even more validity for southern gardeners, because we have so much more choice than those who garden in colder climes.

The Burford holly is the most widely planted in southern gardens. *Ilex cornuta* 'Burfordii' is a fine shrub with glossy foliage and red berries, but we have seen too much of it. Because it is inexpensive and fastgrowing, many builders use it in their instant landscaping. Contractors don't pay attention to the fact that the ultimate height of a Burford holly is approximately

30 feet—an inappropriate shrub for planting beneath a window. 'Burfordii' has its place in the landscape, but it should not be used against the house, where it demands vigorous and frequent pruning to keep it below the roof-line and under the windows. Why not plant *I. c.* 'Burfordii Nana', which slowly grows to modest size, or the even more dwarf *I.c.* 'Rotunda', with a mature height of 3 feet. (Tuck this clue into your memory. Any time you see "nanus" in a name, that plant will be a dwarf or small variety. "Pumilus," "pygmaeus," and "pusillus" are a few other botanical Latin terms that indicate a dwarf plant.)

The blue hollies, *I. x Meserveae*, developed by Catherine Meserve when she crossed the beautiful English holly, *I. aquifolium*, with the extremely hardy Asian *I. rugosa*, have become popular in recent years as lovely specimen plants. These hollies are dioecious, another botanical term which means that the male and female flowers are borne on separate plants. Unlike the Burford hollies that produce fruits without fertilization, for every few 'Blue Princess' hollies you plant, you must add one 'Blue Prince' or some other male holly. Also, be sure to buy from a reputable nursery that has the male and female plants clearly identified.

For low-growing, fine-leaved evergreen shrubs, *I. crenata* 'Helleri' has been planted for many years. *Ilex crenata* (Japanese holly) is another species that will grow to 20 feet or more, but a number of its compact forms, including 'Helleri' and 'Microphylla', are on the market. This holly is grown as a foliage plant, not for its unobtrusive black berries. For the same sites, one nurseryman in our area prefers *I. vomitoria* 'Nana', a dwarf form of our native yaupon holly. She describes it as having a more "modern" look. It also has the advantage of being more drought resistant. I have seen attractive dwarf yaupons grown without pruning and a tiny yaupon hedge severely pruned and used as the border for a garden of antique roses, much as Elizabethan-style herb gardens are often edged with dwarf box.

Fred Garrett, director of the landscape gardening program at the Sandhills Community College in the Southern Pines area, is enthusiastic about *I. glabra* 'Compacta'. He feels that it is an outstanding substitute for boxwood in landscaping projects. This holly is an attractive, bushy, relatively low shrub with handsome, glossy foliage, and it has far fewer pest and disease problems than boxwood.

By the way, the college has one of nineteen official holly display and test gardens around the country. It has a rich collection of three hundred and forty cultivars and thirty different species on display behind the horticulture building. The plants, donated by holly collector Fred Ebersole, are all labeled, and a visitor can compare foliage types, sizes, shrub and tree forms and berries. Dr. Ebersole and Virginia Morrell, in cooperation with Fred

Ilex glabra 'Compacta'

Garrett, have written an extremely useful pamphlet about hollies. It provides cultural information, a list of the official display and test centers and an extensive chart describing many of the cultivars and species by height, growth, form, color, leaf size, serration, branching habit, and berry color. To obtain a copy of this pamphlet, send fifty cents and a self-addressed, stamped envelope to the Holly Society of America, Inc.

Official Holly Arboreta and Experimental Holly Test Centers for the South

Agricultural Experiment Station
Arboretum
University of Tennessee
794 Bethel Valley Road
Oak Ridge, Tennessee

Callaway Gardens
Pine Mountain, Georgia

Clemson Horticultural Arboretum
Clemson University
Clemson, South Carolina

Sandhills Community College
Southern Pines, North Carolina

U.S. National Arboretum
Washington, D.C.

In addition to the evergreen hollies mentioned and the many others that are on the market, some deciduous hollies make lovely additions to our southern landscapes. *Ilex decidua* (the native possum haw) carries a generous supply of red berries on its graceful, bare branches for most of the winter months. Another attractive deciduous holly is *I. verticillata* (the winterberry). Both of these hollies are dioecious, so you need both male and female plants for a heavy fruiting. While the species are good plants, several named cultivars are even better, so when you are in a nursery shopping for these hollies, seek out *I. verticillata* 'Sparkleberry' (a relatively recent introduction from the National Arboretum), 'Christmas Cheer', and 'Winter Red', or *I. decidua* 'Warren's Red', 'Sundance', 'Pocahontas', or other named selections. 'Glow' and 'Harvest Red' are both good fruiters with the bonus of interesting and attractive fall leaf color. Many berried shrubs, including the hollies, are not only beautiful, but they attract birds to the garden.

Billowy evergreen boxwood shrubs epitomize southern gardening. English boxwood (*Buxus sempervirens*) was brought to this country by early settlers and has been used for hedges, edging plants, and specimen shrubs ever since. While the skillful landscape designer can use boxwood with a contemporary house, box does carry with it the connotation of colonial days. We can see wonderful old examples of boxwood usage at Williamsburg.

Boxwood plants can be pruned and shaped or allowed to grow naturally. Over the years a number of different subspecies and cultivars of *B. sempervirens* have been identified. Today we can grow boxwoods that are as large as a small tree or so minute that the shrub only grows ¼ inch per year.

Although thirty to forty species of boxwoods exist in the world, only a few are available commercially. The many varieties of *B. sempervirens*, the finer-leaved *B. microphylla* and its cultivars, and *B. harlandii* and some hybrids are the only boxes of importance to southern gardening.

Boxes are reasonably flexible in their requirements. They will grow in sun or partial shade, in almost any type of soil. Like many of our plants, they need more water if they are grown in full sun, and they will respond enthusiastically to soil that is amended with compost or other humus material. Prune and feed them in the early spring. They are not voracious feeders. In fact, one expert recommends not feeding them at all. Since they are shallow-rooted, if you do add fertilizer, don't cultivate around the shrubs. Water it in or let the next rain do that for you.

Several pests, including a leaf miner, occasionally bother boxes. The most common problem is an attack of spider mites, particularly during one of our droughts. Try to catch all problems in the garden early. Identify the pest or disease and treat appropriately.

A billowy, sixty-year-old boxwood hedge, an attractive backdrop for
bulbs, perennials, and annuals

Although boxwoods do flower, the flowers are so insignificant that most
of us don't even notice. However, some gardeners find the pungent odor of-
fensive. It must be a peculiar chemical the plant exudes—one to which only
some noses are sensitive—because I am not at all aware of it when the box
blooms in our yard.

Although ours is not an Early American type of house, I want a large
boxwood or two, simply for the holiday trimmings. While early spring is
the traditional time for box pruning, I wait to prune these shrubs until December and use the clippings for wreaths and flower arrangements. Boxwood provides an attractive, long-lasting, fine-leaved evergreen for holiday
decorations.

I also have collected a couple of the dwarf forms of boxwood that are
suitable for small rock gardens or trough plantings. *Buxus sempervirens* 'Vardar Valley' is an attractive, compact, and low-growing plant that has only
grown about 12 inches in seven or eight years in my garden. Paul Jones, a
curator at Duke Gardens and a specialist in woody plants, commented that
my plant is not typical because 'Vardar Valley' usually grows 4 to 6 inches a

year. (Perhaps the plant I bought was not properly labeled.) *Buxus microphylla var. compacta* ('Kingsville Dwarf') is even smaller. During the same time span, it has only reached a height of 4 inches—a tight little bun.

For those of you who have the space and want a boxwood tree, seek out *B.s.* 'Arborescens'. You may find this plant marketed as American boxwood, although there is nothing American about it. There are also golden boxes, prostrate boxes, weeping and contorted boxes on the market. It seems that there is a boxwood for every taste today.

To assist gardeners in locating the more unusual boxwoods, the American Boxwood Society has published *The Buyer's Guide for Boxwood*. It costs $3.00, postpaid. This guide contains two lists. First, many of the nurseries in the country that offer boxwood are listed. Most are in the South. Then the known boxwood species and cultivars are listed, along with the identifying numbers of the nurseries offering each box. This guide is not dated, and like all source guides, it needs revision and updating.

In addition to boxwoods and hollies, the other extensive group of evergreens that are extremely valuable in today's world of smaller gardens, condominium patios, and apartment balconies are the versatile dwarf conifers. Their diversity of texture, form, and color makes them anything but a dull green background. Mind you, "dwarf" is a relative term, as anyone who has visited the mature Gotelli Collection of dwarf conifers at the National Arboretum knows. There many of the shrubs tower well above one's head. However, as a group, the dwarf conifers are small and slow growing. Unlike the Burford holly, which will shoot past your windows quickly, the appropriate dwarf conifer will stay in scale for a couple of decades.

With more than 2500 cultivars on the market, you can choose slim verticals, like *Juniperus virginiana* 'Skyrocket', ground-carpeting junipers like 'Bar Harbor' or 'Wiltonii', compact balls of *Chamaecyparis obtusa* 'Nana', or the beautiful, upright, golden 'C.o. 'Nana Aurea', or even gracefully weeping or fastigiate forms.

If you are looking for a slow-growing, prostrate evergreen, the bird's nest spruce (*Picea abies* 'Nidiformis') is one of the most commonly available forms. The main branches rise from the center and arch gently to the outside, thereby forming the "nest." After many years, the bird's nest spruce will cover a large area. However, if you want a truly miniature variety for a trough garden, window box, or bonsai, the pygmy form 'Little Gem' will not grow more than 12 to 16 inches in twenty years.

The bird's nest spruce and all the other dwarf evergreens came into existence in one of several different ways. Some were raised from seed or from cuttings of alpine plants. Others were propagated from a witches' broom, a

Pinus thunbergiana 'Yatsubusa'

Juniperus rigida 'Blue Tosha'

Picea pungens 'Globosa'

A collector's garden of dwarf conifers

roundish mass of congested growth in a conifer. Branches, needles and cones on a witches' broom are miniaturized versions of those on the parent plant. If cuttings are taken from this unusual branch, the new plants will have the dwarf characteristics of the witches' broom.

Experts still seem to disagree about the causes of witches' brooms—perhaps a virus or trauma, spontaneous growth, or genetic fault. These growths, also known as hexenbesen, have been associated with tales of cemeteries and ghosts. (I've been told that here in the South, hexenbesen are found only near cemeteries!) Sometimes, even, a witches' broom is found on a dwarf conifer. That minute 'Little Gem' mentioned earlier was created in just that way, propagated from a cutting of a witches' broom found on a bird's nest spruce. (Conifers propagated from witches' brooms are generally sterile, although occasionally one will produce viable seed. In *Manual of Dwarf Conifers*, Welch says, "We are told that Nature preserves her species by making her freaks sterile.")

Dwarf conifers may also crop up among ordinary seedlings. In a field of pine or juniper seedlings, a nurseryman may notice one or two plants that appear perfectly healthy but miniaturized. The canny nurseryman will save these variant seedlings, propagate them, and introduce them, if they are distinctly different from other plants on the market.

There is one other source for these dwarf evergreens. Alpine plants, growing above the tree line in mountains around the world, are hardy, tenacious, and generally stunted in growth. Frequently, conifers propagated from dwarfed plants seem to maintain the dwarf characteristics when grown at lower altitudes.

While these plants may not do as well as other dwarf conifers here in the South, dwarf conifers in general are becoming more and more popular because of their slow growth and ease of cultivation. They are not at all fussy about soil and will grow in a wide range of conditions. If you are dealing with the worst of our red clay or total sand, do amend the soil with a generous helping of compost.

Generally, you don't need to feed dwarf conifers. You are not trying to promote lush growth and large plants. If they are growing in an area which drains very rapidly, you may need to provide an occasional boost of a low-nitrogen fertilizer. Because of our excessively hot, dry summers, there's no plant you can put in the ground and forget. These evergreens will need regular watering, particularly during the first year while they are getting established.

Although some junipers tend to be afflicted with red spider mites during the driest weeks of summer, dwarf conifers have the added advantage of generally being pest-free. They are simply charming, low-maintenance additions to the landscape. You can plant them in full sun or partial shade. Shrubs with yellow variegation should be in full sun to maintain the color. In shade, you will lose most or all of the variegation. All green ones will do well in sun or light shade.

Finding dwarf conifers to buy is not always easy. Some of the most common, like the bird's nest spruce, the Alberta spruce, and mugo pines, are found in many nurseries. For more rare dwarf conifers, you may have to order from distant specialists. Some nurserymen have stopped carrying them because customers were unwilling to pay more money for a quality, smaller product. We have to understand that it takes more years to grow a good dwarf conifer 3 feet high than the ordinary species and be willing to pay for it. Seek out these choice, slow-growing plants.

Another evergreen shrub you may find a place for in your yard is the gardenia (*Gardenia jasminoides*). During teenage prom years, my favorite corsage was always this fragile, perfumed flower. Gardenia fragrance is potent. To some people it is sickishly sweet; I find it delicious. In the warmer parts of the South, the entire plant has much to offer. It can grow up to 6 feet high and carries its fragrant, double flowers on glossy, evergreen foliage.

Much as I enjoy gardenia flowers, I have found the plants to be marginal here in zone 7. There were two gardenias in our yard when we moved here. They bloomed only once in the first four years. They were killed to the ground three of those four years. I have eliminated them both. They were much too unrewarding to give them garden space any longer. Other zone 7 gardeners may love gardenias and be willing to go to extremes to shelter and care for these shrubs. One gardener, only slightly east of us, builds a large barricade of burlap around her gardenia each winter and fills the enclosure with dry leaves. The same winter my last plant went to the ground, hers survived and was floriferous that spring. Zone 8 gardeners can plant gardenias with more confidence.

So much of gardening is a matter of preferences and prejudices. The older we are and the more years we have gardened, the more pronounced are both the preferences and prejudices. Despite the fact that aucubas are widely used as landscaping shrubs in our area, I loathe them. My keen dislike of these shrubs comes from my California years. There, my husband and I inherited a row of variegated aucuba (*A. japonica* 'Variegata') along the front of the house. They were plagued with aphids that secreted a honeydew resulting in a black, sooty type of mold on the foliage. They demanded frequent maintenance to be at all attractive.

What can I say that is kind about these evergreen shrubs? Aucuba foliage is long lasting in flower arrangements, and the variegated forms often add a desired touch of yellow to a bouquet. I used to use aucuba in church arrangements, because the foliage is relatively large. The narrow, toothed leaves can be as much as 7 or 8 inches long. Like many of our other shrubs, a number of different cultivars of this one species are on the market—plain green, boldly variegated, or spotted foliage, large or compact plants. Aucubas are easily propagated from cuttings and easily grown—just plant them and water them. Like some of the hollies, they are dioecious, so you need to plant both male and female shrubs if you want the red or white berries. The best site for an aucuba is in light shade.

While I feel aucubas are used all too frequently, I think we don't plant enough mahonias. With their whorls of notched leaflets, they are handsome, evergreen plants. The most commonly grown species is *M. aquifolium* (the Oregon grape). It produces modest spikes of yellow flowers in late winter, followed by decorative bunches of large, blue-black berries later in the spring. It is a "must" plant for anyone who is trying to develop a twelve-month, flowering garden. We also find *M. bealei* (the leatherleaf mahonia) in many of our nurseries. It is another upright evergreen shrub worth cultivating. *Mahonia repens* is not widely available as a plant, but I have raised this ground cover mahonia from seed.

When I visited the Rancho Santa Ana Botanic Garden in February 1987, I admired the most handsome, floriferous mahonias I had ever seen. They

An Oregon grape in winter flower. Later in the season, these shrubs are covered with clusters of grapelike berries.

were specimens of a named cultivar, 'Golden Abundance', a chance seedling. That garden displays ten species, some of which would not be hardy here. It often takes a while for plants popular on the West Coast to find distribution here. I hope the hardy mahonias make the trip soon and become commonplace in our nurseries. 'Golden Abundance' is certainly a superior clone. While those mahonias were thriving in full sun in the Los Angeles area, in our part of the country, they perform best in light shade.

Like many plants, the mahonias will be more compact and more floriferous the more sunlight you give them. They will bloom more sparsely and become leggier, the more shade they receive. If you have a completely wooded lot, as we do, then you will not be able to offer any plants full sun. On the other hand, if you are beginning to landscape a totally open field, select trees and shrubs that will tolerate full southern sun and then, as the trees begin to provide light shade, add shrubs like mahonias and aucubas. As with house plants like African violets, you will have the most handsome shrubs if you give them as much light as they can stand without burning.

For some reason, I have always lumped pyracanthas and cotoneasters together in my mind. Both are small-leaved evergreens with colorful red, orange, or yellow winter berries. Although there are some cotoneasters that make large shrubs or small trees, and some of the species are deciduous, the cotoneasters we are most apt to find in our nurseries are the evergreen, low, ground-covering types. For a compact round mound with bright red winter berries, I like *C. congestus*. The rockspray cotoneaster (*C. horizontalis*) goes up about 2 feet and then spreads out in a fishbone pattern that ultimately will cover about 5 feet. It has red berries also, and is described as semievergreen—the farther south we plant it, the more evergreen it will be. *Cotoneaster dammeri* and *C. salicifolia* 'Scarlet Leader' are other desirable, low, ground-covering cotoneasters.

More vigorous and spreading is the cranberry cotoneaster (*C. apiculata*), which is wonderful if used on banks or areas where you want to obstruct foot traffic. It mounds up on itself and creates a congested, impenetrable barrier. Like the little *Rhododendron keiskei* 'Yaku Fairy', the leaves are green during the summer and turn to a rich wine color in the fall. *Cotoneaster apiculata* is generally too large and fast growing for garden placement, but in the right location, it is a splendid plant.

The cotoneasters will thrive in the sun and tolerate light shade. They are easy to propagate from cuttings. Their main drawback is their susceptibility to fire blight. It is an occasional bacterial problem that attacks apples, pears, quinces and a few other plants. (See the chapter on pests and diseases.)

Pyracanthas are close relatives of the cotoneasters—both are members of the rose family, *Rosaceae*. Like cotoneasters, the pyracanthas have brilliant berries, but they also carry thorns—hence the common name, firethorn.

Most of the pyracanthas make large vertical shrubs or small trees. One that had been shaped into a tree form bloomed and fruited for a couple of years outside our bedroom window here. The cardinals used it as a stopping place, en route to the window feeder. However, it succumbed during one of those winters where tender growth had not been hardened off and then we were blasted with cold.

Just now, I am espaliering two *P. coccinea* 'Teton' shrubs on a brick wall. I'm using an informal pattern, but I have seen pyracanthas shaped into symmetrical espaliers, like the Belgian fence design, a fan, or tiers of horizontal branches. These shrubs do not need heavy pruning. Usually, just a trim once a year, after flowering, will be adequate.

You will be able to find a selection of named varieties of pyracantha in your nurseries. Many of them are cultivars of *P. coccinea*, like *P. c.* 'Teton'. Forestfarm, in Williams, Oregon, offers a variegated form of this species named 'Harlequin'. *Pyracantha Koidzumii* is another attractive species that does well in the South, and it also has a considerable list of cultivars on the market. *Pyracantha K.* 'Victory', with its bright red berries, is one variety specifically recommended for espaliering. There are other species in existence, but few are available commercially. Like the cotoneasters, pyracanthas are also susceptible to fire blight.

If you are looking for an absolutely pest-free, problem-free, flexible evergreen shrub that will thrive in sun or shade, plant an *Abelia x grandiflora* or one of its cultivars. This hybrid abelia, a cross between two Chinese species, *A. chinensis* and *A. uniflora*, is not showy or splashy. It is a reliable shrub of modest charm. The glossy small leaves on arching branches are attractive throughout the year, and the small, white flowers add a certain beauty during the summer months. Abelia 'Edward Goucher' is a compact, desirable cultivar that has pink flowers. 'Edward Goucher' has three species in its parentage, for it was developed by crossing *A. x grandiflora* with *A. schumannii*.

The only care I give the abelias in our yard is some pruning after flowering and an occasional handful of balanced fertilizer, because they are competing with tree roots. The dwarf *Abelia floribunda* 'Frances Mason' in the scree garden gets no food. It stays glossy, compact, floriferous, and golden throughout the year—a charming little shrub.

While I enjoy the free-flowing character of abelia's arching branches and allow my shrubs to keep their natural form, it is possible to create an attractive hedge, using abelias. When I first saw an abelia hedge, I thought it unattractive, but I have changed my mind. With heavy shearing, an abelia hedge can be tight and compact and glistening with a generous sprinkling of flowers. If you are creating a hedge of abelia or any other shrub, remember that you should prune the shrubs with a wide base tapering to a relatively narrow top, so that the bottom of the hedge will get plenty of light and stay vigorously full of growth, rather than sparse.

One shrub I won't plant in my yard is the photinia. It is susceptible to several pest and disease problems. I first became acquainted with photinias in our California garden, where the previous owner had lovingly planted a Chinese photinia (*P. serrulata*) and pruned it into the form of a small tree. When allowed to bloom and fruit, it was quite attractive. When pruned as a hedge, as is so often the case in the South, it loses both flowers and fruit. In our area, *P. x Fraseri*, an evergreen with red new foliage, is the most widely planted photinia, much overused. The Fraser photinia is a cross between *P. serrulata* and the Japanese photinia, *P. glabra*.

It's not the red top that offends me, because I treasure the cultivars of *Pieris japonica* (the Japanese andromeda) that put out reddish-bronze new growth. These ericaceous plants are easy to grow, and they have elegant foliage and extremely decorative fountains of small flower bells in early spring. At the North Carolina State University Arboretum, Dr. J. C. Raulston has quite a collection of pieris cultivars, each more lovely than the last. While most of the pieris varieties have white flowers, he has collected cultivars with pale pink and also deeper pink panicles of flowers. *Pieris j.* 'Shogo' is particularly lovely. I also like other species, *P. yakusimense* and particularly *P. Forrestii* with its extremely red new growth. In our garden, hybrid varieties *P.* 'Mountain Fire' and *P.* 'Flamingo' are thriving. We even have a southeastern native, *P. floribunda* (the fetterbush), which takes to garden culture nicely. Instead of the waterfall effect of the flower stems on the other species, our native pieris holds its flowers upright in an attractive manner.

There are a number of other charming evergreen shrubs for southern gardens, like daphnes and *Danae racemosa* (the poet's laurel), which is so lovely in flower arrangements. Daphnes are wonderfully fragrant but touchy. *Daphne odora* will thrive for a number of years and then die without apparent cause. That happens to be one of the shrubs I am determined to have, so I replant. Of all the daphnes, the variegated hybrid 'Carol Mackie' seems to be the most resilient and long-lived in the Piedmont. *Daphne caucasica* is a deciduous species that does well in the South and blooms over a long period of time. And we can grow barberries, leucothoes, cleyeras, ligustrums, wax myrtles, raphiolipsis, osmanthus, and the leatherleaf viburnum (*V. rhytidophyllum*). The number of desirable and attractive shrubs will continue to increase, as breeders develop better cultivars of shrubs we are already growing, and as plant collectors introduce new material.

While the emphasis is on evergreen material for landscaping purposes, a great many floriferous, deciduous shrubs can contribute considerable beauty to our gardens. Since I am working toward a twelve-month garden and also a fragrant garden, I treasure the witch hazels that bloom in the winter months. The deliciously sweet, twisted yellow or red flowers appear along the bare stems before the foliage appears. *Hamamelis mollis* (the Chinese witch hazel) is an attractive yellow species. Even better, seek out its more richly colored cultivar, 'Pallida'. Or select desirable hybrid forms like 'Diana' or 'Arnold Promise'. We even have southern natives, *H. virginiana* and *H. vernalis*, that are reliable and interesting, if not as spectacular as some of the hybrids.

Witch hazels are easy to grow. They will flower best in full sun, but do well in partial shade. They do appreciate regular waterings. The real problem with these shrubs seems to be finding them. Our local nurseries are just beginning to carry a few.

Witch hazels are not the only shrubs that are sometimes hard to obtain. When we moved south, I searched in many nurseries to locate *Viburnum x Burkwoodii*, a cross between *V. Carlesii* and *V. utile*. Now, several years later, some of the nurseries in my own area are offering this wonderfully fragrant shrub. It perfumes the entire yard when it comes into flower. I always break off a sprig and enjoy it at my desk, too. As a delightful bonus, *V. x carlcephalum* was already growing in the yard. The blooms of this large shrub open just as *V. x Burkwoodii* is going past, so we enjoy an extended period of that same delicious fragrance. *Viburnum x carlcephalum* shares one parent with *V. x Burkwoodii*, for it is a cross between *V. Carlesii* and *V. macrocephalum*. I've also planted a small start of another *V. Carlesii* cross, the fragrant *V. x Juddii*.

In the woods, I have left a number of the native viburnum, *V. acerifolium* (arrowwood). They produce modest heads of nonfragrant flowers, followed by attractive groups of black berries. Some gardeners plant the huge and showy *V. macrocephalum* 'Sterile', which produces large snowballs of flowers. If I were to add one of the nonfragrant viburnums to our yard, it would be the double-file viburnum, *V. plicatum* 'Mariesii', with its gracefully arching branches covered with flattened flowers all along each stem.

The viburnums are an easy genus of shrubs, seldom bothered by any pest or disease. Just plant them and water them to establish them well.

The list of spring-flowering deciduous shrubs is extensive. You can use any one as a specimen, combine them, create mixed flowering hedges or drifts of yellow forsythia or sparkling white deutzia. Old favorites like spirea, calycanthus, weigelia, callicarpa, chaenomeles, hibiscus, kerria, and philadelphus vie for our attention with more recent arrivals on the horticultural scene—introductions like corylopsis, enkianthus, chimonanthus, and stachyurus. Each has its own charms, its own virtues, and all are easy to grow. Plant them, water them, and prune them after flowering, except for those you also treasure for their fruits, like callicarpa and quince. Let me

Pieris japonica 'Shojo'

Pieris yakusimense

An old-fashioned flowering almond

Cydonia 'Spitfire'

Chaenomeles japonica 'Toyo Nishiki'

Deutzia bloom

suggest that whatever shrubs you are adding to your yard, you seek out the newest, most vigorous and floriferous cultivars. We all have limited garden space, and it does not cost much more to buy the best. While I used to take any stray sprig home, root it, and plant it, I have become much more selective over the years. It takes just as much effort to care for an inferior plant as it does for the superior ones. Plant the best.

If lilacs were favorite spring shrubs of yours in northern climes, recognize that most of them will not do well here in the South. If you are determined to have a lilac in your yard, seek out the few varieties that are recommended for your zone. Rather than familiar *Syringa vulgaris* cultivars, consider *S. meyeri* 'Palibin' and *S. patula* 'Miss Kim'. Our gardens will be most attractive and successful if we plant those shrubs that thrive, rather than those that sulk and barely survive.

Hydrangeas are an extremely rewarding group of shrubs that provide considerable beauty with little care. Probably your mother or grandmother had *H. paniculata* 'Grandiflora' growing in the backyard or beside the porch. At my mother's home in Maine, several of these shrubs grace the back of the house. I must admit, I've always taken them for granted, but in 1985 I took a fresh look at the pee-gee hydrangeas and found much to commend them.

What more can we ask of a flowering shrub than to bloom in early summer with large balls of white flowers that slowly turn soft pink and then bronze by autumn? The flowers remain on the stalk until hit by a heavy frost. These flowers cut well and are long lasting throughout the growing season. Withhold water from the vase and they even turn into interesting dried material for use during the winter.

The gem of the genus, however, is a plant I didn't discover until we moved to North Carolina. The first June we were living in Chapel Hill, I almost blocked traffic on Franklin Street one day as I slowed to a crawl to admire a gorgeous shrub covered with white pyramidal panicles held above elegant foliage. Each leaf looked like an oak leaf, and I soon learned that this shrub is named the oak-leaf hydrangea (*H. quercifolia*).

The oak-leaf hydrangea is a species native to southern states like Florida, Georgia, and Mississippi. Despite its origins in the deep South, it is totally hardy in zone 7 and is successfully cultivated as far north as New York City.

Like many of the hydrangeas, it thrives in partial shade and is decorative from spring until frost. The foliage is always attractive, whether in summer green or fall wine coloration. The flower heads survive until frost, and I find them attractive even in their senescent beige. Desirable cultivars, like *H. q.* 'Snow Queen', are even more attractive than the species.

Sometimes in a nursery or an old-fashioned garden you will find a lace-

Above: An oak-leaf hydrangea in the landscape. *Left*: The attractive head of a pee-gee hydrangea, showing both sterile and fertile flowers.

capped hydrangea. I was captivated by a blue lace-capped hydrangea in one lovingly tended southern garden. The lace-caps have flat flower heads. The generous center of each head is filled with tiny flowers and all is edged with large, sterile ones, like the flowers of Viburnum 'Mariesii'. The cuttings that gardener shared with me rooted easily.

Here we can also plant the florists' hydrangeas, the hortensias. These have been developed by European breeders, using *H. macrophylla* and its close relatives. Hortensias ranging from white to blue and pink—or even deep red—have been selected and introduced.

We can manipulate the color of pink or blue hydrangeas by changing the pH of the soil. In early springtime, before flowering, water in aluminum sulphate to maintain a blue color. If you want a pink hydrangea, add a generous dose of lime around the base of that shrub.

And what would our southern summers be without crape myrtles? Deciduous crape myrtles, hardy as far north as Maryland, have been reliable plants in the South since they were introduced to American gardens by André Michaux, a French botanist who explored our East Coast between 1785 and 1796, looking for trees that could be raised for timber in France. While he was collecting and shipping thousands of oak, magnolia, and other American tree species to France, he introduced a number of valuable plants to the United States. The list includes *Ginkgo biloba*, *Albizzia Julibrisson*, and *Lagerstroemia indica*, the crape myrtle from China.

Today we can buy crape myrtles by color—red, white, pink, lavender, and purple—or by cultivar name, like 'Dixie Brilliant' (red), 'Pink Lace', and 'Weeping White'. In addition to the large crape myrtle that can be pruned either into a large bush or a small tree, dwarfs have been on the market in recent years. For the most choice ones, purchase cultivars, particularly the recent, mildew-resistant introductions from the National Arboretum. For fun, raise a batch of the seedlings yourself. They are instantly rewarding, because, unlike most shrub seedlings, they will bloom the first year from seed.

Crape myrtles need full sun but are not demanding about the soil. Although they are very drought resistant once established, be sure to water them regularly the first year. If you give them a little food when they first begin to flower in midsummer, that will encourage additional flowering. The only pest that has bothered them in our garden is the Japanese beetle. I do find it annoying that the old crape myrtle that was here in the yard needs pruning at its base several times during the growing season to remove the generous supply of suckers. I'm grateful that the dwarf varieties do not have the same propensity.

The list of valuable and attractive deciduous shrubs is lengthy. In addition to the genera mentioned, there are also a number of other shrubs, like fothergillas, that are rare and difficult to obtain, or slightly peculiar ones, like Harry Lauder's walking stick, *Corylus avellana* 'Contorta' or *Cornus alba* 'Sibirica', that we may select for a particular location. The corylus is a shrub every flower arranger will want to plant and cut for its contorted branches, and the cornus produces interesting vivid red stems in wintertime.

As with the evergreen shrubs, we are sure to see more and more attractive deciduous shrubs of quality coming on the market each year. I treasure much of the old material and look forward to trying new and different shrubs in my yard in the years ahead.

5

Azaleas, Rhododendrons, and Camellias

If there is one plant that epitomizes spring in the South, it is the azalea. Even nongardeners have at least a few 'Hinode Giri' or 'Coral Bells' azaleas near their front doors. Thousands of visitors attend azalea festivals in Wilmington, North Carolina; Norfolk, Virginia; Mobile, Alabama; and a host of other southern cities. Callaway Gardens at Pine Mountain, Georgia, is famous for its 20-acre network of azalea trails with more than 700 different species and cultivars on display. The three great plantation gardens of Charleston, South Carolina (Magnolia Gardens, Cypress Gardens, and Middleton Place Gardens), are at their floriferous best in early April, when the peak of azalea bloom occurs. For a few weeks, azaleas color the world.

Knowledgeable gardeners have discovered that those weeks of bloom can be extended into several months of flowering by careful selection of azalea species and cultivars. In fact, we can plan an extended season in two types of azaleas, both the evergreen and the deciduous.

Evergreen azaleas were introduced into the United States from Asia in the early 1800s. The first Southern Indian hybrids (Indicas) were displayed at Magnolia Gardens near Charleston, South Carolina, in 1840. They have large, showy flowers and are hardy for the Deep South, but very marginal in zone 7. For example, a number of us have 'George Lindley Tabor', the hardiest of the Indicas, planted in our Piedmont gardens, but it never makes the abundant show of those handsome, white-blushed, lavender-pink flowers with their magenta blotches that it puts on in Charleston. The buds are frequently blasted by a frost, and during our worst winter, the plants in my garden went to the ground and one of five died.

Most deciduous types, however, are American natives, from the hills, woodlands, and swamps of the southeastern United States. Like the prophet who receives little respect in his own hometown, deciduous azaleas have not received much attention until recently, when the whole gardening community has become aware of the possibilities and delights of gardening with native plants. Many of these natives are wonderfully fragrant and all of them produce spectacular flowers. By careful selection of species and hybrids, we can have native azaleas flowering in our yards from late March until September.

Natives are also more shade tolerant than the evergreen azaleas, a boon to those of us who are developing woodland gardens. In fact, azalea expert Fred Galle says that those deciduous azaleas that bloom after Memorial Day must have some shade.

Galle, who retired from Callaway Gardens in the early 1980s after working with plants for thirty years there, is knowledgeable about and interested in the entire world of plants, but he is particularly involved with azaleas, both natives and evergreen hybrids.

In retirement, he completed what is truly a magnum opus, *Azaleas*, which will be the definitive book on these flowering plants for many years to come.

Much of what I know about deciduous azaleas, I learned from Fred Galle. In one lecture I attended, he sorted out the seventeen species by sequence of bloom, which is a useful way of looking at them, I think.

In order to comprehend the names, please understand that rhododendrons and azaleas are closely related. In fact, all azaleas are rhododendrons, but not all rhododendrons are azaleas. Some botanists have wanted azaleas to have their own genus, but at present, all are in the genus *Rhododendron*. This genus belongs to the botanical family *Ericaceae*, so you will often see these plants—along with blueberries, heaths, trailing arbutus, mountain laurel, and a large number of other plants, referred to as ericaceous plants.

Our Piedmont azalea, *Rhododendron canescens*, is usually the first to flower in late March or early April, depending on the year and on the geographic location. Its fragrant flowers may range in color from clear white to deep pink. It is not a stoloniferous plant producing runners, but some stoloniferous forms have been found, probably natural hybrids with other wild azaleas.

In fact, it is this tendency of wild azaleas to interbreed with one another that really challenges the botanists when it comes to identifying the different species. At any time during the flowering season, several species of azaleas may be in bloom and hybridizing with one another.

Things really get complicated when we have what Galle describes as a "telescoping" season, an unusual spring when many of the species are in

A *Rhododendron austrinum* hybrid   *Rhododendron alabamense*

Rhododendron speciosum   *Rhododendron bakeri*, a selection with narrow petals

A deciduous hybrid of unproven parentage (all photographs on this page by Fred Galle)

Top and bottom: *Rhododendron prunifolium* flowering in July
in Georgia. *Center*: A pastel form of the vivid plum leaf azalea.

bloom at the same time and can therefore cross-pollinate. Sorting out the species and their natural hybrids is a job for the experts.

Blooming at the same time as the Piedmont azalea is *R. austrinum* (the Florida azalea). While the typical color of this fragrant species is a rich golden yellow, it can be quite variable. One desirable selection is 'Millie Mac', whose yellow bloom edged in white carries long, pink anthers and stamens and has pink on the outside of the flower neck. Another deciduous azalea I admire is 'My Mary', a low, fragrant, light-yellow austrinum hybrid. This was developed by the late George Beasley, innovative breeder of deciduous azaleas at Transplant Nursery in Lavonia, Georgia. This choice hybrid was named for his wife Mary, who now carries on the business with her son Jeff and family.

At Callaway Gardens, the next azalea to flower is the Alabama azalea (*R. alabamense*). This native is a low (3-to-6-feet high), stoloniferous plant. It is another fragrant, variable azalea with flowers from white through tints of pink. The most luscious color form I have seen was a white flower on which each petal was tipped with pink.

The Oconee azalea (*R. speciosum*) flowers just before or along with the Alabama azalea. Some springs, all four of the species mentioned are in bloom at the same time, and they all hybridize readily with one another—a taxonomic nightmare. We gardeners can just reap the benefits and enjoy the color combinations and other genetic blendings.

While the nonfragrant salmon, pink, or yellow flowers of the Oconee azalea occur naturally only in woodlands in a 50-mile-wide band that stretches through Georgia and into South Carolina, as a cultivated shrub, this native azalea does well throughout most of the South.

The coastal azalea (*R. atlanticum*), native from Delaware to South Carolina, has white flowers that are wonderfully fragrant. It is low growing and extremely stoloniferous—one plant, typically, could fill a room. Supposedly somewhere in the sandy soils of New Jersey there is one coastal azalea plant that covers more than an acre. Obviously it is not the azalea to plant in a narrow bed near the front door, but if you do have wooded acres, it's worth giving *R. atlanticum* its space for the wonderful flowers and fragrance. It is usually not as vigorous in heavier soils. Also, it and all the other stoloniferous azaleas and other shrubs can be controlled by root pruning—cutting off the stolons with your spade once or twice a year.

Rhododendron vaseyi (the pink-shell azalea) is a North Carolina native, found not near the coast but in the mountains. It has adapted to cultivation nicely and grows happily in many gardens. It is another of the deliciously fragrant azaleas, and the flowers are unique—each pink flower has a very short tube, and the petals are split almost to the calyx, giving the appearance of separate petals. I was surprised and delighted to discover *R. vaseyi* flowering in our woods the first spring we were in our house. It creates a tall cloud of pink behind some evergreen shrubs. A white form of this plant, called 'White Find', is also on the market.

The pinxterbloom azalea (*R. periclymenoides* [syn. *R. nudiflorum*]), a medium-tall shrub that is native over a very wide range from New England to the South, carries slightly fragrant white or pink flowers. Jim Darden, author of *Great American Azaleas*, notes that it is the best and most spectacular deciduous azalea for the coastal plains.

Rhodora (*R. canadense*) is one American native we are not apt to grow. It is the plant that gives that lovely springtime flicker of pink to the edge of the pine woodlands as you drive on the byways of Maine. Native from Labrador to New Jersey, rhodora prefers a colder climate than we can offer here.

The flame azalea (*R. candulaceum*), which thrives in the South, is the most spectacular of all. Because it is a natural tetraploid, having twice the number of chromosomes as the other species, its flowers are larger than other native azaleas. And its color range is very rich—orange, yellow, scarlet, deep red, apricot, and many shades in between. The flame azalea is upright, tall, nonstoloniferous, and nonfragrant. It flowers in May or early June.

Blooming at the same time is the sweet azalea (*R. arborescens*). Galle describes this shrub as the best of the native white azaleas. Its fragrance is much like heliotrope, one of the strong scents that gardeners seem to love or to loathe. If you plant this upright, white azalea, note that it comes from streamside locations, not from dry hillsides, so be sure to put it in an area you will keep well watered.

The sweet azalea often hybridizes with *R. viscosum* (the swamp azalea). As you would guess from its common name, this low, stoloniferous native really likes to have damp feet, but it does adapt to average garden soil. Although usually white, some pink and even yellow forms have been found among its hybrids.

If you want to extend the azalea flowering season even longer in your garden, add a Cumberland azalea (*R. bakeri*). At Callaway, the Cumberland azalea flowers in early July with small versions of the richly colored flame azalea blossoms. Latest of all azaleas in the Callaway collection is the plum-leaf azalea (*R. prunifolium*), which displays its orange to red flowers in July and August. Occasionally individual plants bloom as late as October.

You probably will find a few of these native species of azalea in your local nurseries. Our recent resurgence of interest in native plants has included these shrubs, so today a number of nurseries that would not have carried any deciduous native azaleas in the past may have *R. vayesi* or *R. candula-*

ceum along with their Exbury hybrids or seedlings. The more unusual species, you will have to order by mail.

Handle them as you would evergreen azaleas. Dig generous holes, supplement your soil with liberal amounts of rich organic material like compost or leaf mold, *plant high*, mulch well, and keep the plants particularly well watered during the first year while they are getting established.

Then luxuriate in the long season of azalea bloom you will have created. Deciduous azaleas can delight you from early spring until fall. I don't mean to suggest that our native species are the only deciduous azaleas to grow. Some fine hybrids, like the Knap Hill and the Exbury series, were developed in England. The vivid orange 'Gibraltar' is probably the most famous and popular Exbury, but there are a number of other fine ones.

If you want to propagate your own, remember that the deciduous azaleas are easy from seed, generally difficult from cuttings.

The evergreen azaleas, on the other hand, are quite easy from cuttings. Expert propagators have put roots on these cuttings any time of year. We amateurs should do it at the most opportune time of the year, which is dur-

Evergreen azaleas decorating the southern landscape at Magnolia Gardens in South Carolina

ing mid-to-late summer. The early blooming types are ready first, as you might guess. The ideal cutting is taken when the branch is on its way from lush new growth to woody material. It will not bend in your fingers, it will snap, and you can feel the fat little promise of the new flower bud at the tip end, which you will pinch off as you stick the cutting.

The term "evergreen" is a general one. As Galle puts it, azaleas "often straddle the fence." A number of azaleas are evergreen in hot areas and deciduous in cooler climates, like many of our herbaceous perennials.

As with native azaleas, you can have a considerably extended season of bloom with hybrid azaleas by selecting different evergreens to plant. The first to flower are the prolific, small-flowered Kurumes, the most commonly grown azaleas here in the Piedmont. The group includes 'Hinode Giri', probably the most widely planted red azalea in the country; 'Hershey Red' and 'Hino Crimson', two other popular reds; 'Pink Pearl', grown since the 1800s in Japan; 'Coral Bells', the pink azalea in almost every southern yard; 'Sherwood Red', more of an orange-red than 'Hinode Giri'; 'Old Ivory', a hose-in-hose, creamy flower; 'Snow', the most common white, which has the unfortunate habit of clinging to its spent flowers as they brown, and many others.

As the earliest azaleas are beginning to fade, you can have some of the midseason shrubs coming into flower. The Southern Indicas are in this group of azaleas. While they are risky here in the Piedmont, they are more and more reliable the farther south you garden. Be sure to plant some if you are gardening in zone 8. Light pink 'Pride of Mobile' is one of the more bud-hardy in the group. I've already mentioned that I like 'George Lindley Tabor'. Pale pink 'Duchess of Cypress', with its wine-colored splotch, and late-flowering 'Criterion', with violet-red flowers edged with white and carrying a deep wine blotch, are also both handsome plants.

Most of the Glen Dale group of hybrids, too, are considered midseason. B. Y. Morrison developed the Glen Dale hybrids while he was working for the U.S. Department of Agriculture at the Glen Dale station in Maryland. He was seeking large-flowered azaleas that would be hardy as far north as Washington, D.C. His was the most extensive breeding program the country has ever seen. Galle faults him in only one way. He named and introduced too many of his progeny—roughly 500. Only a small percentage of those Glen Dale hybrids are now on the market. Galle feels that 'Glacier' is the most important in this group. 'Glacier' provides a good white flower blooming right after 'Snow', and it is also noteworthy because of lush and vigorous summer foliage, followed by excellent fall foliage color. I like 'Copperman', with its coppery orange-red flowers, if it is planted far away from the many pink cultivars.

A mature planting of evergreen azaleas used informally along a woodland path

Pericat hybrids, developed for greenhouse growing by Alphonse Pericat of Collingdale, Pennsylvania, are also fine plants for zones 7 and 8. When I omitted mention of this group of cultivars in a newspaper story, a nurseryman wrote to tell me that he feels that purplish pink 'Madame Alphonse Pericat', with its dark blotch, 'Pericat Salmon', and double, deep pink 'Pinnochio' are well worth growing here.

The Back Acres hybrids were developed by Morrison, originator of the Glen Dale azaleas, after his retirement from the U.S. Department of Agriculture. As Jim Darden says in *Great American Azaleas*, "The Back Acre azaleas produce some of the most fantastic and astounding color combinations ever seen." This group of midseason to late azaleas thrives in our summer heat and humidity. One called 'Debonaire', with a light pink center and deeper pink edges, is luscious.

Satsuki and Robin Hill cultivars are even later varieties we can plant to extend the season. Azalea hobbyists generally are very enthusiastic about the Robin Hill azaleas. Breeder Robert Gartrell developed some lovely soft pastels in his hybrids. 'Nancy of Robin Hill' and 'Watchett' are two particularly beautiful varieties. The latter is a luscious, soft, yellowish pink.

If your taste runs to the miniature, seek out 'Wild Time', a hybrid from *R*.

linearifolium, a Japanese species. It is a good pot plant or rock garden specimen, wider than high, covered with light pink flowers, each less than ¼ inch in size. A white form is also available.

Polly Hill of Massachusetts developed and introduced the North Tisbury hybrids, low ground covers that may grow 18 inches high and 6 to 8 feet wide in twenty years.

Thirty years ago, hybridizers at Beltsville, Maryland, carried out a breeding program aimed at developing small azaleas, and they introduced a group called the Beltsville Dwarf Azaleas. Galle says that at the time, Americans were not ready for dwarfs. The only market then was for large flowers. Tastes, times, and garden sizes have changed. Many of us now are interested in dwarf plants, and Galle finds them charming. He keeps pots of 'White Nymph', 'Pink Elf', 'Salmon Elf', and 'Snow Drop' outside until after Christmas. Then he brings them in for indoor flowers before the outdoor garden begins to bloom.

Relatively new on the market are azaleas for hanging baskets. 'Pink Cascade' is just that, a wonderful flow of flowers tumbling 4 feet below a basket. We cannot expect to winter these varieties hanging on our eaves. Take them down, and heavily mulch the pots. Here in zone 7, I suspect we would do better to store the pots in a cold frame for the winter.

While I have touched on the major groups of azaleas, there are a number of minor groups and literally hundreds and hundreds of varieties on the market. If you are seriously interested in these plants, I would urge you to invest in Galle's book. For beginners, the Darden large format paperback, with its many pages of color photographs, offers a good introduction to many of the cultivars.

When you are planning to plant any azaleas, have a soil test taken, just as you would for a lawn area or a vegetable garden. Azaleas, rhododendrons, and camellias all prefer acid soil, which is seldom a problem in this part of the country, where much of the ground is acid. If your reading is higher than a pH of 6, the testing laboratory will recommend that you acidify the soil by adding sulphur.

When you take any containerized plant out of its pot and put it in the ground, it is wise to score the sides of the root ball to cut any encircling roots and to encourage new, fine feeder roots to form. When planting azaleas, Bob Welshmer introduced me to butterflying. He takes the plant out of the can and, from the bottom of the root ball, he cuts upward about two-thirds of the way, dividing that ball into halves, which he spreads or "butterflys" and plants. Azaleas are shallow rooted and this system works very well, as his beautiful garden attests.

Watering and mulching are very important in the first year or two. Our old established plants that have been in our woods for more than fifteen

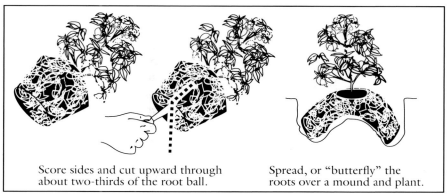

Score sides and cut upward through about two-thirds of the root ball.

Spread, or "butterfly" the roots over a mound and plant.

Butterflying an azalea

years receive no water other than our limited rainfall, and they thrive and bloom. New ones will wilt and die if not watered regularly.

If you are new to the South, you may have to change some of your ideas about watering. Here, it is often necessary to water our gardens in midwinter—an unheard-of practice in Massachusetts or Minnesota. Learn to monitor your garden. If you have had several weeks of mild weather without rain, even if it is December or January, it is time to get out the hose and thoroughly soak your garden, paying particular attention to newly planted trees, shrubs, and perennials. During our two devastating winters of 1983–84 and 1984–85, gardeners who had watered their plants before the sudden drop in temperature lost very few plants.

Water, too, can be a tool to save blossoms threatened by a late frost. I first saw this technique used by a California orchid grower in Santa Cruz who turned on his sprinklers when his blooming cymbidium crop was threatened by frost. Here, an azalea hobbyist uses water to protect his azalea buds. The trick is to leave the sprinklers on all night, letting a coating of ice build up on the plants. During the next day, the ice will melt and the buds will be unharmed.

I water newly planted shrubs in with a dilute solution of water-soluble fertilizer. Old, established plants get a liberal feeding of 10-10-10 in late February or early March. I am overly generous because our shrubs are growing in heavy competition with tree roots. In a garden with a rich loam bed, your azaleas may need little or no feeding. Galle emphasizes that more azaleas are killed by overfeeding than by lack of fertilizer. The same is true for rhododendrons and camellias.

In a garden setting, you will probably want to prune your azaleas to keep them in scale with the other plantings. Prune either while in flower (enjoy the branches in the house and share with friends) or immediately afterward.

If you wait until later in the season, you will cut off the flower buds for the following year. I prune the azaleas around the small garden pool behind the house, but I allow those in the woods to grow without constraint. There, I only remove damaged branches. Whatever you do, don't chop your azaleas into little boxes or balls. Gardeners who butcher these shrubs in this manner lose most of the bloom and all of the charm of their azaleas.

Containerized plants can be planted and evergreen azaleas can be transplanted any time from midfall until midspring. More and more, the nursery industry in the South is trying to persuade the gardening public to do the bulk of their planting in the fall, so that all plants are very well established before the next summer's heat wave. However, azaleas are among the most flexible of our plants, and sometimes it is helpful to purchase them in flower to make the appropriate color designs in your garden. The orange varieties really clash with the pinks. The later in the spring that you plant any tree, shrub, or perennial, the more attention you must give to regular watering that summer.

The deciduous azaleas should only be transplanted while dormant, during the winter months.

If you are looking for compatible small trees to plant with your azaleas, remember cut-leaf Japanese maples. Maples and azaleas are very attractive together, and they will both thrive in light shade or filtered sunlight. I notice that a number of southern retail and wholesale nurseries grow their collections of containerized azaleas, rhododendrons, Japanese maples, and camellias beneath carefully spaced, tall, deep-rooted pine trees.

However, while azaleas and camellias are thoroughly southern plants, well adapted to our heat, rhododendrons thrive in cool, moist climes. Most of the country's rhododendron nurseries, hobbyists, and display gardens are in the Northwest, the misty, coastal areas of Washington and Oregon. Our southern mountains are good growing areas for rhododendrons. A number of fine growers, like Dr. John L. Creech, former director of the National Arboretum, have chosen to retire and grow their rhododendrons in the cool mountain area of North Carolina, near Asheville and Hendersonville. But the lower sections of the South are somewhat hostile growing areas for rhododendrons. Some research suggests that it is the hot, humid nights that cause more of our summertime garden problems than the terribly hot days.

Nonetheless, many southerners attempt to have rhododendrons in our gardens and rhodies are on display in public gardens as far south as Atlanta, Mobile, and Birmingham. I understand why a Connecticut gardening friend sneered at our runty 'Scintillation'—his is almost three times the height and five times more luxuriant. Still, I love the sparkling, crystalline pink flowers of 'Scintillation', and I treasure every truss.

If you are determined to grow some rhododendrons in zones 7 and 8, then try to find out which varieties are most successful in your area. Visit the gardens of local collectors and public plantings. Join the nearest chapter of the American Rhododendron Society. We do have a few southern chapters: one in Georgia, two in Alabama, one in Virginia, and one in South Carolina, in addition to the Piedmont chapter, which is based in Charlotte, North Carolina. (Contrast those numbers with the sixteen chapters in Washington and Oregon.) Attend a show and see which cultivars are on display.

When we first moved here, we met a gentleman who had been growing rhododendrons for thirty years or more in this area. He had failed with a number of varieties, but he recommended 'Boule de Neige', 'Mars', 'The Honorable Jean Marie de Montagu', 'Dr. Stocker', 'Nova Zembla', 'Anna Rose Whitney', and 'Vulcan' as particularly good candidates for the Piedmont. I already knew that 'Roseum Elegans' would thrive, because there was a large one that was at least fifteen years old growing in our yard. (Jim Darden notes that 'Roseum Elegans' and its sports are the only varieties that will endure the heat in our sandy coastal soils.) We have added old, reliable 'P.J.M.', desirable for its compact size, early blooms, and floriferousness. A number of southern gardeners have told me that *R. yakusimanum* and its hybrids are resilient rhododendrons for the South. Since it is one of the most beautiful species, I'm happy to plant yaks.

Summer stress seems to be the problem, when raising rhododendrons in the South. Stress causes many people to have a higher than normal blood pressure, which in turn leaves them more vulnerable to strokes, heart attacks, and related problems. Stress is just as damaging to plants, and rhododendrons seem to be among the most affected plants. When we have weeks of heat in the nineties, no rain, and then a storm, pathogens seem to flourish in our rhododendrons.

Sometimes we have a rhododendron with a branch or two covered with drooping, dying leaves. Pruning the shrub back to good, healthy, white wood is the recommended treatment for the occasional branch succumbing to this dieback.

However, if the entire plant droops, although well watered, suspect root rot, most commonly caused by fungus *Phytophthora cinnamomi*. This fungus, which affects camellias and a number of other woody plants, can be devastating to rhododendrons. If you suspect its presence, you can verify your suspicions by scraping through the bark just above the soil line, using your fingernail or the tip of a knife. If the tissue under the bark is brown or reddish brown instead of healthy white, the plant is a victim of root rot and ready to be discarded. (Don't scrape unless you are quite sure the plant is headed for the trash heap, however. Any wound leaves a healthy plant vulnerable to fungus problems.)

The reliable and floriferous *Rhododendron* 'Roseum Elegans'—perhaps the best rhododendron for the South

While it is perfectly safe to replant in a hole from which you have removed a plant with dieback, it's undesirable to plant a rhododendron into the ground from which you removed a phytophthora-infected plant. The soil will still contain spores of that fungus, which may or may not attack the next plant.

Those of us who have a rhododendron stricken with root rot would like to have a fungicide that would cure the diseased plant. Unfortunately, to date no such product is on the market. However, in the 1980s, some expensive but effective preventative fungicides, like Aliette and Subdue, have become available. Many rhododendron hobbyists are using Subdue, which is available in reasonably small packages. Aliette is not yet available for home gardeners. Dr. Michael Benson, a scientist at North Carolina State University who has done considerable research on the subject of root rots and fungicides, says, "In the South, the fungus survives and lives in the soil. The same fungus can be killed further north, if the soil freezes. Chemicals like Aliette and Subdue prevent the growth and development of the pathogen. They do not kill it. The roots are still infected. The symptoms go away."

He noted that these products are much more feasible for use in a nursery full of container plants than in a home garden where the plants are grown in the ground. "If you introduce an infected plant to your site, you will always have the pathogen," he said.

Otherwise, the best thing we can do for our rhododendrons is to provide good drainage. Every expert, every nurseryman, every garden writer will say "plant high." Don't just dig a large hole and amend the soil—literally plant the rhododendron higher than the surrounding soil.

I thought we were planting our ericacious shrubs high until I visited a rhododendron nursery an hour south of here. The rows of plants looked as if they were set on top of the ground. They were growing in huge mounds of soil and were watered with a drip irrigation system. The appearance was totally unaesthetic, but the nurseryman was not losing many plants to fungus problems.

Planting your rhododendrons in raised beds is one solution to the drainage problem. If that is impossible, plant your shrubs high—what seems absurdly high to anyone who has gardened in northern states. Then mulch well.

Experience has taught me that frequently small plants I have started from seed adapt better to my garden, my culture, than older, purchased plants, so I am experimenting with rhododendron seedlings. While I know it may take ten years or more for rhododendrons to bloom from seed, if one starts a few each year, then after the first ones begin to bloom, the production line is rolling, and each year should provide more flowering shrubs. I was thrilled when my first rhododendron seedling bloomed in the spring of 1987. Two little plants of *R. keiskei* 'Yaku Fairy', started in 1983, produced a few pale yellow blooms. They are small plants, intended for the rock garden. Other rhododendrons, both species and hand-pollinated crosses, are being planted out along the woodland trails. If this long-range project entices you, join the American Rhododendron Society. The seed list alone is worth the price of membership.

Barry Starling, one of England's most expert nurserymen and a specialist in ericaceous plants, told me how he pricks out his rhododendron seedlings. If I have space to grow only twenty-five plants of one cross, I usually select the largest and sturdiest of the seedlings and discard the rest. Starling deliberately takes a few of the largest, some of the middle-sized, and some of the weakest ones in the pot. The genetic diversity is increased by selecting both strong and puny seedlings from each cross. "My finest hybrid and introduction came from one of those weak seedlings," Starling said.

I laugh when I look at the extremes we go to, in order to raise a few rhododendrons here. I remember visiting a hobbyist in Scotland who was able to plant his hillside with rhododendrons and literally never water them again. Perfect climate, perfect conditions. Nearby, on that same trip, we also visited Peter Cox's nursery, full of rare and extraordinary rhododendrons. If you are interested in these plants, you will want to own his books, *Dwarf Rhododendrons* and *The Larger Species of Rhododendron*. Cox, among others, has been visiting and revisiting China since that country opened its gates to tourists and botanists during the past few years. He has been collecting new species and recollecting old ones that have been lost to cultivation since earlier plant hunters, like Kingdon Ward and George Forrest, collected them. China is a rhododendron paradise: many of the more than 800 species come from that part of the world.

Cox's books are excellent because they are written from hands-on experience, not just from library and herbarium research. He teaches readers a great deal about the native habitats of the species, and this sort of information usually helps us cultivate the species and their hybrids. While Cox's misty Scottish hillside is ideal for rhododendron culture, many of us will continue to raise rhododendrons in the South, in our far-from-ideal conditions. We will plant them in rich, humusy, acid soil, with the best drainage we can provide.

Some camellias, orchids, bamboos, and rhododendrons grow together in the same Asiatic meadows. While the rhododendrons are spring flowering, the camellias provide color and beauty with their fall and winter blooms. We who want twelve-month gardens treasure camellias here. Like the azaleas and rhododendrons, the camellias are shallow rooted and easy to transplant, and they prefer an enriched, friable, acid soil. They also need excellent drainage.

However, and it is a *big* however, the camellias are not as cold hardy as most azaleas. While many Piedmont gardens had old camellias that had bloomed for many years, most of those shrubs were damaged in the winter of 1983–84. Gardeners all were shocked by the number of plants we considered to be hardy that were killed or damaged that year. We were not alone. Gardens throughout the South had injured plants. At Bellingrath Gardens in Mobile, some camellias were damaged and some of the most tender azaleas were killed. Drayton Hastie of Magnolia Plantation and Gardens in Charleston, South Carolina, also lost some azaleas and camellias. Many of the 900 different varieties of camellias there went to the ground in the freeze but came back and were magnificent two years later.

Never mind. That sudden drop in temperature was a once-in-a-century event, said horticulture professors and garden writers, myself included. Surprise! The same disaster struck the following January, killing or damaging many of those plants that had survived the year before. For example, in Durham, North Carolina, the temperature went to $-9°$—the coldest night of the century. Almost all camellias went to the ground.

That second spring, I heard more gardeners say that they would never plant another camellia. However, clichés ring true—hope does spring eternal, and in a year or two, many of us were back planting camellias for their winter beauty.

One University of North Carolina botanist, Dr. Clifford Parks, has been pursuing his hobby of breeding camellias for cold hardiness for more than thirty years. After he looked at the hundreds of seedlings that had died to the ground that second disastrous winter, he decided to emphasize the positive and continue breeding with the hardy ones that survived.

"Don't give up on the broad-leafed evergreens," is his message to all gardeners. If these plants have a chance to harden off, they will survive considerable cold without damage. Parks referred to a period with a temperature of $-1°$ in 1977 that didn't hurt his camellia collection, because it followed weeks of cold weather. It's the freezing zap to succulent, growing tissues that does the damage.

He began his hybridization work by crossing the hardiest forms of cultivated *C. japonica*. He notes that the entire group of cultivated *C. japonica* is not very hardy. Interestingly enough, some of the Asian native species forms are hardier. Wild species collected from the northern border of South Korea are particularly hardy. Some of his crosses, using these wildlings as parents, did the best in his local plantings. 'William Lanier Hunt' and 'Yoi Machi' are particularly fine Parks introductions.

During recent years, Parks has had considerable contact with Chinese botanists. Some Chinese experts visited Chapel Hill, and in 1985, Parks went to China. The exchange of information and plant material continues. Some Chinese camellia species may offer hardiness characteristics to his breeding program.

Parks has already experimented with one Chinese species, *C. oleifera*, crossing it with *C. Sasanqua*. This Chinese species, with its little, white flowers, is grown on plantations as an oil-producing plant in locations as far north as the Yangtze River. The hybrid is intermediate in hardiness and in flower size. Parks says that he needs to select among the seedlings of several future generations in order to get larger flowers and still maintain the hardiness.

Another Chinese species, *C. Chekiangoleosa*, comes from a fairly cold area, and Chinese botanists think that it has excellent possibilities for Parks's breeding program. In 1985 he only had seeds of this species, so it will be a number of years before he sees any breeding results.

Of course every plant breeder has several goals in mind. Not only is Parks trying to attain cold-hardy camellias, but he is also extremely interested in flower size, flower color, disease resistance, and hybrid vigor. As he selects among his thousands of seedlings each year, he is looking for plants that are better in several different ways.

He is growing fifty of the approximately 200 different camellia species extant in the world. Many of these species are too tender to survive outdoors in Chapel Hill and are grown only in the greenhouse. Perhaps the most exciting one he is working with is a Chinese species with a bright yellow flower. With the appropriate crosses and enough generations of selected seedlings, yellow camellias eventually will become available here in the States—a real breeding breakthrough.

To give you an idea of the time involved in camellia breeding, Parks gets his first blooms from a seedling in four years, if it has been grown under good conditions. Those that he plants out in the woods may take up to eight years to flower. However, by grafting the seedlings, he can speed things up and produce flowers in just two years. Space and time are always limiting factors in this painstaking process. The same principle applies to all plant breeding. Professionals have developed techniques to speed up flowering for roses, orchids, rhododendrons, and a number of other plants. The most keen hobbyists can adopt these propagation methods. Most of us, lacking greenhouses, costly light setups, sterile laminar airflow chambers, and so on, do it the old-fashioned way. We root a cutting or start a seed and then let nature take its course, using reasonable garden culture.

If you read the American Rhododendron Society or the American

Camellia chrysantha, a rare yellow camellia from China that offers great promise for generations of lovely yellow camellias to come

Camellia Society bulletins, you become aware that hybridizers are working at both extremes. Some are trying to develop cold-hardy plants (for example, breeders at the University of Minnesota have developed a beautiful series of hardy deciduous azaleas called 'Northern Lights'); others are working to achieve heat-tolerant azaleas and rhododendrons. Like Cliff Parks, Dr. William Ackerman at the U.S. Department of Agriculture in Beltsville, Maryland, is also breeding for cold tolerance in camellias. Fragrance is another goal for him. His best to date are 'Ack-Scent', 'Frost Prince', and 'Snow Flurry'.

The farther south one goes, the more camellias are successful evergreen shrubs for the landscape. They espalier easily—in California, our patio fence was decorated with informally espaliered japonicas. Other than this sort of specific training, camellias seldom need pruning. Shape your plants when you cut flowering branches for your home. Remove any damaged wood. The glossy foliage is attractive year-round, and the flowers are wonderful fall and winter decorations. I love the small-flowered sasanqua blooms that cover large shrubs near the library in our town in early fall.

However, for showy, large flowers, grow japonicas. When H. H. Hume wrote *Azaleas and Camellias* in 1930, he said, "Practically every specimen of

'Jessie Conner'

'Pink Dahlia'

'Margaret Davis Picotee'   Prizewinning show camellias

camellia throughout the country represents the species *Camellia japonica.*"
We have obviously made considerable progress during the past sixty years.
Some of us even grow *C. sinensis* (the tea plant). It makes an attractive
shrub with very small, white flowers.

To manipulate flowering time of camellia blooms, many gardeners "gibb"
their camellias. The most commonly recommended way to use gibberellic
acid on camellias is to break out the vegetative bud next to the flower bud.
Then put one drop of the chemical in the little cup that remains. Flowers
should appear in forty-to forty-five days. Plants vary. If you are a show

competitor and want to time this flower manipulation carefully, keep good records and in a few years, you will be able to schedule your camellia flowering quite accurately.

There are a number of pests and diseases that can bother camellias. Identify the problem and then use the appropriate treatment. Good sanitation, including keeping all the spent flowers picked up, is one of the best ways to minimize problems with petal blight. It's easy to be that neat if you have five camellia shrubs. If you have fifty, it's more of a problem.

Azaleas, rhododendrons, and camellias are not trouble-free shrubs for our gardens, but they are so spectacular in flower that I'm sure most of us want to incorporate all of these plants into our landscaping plans. Of these three large groups of flowering shrubs, the azaleas are by far the easiest plants to maintain, so if you can just plant one, let it be an azalea.

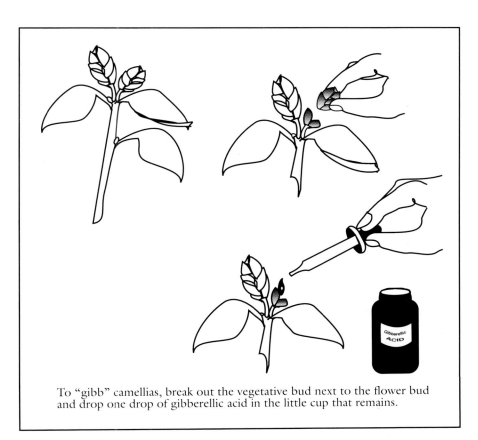

To "gibb" camellias, break out the vegetative bud next to the flower bud and drop one drop of gibberellic acid in the little cup that remains.

Gibbing a camellia

6

Lawn

Poets rarely wax rhapsodic about turf. No one ever wrote, "I think that I shall never see a poem as lovely as a lawn." No wit ever said, "Lawn is a lawn is a lawn is a lawn."

Lawns are not dramatic, exciting, or blatantly beautiful. But they can be lovely—a pleasure to look at and, yes, even to feel. They provide a serene flow of soothing green between house and garden, between garden and woods. Lawns offer a quiet contribution to the landscape, but one which should not be overlooked.

You can picnic on a lawn, play croquet or badminton, sunbathe, establish a children's play area, or practice your golf putts—all active pursuits. Or you can simply enjoy the calm serenity of plain green turf, interrupting and integrating a busy landscaping scene.

When we moved into our home in Chapel Hill, I looked at the front yard and immediately decided that I would eliminate the small lawn there and turn the area between the house and the woods into a rock garden.

Fortunately, I was too busy remodeling the inside of the house that first fall to carry out my landscaping impulses. By the time we had enjoyed our first Carolina spring, I could see great virtue in the simplicity of the lawn. It is a small, green area of turf, one my husband mows in less than fifteen minutes, but it provides a quiet flow between the colorful azaleas by the house, the luscious pink and white arches of the weeping crab apple trees, and the wild flower trails leading into the woods. Like the house, the old lawn needed renovation. Often the lawn at an older home has bald patches, weeds, and sometimes a thatch build-up.

Rather than buying an established house, as we did, perhaps you have built or purchased a brand new home. It needs a brand new lawn to go with it. Where do you begin?

Proper grading is the first step. The contractor will rough-grade the site

A serene Georgia zoysia lawn in July

first. Be sure that he grades the land so that it drains *away* from the house on all sides—there should be a 2–3 percent slope away from the building. Check also that irregularities (unnecessary high spots, abrupt changes in contour, or steep slopes) have been considered, and that building debris has not been buried.

After the rough grading, walk the land and check for low spots. It's helpful to wait until after a heavy rain, because then you can see how the land drains, where water collects and the ground does not drain well at all, or even where there are places that dry out unusually fast. If the drainage problem is severe, you may need to have some drainage pipe installed. For many years, contractors used clay pipe for downspout runoff and all drains. Today, almost universally, drainage construction is done with tough plastic tubing, available at any building supply store. Solid tubing is installed to carry water away from downspouts or window wells. For draining low spots or foundations, perforated tubing is used. All drainage tiles or tubing, laid in a gravel trench, should slope gently away from the house. It's much easier to do this sort of work in the beginning than to tear up an established yard later.

With all drainage problems resolved, the contractor will then do the fine grading, and you will be ready to install your lawn. Begin at the beginning.

Before you plant a sprig, spread grass seed, or lay sod, have your soil analyzed and learn just what amendments you should add.

If your topsoil was removed, you are left with only subsoil, and you want good turf, you will need to add a generous layer of organic material—compost, decayed sawdust, peat moss, manure, or even purchased topsoil—and mix it thoroughly into the top 6 inches. By using manure or topsoil, you will also introduce more weed seeds. If you water thoroughly and let them germinate, you can then control the weeds either by cultivation or by use of a nonspecific, postemergence herbicide like Roundup seven days before you plant the grass. There are many weed species like ragweed and smartweed that cannot survive constant mowing and will disappear as the lawn matures.

You may be facing that bare ground at a time of year when it is inappropriate to start your lawn. Rather than live with the mud or dust, you may choose to plant a temporary cover crop like clover or annual rye for one season and then plow that crop under several weeks before you start the lawn. In addition to slightly improving the soil, a cover crop provides soil stabilization and minimizes tracking mud into the house during those weeks between house construction and the installation of your lawn.

Spread the recommended amounts of fertilizer and lime over your yard and then rototill so these additives are thoroughly incorporated into the top 4–6 inches of soil. Experts recommend that all spreading, whether seeds, fertilizer, or lime, be done in a criss-cross pattern to achieve even distribution.

Hand-rake the area to provide an even surface of small (pea-sized to golf ball–sized) but not pulverized particles, ready to receive your seed, sod, or sprigs. (Pulverized particles will compact, reducing air and water percolation, and should be avoided.) It is important to do the same amount of preparation for sprigs or sod as for seed.

Then decide just which type of lawn you want. Southern gardeners living in the "transitional zone" have considerable choice among lawn grasses.

When we're talking about lawns and lawn grasses, North and South don't meet at the Mason-Dixon Line. They bump against one another and intermingle in a broad band that follows the line between climatic zones 7 and 8 as it squiggles its way across the hardiness map from Virginia, through the Piedmont of North Carolina, and west through South Carolina, Georgia, Alabama, Mississippi, Arkansas, and Texas.

There are no perfect lawns in this middle ground. Approximately half the homeowners raise lawns of northern, cool-season grasses like tall fescue and Kentucky bluegrass. These grasses do well most of the year, but suffer during the hot, dry summer months.

The other half of the homeowners use southern grasses—bermudagrass, centipedegrass, zoysiagrass or St. Augustinegrass—which thrive during the warm months but have trouble coping with winter frosts. The roots don't die, but the lawns brown off unattractively. With severe temperature drops, these grasses may even be killed.

In our area, we see mostly bermudagrass in sunny locations. Centipedegrass is used along the coast. St. Augustinegrass is usually found at the coast or in the deep South. At least one turf expert feels that we should be using a lot more zoysiagrass—attractive and generally easy to manage, although it can be difficult to mow.

My Michigan and Connecticut experiences were showing during that first April when I told my North Carolina newspaper readers that fall is the best time to rebuild a lawn. I soon learned from Dr. Arthur Bruneau, turf expert at North Carolina State University, that I was only half right. Fall *is* the best time to create or refurbish a lawn of northern grasses which grow best under cool conditions. The southern, warm-season grasses, however, should be planted in the spring, because their most active growth takes place from then on through the summer months.

In aiming for the near perfect lawn, or at least a thoroughly satisfactory one, Dr. Bruneau suggests that all homeowners should ask themselves three questions before planting:

1. *What is the environment and the purpose of that particular lawn?* Will you be growing grass in full sun or partial shade? Bermudagrass, for example, will not be satisfactory in shade. How much traffic will this lawn have to bear? Will it suffer wear and tear as a play area for the children? Will it be a lawn intended for occasional strolls, or a patch of green in a landscape design intended for viewing at a distance?

2. *What is your level of expectation?* Do you want a perfect turf? If so, K 31 tall fescue may not be the best choice for you, because it is rather coarse. If you compare your lawn to a well-maintained golf course, will you be satisfied with a good-looking rough, a handsome fairway surface, or nothing less than an elegant putting green? How do you feel about having your lawn brown from late fall until early spring? (Some homeowners have been known to spray a water-soluble dye on their brown, southern grass lawns green for those winter months.) A more common solution to the problem is to overseed a healthy bermudagrass with annual or perennial ryegrass for winter green. Overseeding should be done in zone 7 during the last two weeks of September, and farther south, a couple of weeks later.

3. *How much time, money and effort do you intend to spend on your lawn?* This is the most important question. While no lawn thrives on total ne-

glect, some grasses need much more care than others. Some homeowners select a hybrid bermudagrass turf, fine-textured and handsome, without realizing that it is a very high-maintenance lawn, demanding frequent feeding, watering, and mowing to stay healthy and attractive.

There's a fourth question which you should consider. Do you even want a lawn? At least two prominent plantsmen, Dr. August A. De Hertogh, head of the Department of Horticulture at North Carolina State University, and Frederick Garrett, director of the Landscape Gardening Program at the Sandhills Community College, chose to spread pine straw or bark in their yards in lieu of lawn, an attractive southern alternative. Obviously it's not necessary to plant grass—but probably most of us will opt for some sort of lawn.

I vividly remember a gardener in Detroit, Michigan, who delighted in maintaining a tiny lawn of bentgrass at putting-green perfection. To him, the constant, daily maintenance was worth it for the pleasure he derived from his small patch of perfect turf, which complemented his equally well-groomed rose garden.

Many homeowners want an attractive lawn but not a putting green, I suspect. Dr. Bruneau emphasized considering time, effort, and money because these factors should influence your lawn selection. The money we spend nationwide on creating and maintaining home lawns is astounding. Turf is a major industry in this country. In fertilizers alone, we Americans spend close to $1 billion a year on home lawn care. (This figure includes the professional lawn services.) In 1985, 56 million households participated in lawn care, and the industry estimates that this number has been growing at 10–15 percent a year. When you consider that in addition to fertilizer, lawn care also involves expenditures for fungicides, pesticides, herbicides, seed or plants, mowers, hand tools and in some situations, labor, you can see it is truly a big business—and home lawn care is less than half of the total turf maintenance costs. Golf course superintendents intensively manage their fairways and greens.

If you want an acceptable, low-maintenance lawn, you should choose tall fescue (a northern grass) or centipedegrass (southern). If you admire the attractive, fine-textured appearance of a bentgrass (northern) or hybrid bermudagrass (southern) lawn, be aware that it requires high maintenance. In addition to the necessary daily mowing with expensive equipment, bentgrass is also very susceptible to diseases.

Intended use is important. For example, soccer is popular in our area, as in many parts of the country. Another member of the faculty at North Carolina State University, Dr. Joseph DiPaola, has been trying to educate soccer field managers that southern playing fields, which have been planted in tall fescue, should be of bermudagrass. Bermudagrass can recover well during the summer, while fescue cannot—a characteristic to remember if you are designing a children's play yard.

Newcomers to the South are usually not familiar with the choices in southern grasses. If possible, visit your nearest turf patch display garden. Side-by-side comparisons will help you decide which lawn grasses you find most attractive.

Lawn Grasses for Zones 7 and 8

Grass	Durability	Sun or Shade	Blade Type	Pests or Diseases	Drought Tolerance	Mowing	Height Required
Southern Grasses							
Centipedegrass	poor	sun to light shade	coarse		good	infrequent	1″
Zoysiagrass	good	sun to light shade	fine		high	less than bermuda	.75″
St. Augustinegrass (tolerant of salt spray)	moderate to poor	sun or shade	coarse	many pests	good	moderate	2″
Bahiagrass	good	sun to light shade	fairly coarse		high	moderate	1.5–3.5″
Bermudagrass	excellent	best in sun	coarse		high	frequent	.75–1″
Bermudagrass cultivars	excellent		finer		high	frequent	.75″
Northern Grasses							
Tall fescue	very good	tolerates some shade	medium to coarse	brown patch	good	frequent	2.5–3.5″
Mix of tall fescue and Kentucky bluegrass	very good	shade tolerant	medium to coarse		good	frequent	2.5–3.5″

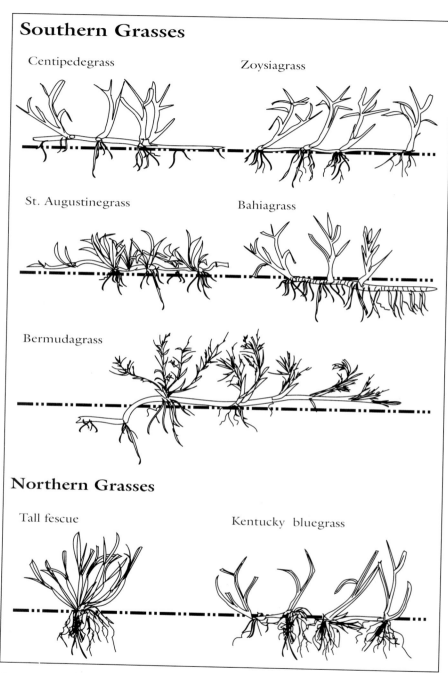

Southern Grasses

Centipedegrass

Zoysiagrass

St. Augustinegrass

Bahiagrass

Bermudagrass

Northern Grasses

Tall fescue

Kentucky bluegrass

Seven grasses for lawns in the South

If you choose a lawn of cool-season grasses, use a blend of tall fescue and Kentucky bluegrass seed in a five-to-one weight ratio. This recommendation comes out of research on tall fescues done at North Carolina State University by Drs. Joseph DiPaola and William Gilbert. Tall fescue grows as clumps and does not spread, which is why the addition of a small percentage of Kentucky bluegrass—a spreader—is recommended to fill any spaces left between the clumps of tall fescue. For a planting in partial shade, Bruneau also suggested adding a small amount (1 pound per 1,000 square feet) of fine fescue seed to the mix.

Two cultivars of Kentucky bluegrass are widely available, 'Kenblue' and 'Glade'. The latter is a bit more shade tolerant, so it is the bluegrass of choice for lawn areas that get some shade. Several other shade-tolerant cultivars are on the market.

K 31 is the standard tall fescue. It has been in use for years and is a proven performer. 'Rebel', 'Falcon', and 'Olympic' are three of several new hybrid, turf-type, tall fescues, and being deeper rooted, they tend to be more heat and disease resistant than K 31. They also have finer blades and darker color, and produce a more attractive appearance. Newer, improved cultivars of all the grasses will continue to come on the market. (In 1987, the NCSU staff was evaluating more than 600 different cultivars in test sites, and similar research is going on at other universities with turf programs.)

If Dr. Bruneau were installing a tall fescue lawn today, he would blend equal parts of K 31 and one of the newest fescues, combining the old reliable with new promise, for a broad genetic base.

If you buy your seed varieties separately, it is important to seed the lawn one variety at a time. Otherwise it is impossible to mix them evenly and get a uniform distribution.

Rather than concocting our own seed mixes, most of us go to the garden center and purchase a ready-made blend. Before you buy any seed, read the package label, which lists the percentages of various grass seeds contained in the mix. Avoid those with annual ryegrass in the blend. Annual ryegrass germinates fast and grows quickly, but it will crowd out the better seedlings, and it will be short-lived.

After you have seeded the lawn, drag a rake lightly over the soil to help the seed make contact with the ground. It is not necessary to bury the seed deeply. If you are planting on a very exposed site or on a slope, a light mulch will help hold the seed in place until it germinates and becomes established. Rolling the lawn is not really necessary, but it is desirable.

If you are ready to seed a lawn and it rains, sometimes a crust forms. If so, go back and break up that crust with your rake before you seed.

Among the southern grasses, common bermudagrass and centipedegrass

U.S. Universities with Turf Programs

Department of Agronomy
Auburn University, Auburn, AL 36849

Department of Agronomy
University of Arkansas, Fayetteville, AR 72701

Agronomy Department
University of Georgia, Athens, GA 30602

Department of Agronomy
University of Kentucky, Lexington, KY 40546-0091

Department of Agronomy
Louisiana State University, Baton Rouge, LA 70803

Agronomy Department
PO Box 5446, Mississippi State University, Mississippi State, MS 39762

Department of Horticulture
University of Missouri, Columbia, MO 65211

Department of Horticultural Science
North Carolina State University, Raleigh, NC 27695

Agronomy Department
360 Ag Hall, Oklahoma State University, Stillwater, OK 74078

Department of Horticulture
Clemson University, Clemson, SC 29631

Ornamental Horticulture and Land Design
University of Tennessee, PO Box 1071, Knoxville, TN 37901-1071

Department of Soil and Crop Science
Texas A & M University, College Station, TX 77843

Department of Agronomy
Virginia Polytechnic Institute and State University, Blacksburg, VA 24060

are frequently established from seed. Hybrid bermudagrasses and the other southern grasses are usually sold as sprigs or sod plugs, and you plant them as you would any bedding plants. The closer the plants, the quicker the coverage.

Both southern and northern grasses are also available as sod, which is much more expensive but provides an instant lawn. It's easy to install—somewhat like rolling out a carpet. I learned this fact several years ago when, with no training or experience, I produced a small, creditable sod lawn beside a new patio at our home in Michigan.

Usually my husband handles such projects, but he was working crazy hours on a new job. I wanted a lawn, so I jumped in and attempted to do it. After preparing the soil, I bought a few rolls of sod and began. I learned that sod installation just takes patience and a sharp knife. Sod is a flexible medium. One can easily shape, trim, and patch. Butt the sod strip edges together for tight seams, and voilà, finished lawn!

Finished, but not established. Whether your new lawn is sodded, seeded, or sprigged, it needs regular, light, frequent watering until good growth begins. The ground should be kept constantly moist, because even an hour's drying can kill sensitive new seedlings. If yours is a seeding of northern grasses, be aware that the tall fescue will germinate in about ten days, while the bluegrass takes from fourteen to twenty-one days. Continue the light waterings until all the seed has germinated.

Once the seed has germinated, or the roots of the sprigs or sod have taken hold, the watering technique changes. Water less often and for a longer period of time, so penetration is deeper and thus more long lasting. Rule of thumb is to give a lawn an inch of water each week during the growing season to have a lush, vigorous lawn. If nature doesn't provide the rain, then man must provide the water. To check how long your sprinkler must run to provide an inch of rain, just set several cans within the sprinkling pattern and measure the contents with a ruler. It will take longer than you think. Water until runoff, allow percolation, and water again until you have applied the necessary amount.

If you water less often and mow high, you can allow your turf to go dormant during the summer. It will look unsightly, but will only need watering once every three weeks during our heat and drought period to survive.

Those gardeners who want to maintain lawn in lush growth should wait to water an established lawn until they see indications of wilt. Three signals are: a blue-green color, footprinting, and curling leaves. Above all, don't stand with a hose and lightly sprinkle. Roots will tend to come to the surface in search of water. You want to encourage them to go deep into the ground. Morning is the ideal time to water, with early afternoon a good second choice. Try to avoid late evening watering. Let the foliage dry before dark to minimize fungal problems. Working people cannot always do household chores at ideal times. If no members of the family are at home during the day, perhaps you might consider putting your sprinklers on a timer.

It is also important to feed the new lawn again four weeks after seeding, using a complete fertilizer like 10-10-10, at the rate of 10 pounds per 1,000 square feet.

All the preparation suggested for installing a new lawn applies to renovating a thin old lawn or one with some bare patches. Homeowners tend to think that they need to reseed each year. With good maintenance, reseeding should only be necessary every three to five years. If a lawn has declined, try to find out why. Is there too much shade? As small trees grow and mature, sunny yards often evolve into shade gardens. You may want to use a suitable ground cover in an area where you began with a lawn. Have you been keeping it too dry? Identify your problem and then remedy it. To repair the old lawn, spade up the bare soil to a depth of 4 inches and then go through the same steps of soil analysis, amending, raking, planting, watering, and feeding. Seed by hand.

Installation of the warm-season grasses is best done in the spring. Centipedegrass and common bermudagrass lawns are frequently created by seeding. The other varieties are vegetatively produced. "Sprigging" is a process that can be accomplished either by tearing sod apart and planting each small rooted piece or by broadcasting the small pieces over the prepared soil and then tilling. The latter method takes more material; the first uses more hand labor.

The final and constant step in lawn care is the routine mowing. How often the lawn should be mowed and at what height varies from grass to grass (see chart). Whenever you mow, be sure to have a sharp blade on your mower. Never remove more than one-third of each blade of grass at one time. If it has rained for a week and the grass is exceedingly long, gradually reduce its height. The plants will go into shock if you remove more than one-third. Never mow wet grass. If you do, you are asking for fungus problems.

Allow the clippings to fall to the ground. They will cause no problem. Actually, as they decay, they will return enough nutrients to the soil that one feeding can be eliminated. According to one study, if you routinely fertilize your lawn four times a year, you can get by with only three feedings if you allow your clippings to break down. The clippings do need to be fine enough to sift down to the ground through the blades of grass.

Remember to edge your lawn along the walks or garden beds. A clean, crisp edge provides the finishing touch and makes the yard look well groomed, just like neatly trimmed sideburns on a man's recent haircut. Of the several edging tools that are on the market, the one my husband has found most convenient to use is the sharp-edged wheel with a smaller wheel that runs along the walk, driveway, or brick-edged garden bed. Toss the trimmings on the compost pile for recycling.

Every yard will have a few places that need trimming by hand. In our garden, I need to use grass shears around some liriope plants that line the demarkation between the lawn and the woods. Find shears that fit your hand and are comfortable. Keep them sharp. A trimmer, like the Weed-Eater, that uses a fast-spinning nylon line to cut grass around trees and beside stone walls or raised beds is a relatively new, handy addition to our collection of garden tools.

Many of us use some chemicals to improve or maintain a lawn. Crabgrass, a coarse, unattractive annual grass, is a lawn nuisance that a well-timed preemergence application can prevent. My husband uses a simple signal. He applies his crabgrass preventative when he sees the first forsythia buds in the spring. Should the gardener's timing be off and crabgrass seedlings be already germinating, there also are postemergence chemicals available that will kill the crabgrass plants. Also, keeping your grass mowed high will help prevent later seedlings from germinating. A thriving turf will shade out undesirables.

Several diseases can damage tall fescue. Brown patch is the most frequent problem for homeowners with fescue lawns. You are apt to have more problems in shady parts of the yard than in the full sun. Watering too little or too late in the day can encourage this fungal problem. Dr. Leon T. Lucas of the plant pathology department at North Carolina State University suggests adjusting the soil's pH to 6.5 and applying no nitrogen fertilizer during the spring and summer months, as part of your lawn management program. In fact, the cool-season grasses should have at least two-thirds of their annual food in the fall, with the additional light feeding in February.

"If turf is properly managed, you greatly lessen the chance of disease," says Bruneau, and these management recommendations apply to all turfs, not just tall fescue. It is particularly important to use little nitrogen on centipedegrass. Lucas recommends providing only one feeding with 5-5-15 early in the summer for that turf.

Since thatch, an undesirable layer of material between the green leaves and the surface of the soil, is most often a problem for heavily managed turfs, such as golf course greens and fairways where heavy amounts of pesticides, fungicides, and fertilizers are used, we homeowners may never be bothered by it. If the soil beneath the grass is healthy, with beneficial microbes at work, then the grass probably will not develop thatch problems.

Some lawn fertilizers today are biologically enriched organic materials that include soil bacteria and enzymes. Test results from studies managed by Dr. Joe Vargas at Michigan State University indicate that one such product, Turf Restore from Ringer Research (called Lawn Restore for the homeowners' market), does indeed gradually eliminate thatch buildup while encouraging green grass to flourish. That the product also gradually eliminated fungal problems was an unexpected bonus. Nature was once again in healthy balance. I suspect we will see more of these products in the future.

Other hopeful signs for the future—today some of the grass seed on the market is coated with both nutrients and a fungicide to get the seed off to a vigorous start. Breeders are continually working to develop better, more disease-resistant turf grasses and also they are looking for more dwarf forms that will need less maintenance.

In the August 1987 issue of *Seedsmen's Digest*, Mike Robinson, president of Seed Research of Oregon, is quoted on the subject of turf grass breeding. "Endophyte-enhancement is another major breeding trend," he said. "Endophytic fungi live within the plant and are transmitted through seed to the next generation. They improve the performance of turf grasses by producing toxins that repel many common damaging insects." He goes on to say that several grass varieties already have these endophytes and by 1989, all of his firm's introductions will carry them. Exciting facets of plant breeding.

But today, using today's hybrids and a commonsensical approach to today's turf management techniques, you can develop an attractive greensward to complement your flower garden, for lawn sports, or just to provide that desirable touch of serenity in a busy yard.

There is one other alternative to a grass lawn that you might consider. Several ground covers are low enough and tough enough to qualify as lawn materials. One gardener in coastal North Carolina has installed a dichondra lawn behind her house. She likes the small, round leaves of this perennial, ground-hugging plant. *Dichondra micrantha* can be planted as plugs or raised from seed and will thrive in the warmest parts of the South, but can't withstand traffic. It needs infrequent mowing.

The same innovative gardener has planted pennyroyal (*Mentha Pulegium*) between large paving blocks in her driveway. This tough mint can easily withstand the traffic and provides a wonderful odor every time a leaf is crushed.

Other herbs used for lawn plantings are chamomile and a number of low thymes. The chamomile lawn does well in full sun and limited traffic. Thymes, on the other hand, are quite rugged, and, like the pennyroyal, provide a heady fragrance when crushed underfoot.

7

Ground Covers and Vines

Ground Covers

The most ubiquitous ground cover in the United States is grass. Frequently, however, we want another type of ground cover in shade, under our shrubs, in the woodland areas, covering bulb gardens, or in many informal plantings. A ground cover can delineate a garden area and also unify its diverse components. Ground covers can be used in narrow spaces or on banks where it would be difficult to maintain grass. Every landscaping plan has some area or areas where a good ground cover would be useful.

Which ground cover to use? The choice is wide. We can grow everything from dainty baby's tears (*Soleirolia Soleirolii*) to romping, rampaging kudzu.

Among gardeners and nurserymen, there is no consensus as to precisely what is a ground cover. One Canadian grower uses the term "carpeter." I like that description, but I find that my own definition is even more narrow. Since we do not enjoy months of snow cover each winter here in the South, and our gardens need to be presentable year-round, I think of a ground cover as an evergreen carpeter that covers the ground attractively twelve months of the year.

However, one large Georgia wholesale nursery includes hostas and day lilies in its ground cover catalog. It's true that, planted in tight patterns, these large, deciduous perennials can cover bare earth for part of the year, but they will never carpet the ground, and they leave us without a cover during the winter months.

Probably the most popular and traditional ground covers are ivy, perennial vinca, and pachysandra. These plants all spread rapidly, cover the ground completely so that a minimum amount of weeding is necessary, and provide an evergreen cover for bulb beds, woodland gardens, and other spots where turf is inappropriate.

When choosing a ground cover for a particular area, consider the shape, size, color, texture, ease of culture, and necessary maintenance of the various plants. Identify the demands of the site. Is it sunny or in the shade? Is it damp and boggy or dry and windswept? Will you be watering this part of the garden routinely, or will the plants have to be drought resistant, once established?

If I could snap my fingers and have all the ivy at our home disappear, I would do it in an instant. Some previous owner carefully selected and generously planted ivy as a ground cover in azalea beds near the house. Maintaining the ivy there is not too difficult. We prune it back severely twice a year. However, it has been allowed to expand into many other parts of the yard. Ivy streamers are now invading the woods, climbing trees, and shooting up the walls of the house. It is harder to eradicate than many other ground covers. In some situations, you can pull it out. The roots are tenacious and hard to dig up. In a location where you can leave the dead roots, Roundup is effective at killing ivy, but it must be applied when the plants are in active growth and repeated treatments are often necessary. If you must remove the large root masses, that's hard work, and scraping ivy tendrils off the bricks of the house is a tedious task.

Having voiced my complaints, let me tell you the good points about ivy (*Hedera helix*) as a ground cover: It will do well in either sun or shade. It survives nicely in woodland areas that are completely unwatered during weeks of drought. (In full sun, it does need occasional watering.) It covers the ground quickly, particularly useful if you are trying to prevent erosion on a slope. It will grow almost anywhere. While it will grow lushly with rich soil and annual fertilization, it grows adequately in poor soil.

Unlike wisteria vines, which can strangle a tree and ultimately kill it, ivy does not usually cause damage to a tree by climbing up the trunk and wandering in the lower branches. Perhaps if the ivy were extremely vigorous and shaded too many leaves on a tree, it might contribute to its decline. Ivy vines climbing an old oak or hickory add to the sense of age and maturity in a garden. This effect may be appropriate in some gardens.

It can also be used to cover fences informally or be espaliered formally in our part of the country.

It is seldom bothered by pest or disease.

It is easily propagated from cuttings.

In specialist catalogs, you may find 100 or more different varieties of *Hedera helix*. If you decide to use ivy, rather than just purchasing a flat of ordinary English ivy, consider using one of the more interesting forms. For example, if you are designing a small garden, select one of the fine-leaved cultivars, like 'Needlepoint' or 'Hahn's Self-Branching'. (Note that even the small-leafed ivies become larger with age and maturity.) Or perhaps one of the variegated forms, such as *H. h.* 'Gold Heart' or white-edged 'Anna Marie'. Should you become a real enthusiast, you can even join the American Ivy Society.

Perennial vinca comes in two sizes. *Vinca major* has relatively large leaves and will shoot 15 to 20 inches high before tumbling over to cover the ground. It is both more vigorous and more tender than *V. minor*, an evergreen, carpeting vine with 3/8-inch, opposing leaves. Both species have lavender-blue flowers that combine attractively with daffodils. Cultivars of both species that offer variegated foliage, double flowers, and other flower colors do exist, but they are infrequently seen in nurseries and catalogs. You may have to hunt for them. A friend just gave me a very attractive rose-purple form of *Vinca minor*.

Vinca major will thrive in the warmest parts of our gardening area. Because of its size, it is appropriate for large garden areas. However, expect it to suffer winter damage in any harsh season and be prepared for it to disappear completely if we get zapped by a 1984–85 type freeze.

On the other hand, *V. minor* is completely hardy. Its evergreen foliage spreads neatly across the ground—the perfect companion plant for bulbs. Although vigorous, it is loose knit, so bulbs can poke up through the vinca runners.

Like ivy, the vincas will grow in sun or shade and they root easily from cuttings. An early pinch will encourage the cuttings to branch.

Unlike ivy, I've never found *V. minor* to be a pest. It spreads nicely but is easily weeded out where it is not wanted. Maintenance is a semiannual pruning and occasional weeding.

The first ground cover I ever planted extensively was pachysandra (*Pachysandra terminalis*), a Japanese import. It was the perfect foil for dogwoods and azaleas in a lightly shaded location.

This plant produces 4-to-6-inch whorls of evergreen, toothed foliage and it spreads rapidly by underground stolons. If you are planting it next to a lawn area, I suggest using one of the many edging materials that are on the market. Any metal or plastic material that goes 4 to 6 inches into the ground will block the stolons from invading the lawn. Otherwise, you will be constantly battling the pachysandra in your grass.

This ground cover propagates readily from cuttings. Plant your rooted cuttings 6 to 8 inches apart and they will quickly fill in and create a solid mass cover. Even faster, find a friend with an established pachysandra patch and judiciously thin it by pulling plants with extensive stolons. Plant these green tops with their stolons, water thoroughly, and these plants will continue to grow as if they had never been disturbed.

While the Japanese spurge is the most widely planted pachysandra, we have a southern species, *P. procumbens*, that several growers have suggested

Lycoris radiata coming up through a ground cover of vinca in early fall. Daffodils bloom here in the spring.

southern gardeners should use more freely. Locating a source may be the major problem. To date, I don't see this pachysandra widely propagated. Andre Viette does offer it in his mailorder catalog.

With a new pachysandra planting—or indeed, any new ground cover planting—mulching thoroughly the first year will help retain water around the plants and will minimize the weeding.

While all three of these ground covers are reliable and attractive tools for landscaping, ivy is the only one that will do an effective job on a bank or a steep slope. Anyone who needs to control erosion, whether on a home site or at a commercial location, wants to use plants that are tough, reliable and quick to take hold of the sloping land.

Years ago, two southern pests were introduced into our landscapes for this very reason. The rampant kudzu (*Pueraria lobata*), a vine that shoots 60 feet or more per season, is often seen covering abandoned houses, cars, roadside trees, and banks in the South. To my amazement, seed of this plant was offered by Park Seed Company until 1987.

Kudzu certainly does do its job of erosion control quickly. It takes over the entire neighborhood. It can be controlled by physically pulling the vines or by using an appropriate herbicide. Underneath the vigorous foliage, fragrant, attractive purple flowers are produced during the summer.

The other plant that we all are constantly weeding out of our woods and gardens is the Japanese honeysuckle (*Lonicera japonica*). The wonderfully sweet fragrance of honeysuckle was one of my first impressions of North Carolina, as we drove up country lanes and byways house hunting in May.

This particular lonicera is both beautiful and fragrant, but it is rampantly invasive. My husband and I continually pull vines from our woods. I have seen it grown attractively in a controlled situation, where it is limited to a tall wire frame and treated like a clematis or other flowering vine. It also does a fine job of holding a steep bank, if you confine it stringently so that it does not go beyond the area where you want it to flourish.

Evergreen, carpeting junipers are so successful that, like the springtime effusion of Bradford pear plantings, they tend to be overused. Every home, bank, or office building that is professionally landscaped seems to have a number of junipers in the planting.

There are good reasons for this enthusiasm for junipers. In any sunny location, junipers will carpet the ground, tolerate almost any type of soil, and thrive with minimal care. The only pests that cause much of a problem with junipers in the South are bagworms and red spider mites during our hot, dry summers. Regular irrigation will minimize the mite problem.

We can choose among a considerable number of attractive, prostrate junipers in a wide color range, from gray-blues to yellow-greens. *Juniperus horizontalis* and its cultivars like *J. h.* 'Bar Harbor' and 'Wiltoni' are excellent carpeters, as are the many forms of *J. procumbens*. Recently I have noticed that some of the landscapers are designing interesting mosaics of different junipers in large plantings, thus avoiding the monotony of an entire bank covered with just one variety. While carpeting junipers are fine in flat positions and attractive hanging over rocks or the edges of raised beds, they truly excel as reliable slope cover.

Junipers are not the only evergreen shrubs that serve well as ground covers. Several cotoneasters, particularly *C. salicifolia*, are used to cover banks; leucothoe is occasionally used to cover a large area; rosemaries that are temperamental in our area are fully hardy farther south, and several have the sprawling character of ground covers; even azaleas are being developed specifically as ground covers. We planted *Rhododendron takahari* recently, and it is beginning to reach out along the ground in an attractive way.

Lily turf (*Liriope muscari*) and its smaller cousin, Mondo grass (*Ophiopogon japonicus*) are plants with clumps of strappy, evergreen leaves. They can be used as borders for walkways, as edgings for garden beds, or as large plantings of ground cover. Which plant you choose depends on the scale of the planting. Liriope, which comes with white or purple flowers, in plain green or variegated foliage, has leaves that are 12–15 inches high.

Mondo grass is finer-leaved and shorter, with its flowers tucked into the foliage. For small gardens or dainty edging, there are several dwarf forms of this plant on the market. There is also a variegated *Ophiopogon jaburan variegatus*. Rarer still is the black-leaved Mondo grass, which is not terribly vigorous and is more of an oddity for a specimen planting in a rock garden than for using en masse as a ground cover.

These southern gems, hardy through zone 6, are flexible and trouble free. I throw a little balanced fertilizer their way once a year, in early spring. They will thrive in sun or shade and need only one bit of special care. The foliage stays evergreen and hangs on until new foliage appears in the spring. Check the plants in late February or early March. If you see the tips of fresh new spears beginning to break the ground, mow off the old foliage with your lawn mower. Timing is important for this maneuver. If you wait too late, you will either have to trim the planting carefully by hand or risk knocking off the tips of the new foliage with the mower.

If you have an area where you want a low, spreading mat that will be covered with flowers in the springtime, look to the phloxes, particularly *P. subulata*. I admit to a strong aversion to what I think of as "mailbox phlox," that vivid cerise variety too often planted on roadsides and around mailboxes in our area.

However, we can choose from a large group of subtle, soft, clear-colored *P. subulata* cultivars that are very attractive. In many instances, nothing is more lovely than a mat of plain white single flowers on the curving, fine-needled phlox branches. For a little color, seek out *P. s.* 'Millstream Coral Eye', lavender *P. s.* 'Millstream Jupiter', or pink *P. s.* 'Millstream Daphne'. I'm particularly fond of the pale pink *P. s.* 'Laura', selected by Linc Foster and named for his wife Timmy, more formally known as Laura Louise.

The first two years I planted the white form of *P. stolonifera* 'Bruce's White', I did not see why other gardeners called it a ground cover. How-

An English hybrid phlox, *P.* 'Boothman's Variety'

Phlox stolonifera 'Bruce's White'

ever, as the planting became established, suddenly it all grew together and truly covered the ground with its neat, rounded leaves throughout the year and attractive stems of white flowers in early spring. Two other attractive *P. stolonifera* choices are 'Blue Ridge' and 'Pink Ridge'.

Because I am partial to flowering plants, I use a number of flowering ground covers in appropriate places. We grow the sedums and sempervivums for their attractive foliages, but they do all flower in one season or another, and some of the sedums spread very quickly. Yellow-flowered *Sedum acre* is the most enthusiastic, the most invasive. Plant it only where you want it to spread for yards. However, I don't deem it a real pest, because it is shallow rooted and so easy to weed out.

Most sedums are hardy perennials, tolerant of a wide range of conditions. If you want to raise the plants to perfection, you will want to research each plant's origin and native growing conditions. However, the sedums that are commonly available will grow in sandy or clay soils, need minimal feeding and can thrive in a nurtured garden or in a location watered only by occasional rains.

Sedums are generally flexible about their conditions. For example, since we have lived in the South, I have become fond of our native stonecrop, *S. ternatum*. I first saw this plant in situ when my husband and I accompanied C. Ritchie Bell, then director of the North Carolina Botanical Garden, on one of his botanical outings in the Smokies during mid-May.

Fairly high up on the Mount Sterling Trail, which climbs out of the beau-

Sedum ternatum, a native stonecrop that thrives in a garden setting

tiful Cataloochie Valley, we saw one rocky hillside—an acre of boulders—covered with *Sedum ternatum*, flecking the hill with a snowfall of white.

When we saw *S. ternatum* in the wild, it had a rather moist site, a vertical position, and minimal soil among the boulders. Here in the Piedmont, it provides an attractive, low, spreading ground cover at the edge of our woods, living in a rich, dry duff where it gets little attention. In memory of Mount Sterling, I planted it in front of a large, lichen-covered boulder, under an established pink azalea. This area is watered only by rainfall.

Each year, one clump divides into ten or so, and I keep spreading it along the edge of the driveway. Eventually we will have a solid mat of the attractive, succulent leaves, bedecked with the sparkling white flowers each spring. But *S. ternatum* is only one of a host of spreading sedums that will carpet the ground. If you want to learn a lot about this genus, study Ronald Evans's *Handbook of Cultivated Sedums*.

The hens and chickens, sempervivum species, come in all sizes, from minute forms of *Sempervivum arachnoideum*, covered with its spider webs, to plants with one rosette that is 4–5 inches across. Both of these genera of succulents are appropriate for hot, dry places.

Arabis is another genus of spring-flowering plants that does well here in the South. In her book on perennials, Pamela Harper recommends *Arabis procurrens*, a flexible, reliable, attractive, and easy plant. I like its small, evergreen rosettes that spread out to make a solid mat. The tiny sprays of white flowers are a nice bonus. *Arabis Sturii* is even more choice and compact. Rockcress (*A. alpina*) produces coarser rosettes of attractive gray-green foliage with toothed edges. It, however, does not make a tight-knit colony. The rosettes extend on stolons for a looser appearance. I did just acquire the variegated form, which is quite attractive, but I don't yet know how vigorous it will be. There is also a pink-flowered form which I have grown. *Arabis blepharophylla* 'Spring Charm' was nice this past spring—the rosettes had a reddish tinge and the flowers are pink. In the nursery, I have seedlings of another species, *A. cypria*, but, of course, no experience yet.

I tend to do that in my southern garden. Anytime I find a genus that I like and that thrives here, like aquilegia or campanula or arabis or hosta or epimedium, I try to collect as many species and cultivars of that genus as possible.

Ajugas (the bugle weeds) are grown more for the foliage than the flowers. However, when the ground near some daffodils is a sheet of small blue-purple spires, the combination is very effective. Ordinary ajuga, *Ajuga reptans*, is one of those plants to use with caution. It is very vigorous and will spread over large areas quite quickly. It is ground hugging and evergreen. The round rosettes bronze up a bit in the wintertime. Ajugas will grow in sun or shade and they will tolerate considerable neglect. Like many of the tough plants that survive without much water, they will really perform for you if you give them regular waterings. In a nursery condition, one grower commented that his ajugas seem to need more water than other ground covers. There are a number of cultivars with variegated or bronzed or burgundy-colored leaves and others with pink, white, or purple flowers. Some of the more interesting ones are gradually becoming more widely available. A very choice one that is difficult to locate is *A. metallica crispa*. It is not stoloniferous, like the others, and its foliage is puckered and metallic, as the name suggests. In an isolated spot, I also am growing a very vigorous deciduous pink ajuga with light green leaves. It can take over its particular corner of the world, but I won't let it into any other part of the garden. It is attractive covering the ground beneath white azaleas. One gardening friend noted that it is important to shear the flower spikes from ajuga before it goes to seed. Otherwise, you may discover a large patch of seedlings in the middle of your lawn.

As we are designing gardens or small plantings, we are always considering compatibility—physical compatibility (we don't plant marsh marigolds with cholla) and visual compatibility. On one edge of the driveway, there is an aged 'Coral Bells' azalea in front of a huge, lichen-encrusted boulder. This is a location away from the house, where being leaf strewn during the winter months looks natural at the edge of the woods, and I do use an herbaceous perennial as a ground cover there. The variegated, silvery foliage of low *Lamium maculatum* 'Beacon Silver' is wonderful in combination with that old rock. 'Beacon Silver' has short spikes of pink flowers that bloom after the azalea. Even better might be the newer form, *L. m.* 'White Nancy', with its white flowers.

If you want a vigorous, deciduous, variegated ground cover that will take over an area quickly, plant the silver-edged goutweed (*Aegopodium Podagraria* 'Variegatum'). I think of this plant as a weed, but it can be effectively used, if well controlled.

Hypericums come in all sizes, from large shrubs down to minute treasures for the rock garden. *H. calycinum* is a fine ground cover, described as semi-evergreen in zone 7. It is one of those plants that is more evergreen, the farther south it lives. It spreads by stolons, prefers a light soil and is particularly useful in holding a bank in front of shrubs. The decorative, sizeable, yellow flowers are a nice summertime plus. I have never seen it covered with bloom, but rather it offers a sprinkling of flowers over a long period of time.

In shady, informal settings, like woodland trails or wild flower gardens, closely planted evergreen ferns make natural and attractive ground covers. The Christmas fern (*Polystichum acrostichoides*) is native to much of eastern North America. It is widely planted in our area, but it is only one of a number of evergreen ferns, like *Dryopteris intermedia* (the evergreen wood fern) and *Polypodium virginianum* (the common polypody), that are attractive throughout the year.

For a large-leafed, evergreen ground cover in a shady nook, the cast iron plant (*Aspidistra elatior*) is wonderful. For Northerners, it is a house plant. It is marginal in zone 7 (some gardeners grow it successfully in a sheltered place) but the farther south your garden, the more reliable it is outside. And as a house plant or an outdoor plant, it survives with less light than almost any other plant I know. No flower arranger would be without this foliage that is so attractive and malleable. Just keep the slugs and snails away.

Another house plant that is completely hardy here is the strawberry begonia (*Saxifraga sarmentosa*). It is neither a strawberry nor a begonia, but carpets nicely and spreads its silvery rosettes by stolons, much like a strawberry plant. It does well in our acid woods, but does need regular moisture.

For sunny spots where you want a low blue-gray grass, the clumping *Festuca glauca* can be planted closely to cover the area. The choices of appropriate plants to use as ground covers go on and on. Wholesalers of ground covers are continually looking for new and interesting plants with potential. In the last few years I have seen saponarias, anagallis, dwarf blueberries, Peruvian verbena, and two hardy ice plants, *Delosperma nubigena* and *D. cooperi*, either reintroduced (sometimes growers overlook and forget about old plants of recognized virtue) or brought to the American market for the first time. I'm sure this pattern will continue.

Vines

I've already mentioned ivy, vinca, and other vines that are commonly used as ground covers. Many vines, like the Virginia creeper (*Parthenocissus quinquefolia*, which is usually scrambling up telephone poles or covering stone walls, are not thought of as ground covers, but at Orton Plantation on the coast of North Carolina, I have seen Virginia creeper used very effectively in a contained bed.

In addition to their possible function as ground covers, vines can provide shade for a porch or patio, add flowering beauty to the garden, cover ugly fences, or soften brick walls. They can be trained up a post to add a desirable vertical touch to an otherwise uninterestingly flat garden. Some, like grape and kiwi vines, even provide a harvest, along with their decorative value. There are both evergreen and deciduous vines that we should consider as candidates for our landscaping plans.

If we were narrow enough of focus, we could limit ourselves happily to just one genus of vines. There are more than 200 species of clematis in the world, both evergreen and deciduous. Some bloom in the spring, some in the summer, and others in the fall. An occasional one, like the hybrid 'Mme. Le Coultre', produces a huge bouquet of large white flowers in the springtime and then rewards us with occasional flowers throughout the season.

New to me in the South is the vigorous evergreen, *C. Armandii*. The glossy foliage is rather coarse, as clematis foliage goes, but it is a marvelous drapery for a fence or arbor, covered with deliciously fragrant white flowers in the springtime. Give it space and let it decorate your garden, in flower and foliage. A pink form, *C. A.* 'Farquhariana' exists, but it is not easily located.

About seventeen years ago, as we were traveling the back roads of Connecticut on the way to Boy Scout camp, I suddenly shouted "STOP!" My husband screeched to a halt, and I ran back to admire and photograph a magnificent *C. x Jackmanii*, covered with rich purple flowers from the ground to the porch roof of that farmhouse. That was my first encounter with clematis, and I've been growing them ever since.

Clematis do as well in the South as they did in Connecticut. *Clematis* 'Nelly Moser', *C.* 'Gypsy Queen', or *C.* 'Henryi' is covering every lamppost or mailbox support. Many gardeners here also rejoice in the exuberance of Virgin's Bower, the native *C. virginiana*, which covers its vines with small white flowers in late summer and early fall, or *C. paniculata*, also replete with white flowers in late summer.

All clematis are easy to grow, not "difficult" or "challenging." Perhaps they have been so described because they are slow to establish. Plant them in good soil, water and feed regularly, and they will be magnificent in about three years. Mulching well helps. One local collector raises his vines in the rock garden, on the barn wall, on cedar posts in his perennial beds, and on the pergola posts to shade the east and west ends of his house. Since clematis need to twine their petioles around something, he covers all posts with chicken wire. He has never experimented with the British method of allowing clematis vines to climb into roses, trees, and shrubs. (Pamela Harper does use that method in her Virginia garden. She raises clematis on her camellias.)

While many authorities say that clematis need lime, Christopher Lloyd, who has written the most authoritative book on the subject, *Clematis*, says that there is no evidence clematis need lime. Mine just get a February handful of 10-10-10, and they seem quite content.

If you have purchased a home with some clematis vines on the fence, you may be mystified about pruning. Some of the clematis go to the ground each winter; others bloom on old wood. If you don't know which varieties are growing in the yard, wait a year to see what the growing and flowering patterns are. To be very simplistic about clematis pruning, let me suggest that if you have an herbaceous variety that goes to the ground, come late fall, simply cut off the existing vines above ground level and pull them off the trellis or fence. New wood will develop in the spring and the plant will flower on that new wood.

For those that flower on old wood, prune the vines back to keep the plant in a desirable shape. Old wood will break on clematis, but if you ignore the plant for ten years and then decide to shape it up, it may refuse to break and instead, die on you. Lloyd recommends yearly pruning for all clematis. For an entire chapter on clematis pruning, let me refer you to his book.

Clematis is one of the few plants that I allow to develop seed heads. Those fluffy whorls are almost as decorative as the flowers. While it is not desirable to raise seedlings of hybrid plants, as you will usually get an inferior product, it is easy and satisfying to raise clematis species from seed. *C. crispa* is one of our southeastern natives that is lovely. It produces its blue flowers from Virginia to Texas. This year I have a vigorous seedling of *C. tanqutica* by the front porch. I can't wait to see its first golden yellow bells. Still on my "want list" is *C. texensis*, with its nodding, scarlet flowers.

While I am obviously enchanted with clematis species and cultivars, there are a number of other delightful vines for use in home gardens. Native campsis (bignonia) and Japanese honeysuckle are both regarded as dreadful pests. However, under strict cultivation, their beautiful flowers and the wonderful honeysuckle fragrance of the lonicera make both nice additions to a large garden. The most effective way I have seen these plants controlled is to train them up a tall post encircled with chicken wire. They climb vigorously and then the vine tips and flowers spill back toward the ground in a wonderful fountain of color. There are other honeysuckles, like *Lonicera x Heckrottii*, that are desirable additions to large gardens. The leaves of *Lonicera flava* cup the flower clusters in an attractive way.

Another way to cultivate the campsis varieties—and some choice cultivars are on the market—is to take several vines and stake them. The first year prune to 5 or 6 feet, whichever height you wish to establish for your "tree." Allow the vines to grow and flower in a weeping circle each year, but each winter, prune severely back to the tree form you have developed.

In the North, wisteria was a choice plant. Here, I see so many escaped vines racing 80 feet up roadside trees and ultimately killing the trees that I think of it as a problem. Again, it is a beautiful plant if kept under strict control. Walk under the wisteria gazebo at the Sarah P. Duke Gardens when it is in full bloom, and you will be sure you have never seen such glory. Then note the heavy steel framework of that gazebo, needed to support those old vines.

We also walked beneath a marvelous old wisteria in a courtyard in Charleston, South Carolina. It too had a sturdy metal support. If you choose to raise a wisteria, don't plant it against the house, where the vine

Wisteria trained into a graceful tree form

tendrils literally can raise the shingles, but give it a strong support and prune it vigorously each year. Never let it get out of control. At Hidcote, in England, there is an ancient and magnificent wisteria growing the length of a garage roof. It is tightly pruned.

Wisteria is another vine that can be trained into tree form. You can purchase trees or train one yourself, much like the campsis. These trees make lovely specimens in a lawn setting. There can be one problem. Some gardeners find that trees in a lawn do not bloom well. That lack of bloom is usually caused by too much nitrogen fertilizer, which the lawn needs, encouraging the wisteria to put out leafy growth, not flowers. Either hold back on lawn food or find a more appropriate place for the tree—as a centerpiece in a large perennial garden, perhaps—where the feeding program will encourage bloom.

Gelsemium sempervirens (the Carolina jessamine) is another popular flowering evergreen vine that is useful as a screening plant, growing vigorously on fences or display posts. The profusion of fragrant, single yellow flowers is produced in early spring. An attractive double form is also on the market. This vine is a pest-free native plant, highly desirable.

Another yellow-flowered vine for zones 7 and 8 is the yellow star-jasmine (*Trachelospermum asiaticum*). This relatively slow-growing vine should be planted where visitors will pass by and appreciate its fragrance.

In some situations, the gardener does not care about flowers, but simply wants a reliable evergreen vine. In addition to ivies, there are also several euonymus vines, from coarse to fine, that serve to cover bare stonework, walls, or screen porches. *Euonymus Fortunei* offers a long list of selected clones. The foliage of *E. F.* 'Colorata' turns an attractive reddish hue in the fall. Tiny *D. F.* 'Kewensis', its leaves only ¼ inch, grows slowly and should be used in plantings of appropriate scale—perhaps as ground cover for miniature bulbs in a part of the rock garden.

In the warmest parts of our area, the dwarf fig (*Ficus pumila*) makes a beautiful tracery on brick walls. I've admired it south of here, but it is not hardy in the Piedmont except in very sheltered sun traps.

Not only do we treasure the evergreen vines, but many of us are using a number of deciduous vines to advantage. Fruiting vines, like grapes and kiwis, are grown on arbors or trellises in a number of southern gardens. One friend has trained *Actinidea chinensis* (kiwi) vines up to the second floor of her home and then along a support system the length of the house. These vigorous deciduous vines shade the ground floor windows during the hot summer months. If you want kiwi fruit, remember that you must plant both male and female vines or purchase the new, self-pollinating, hardy kiwi 'Issai', which recently came on the market.

One vine that is supposed to be magnificent is the climbing hydrangea (*H. anomala petiolaris*), frequently sold as simply *Hydrangea petiolaris*. My three-year-old vine is about 12 inches long, just beginning to creep up its tall oak tree. I recognize that it is getting severe competition for water and food from the vigorous tree roots in the area, but climbing trees is supposed to be its forte. I hope I live long enough to see it climb 50 feet into the tree and be covered with white flowers in late spring, as I have seen described in other gardening books.

Polygonum Aubertii, the very vigorous fleece vine or silver lace vine, produces abundant sprays of white flowers during the summer. If, as John Elsley says in the Wayside catalog, it will cover a barn in two years, you can tell that it is a rampaging vine. You may have a barn you want to cover. . .

Along the roadsides in zones 7 and 8, you may find *Passiflora caerulea*, one of the passion flowers. Most of these vines with their beautiful flowers are tropical and tender, but this blue one is relatively hardy. Woodlanders, a nursery in South Carolina, offers a choice white form. I think we ought to cultivate this vine more often. It's lovely and trouble free.

Like poison ivy, wild grape vine, Japanese honeysuckle, and kudzu, our native smilax (*S. rotundifolia*) is a vine you will probably spend considerable time trying to eradicate. However, *Smilax megalantha*, an attractively red-fruited species from Japan, is a desirable, vigorous vine.

Bittersweet (*Celastrus orbiculata*, [Oriental] or *C. scandens*, [American]) is another vine that gardeners regard as either a gem or a pest. I get readers' questions about how to grow it and how to kill it. Both species are vigorous and can strangle shrubs, but if controlled, they produce their beautiful red and yellow fruits in time for Thanksgiving decorations in the fall. Both male and female plants are necessary for flowering and fruiting. If you want to grow this vine, purchase your plants from a nurseryman who propagates and segregates the two sexes and control your plantings by vigorous pruning.

As with the numerous ground covers, nurserymen are experimenting with new varieties, and they will continue to introduce additional attractive and interesting new vines in the years ahead. I think vines are often overlooked when people plan garden designs. Keep them in mind as interesting ingredients in your overall landscaping plans.

8

Bulbs

For power-packed gardening potential, nothing beats a flowering bulb. There, in one neatly wrapped package, are the roots, flowers, and leaves, ready to flourish with the slightest encouragement. Some bulbs, in fact, need no encouragement. A colchicum will flower if you place it on a saucer or the shelf. Amaryllis often begin to put up their large buds while sitting in the garden center's bin. Paper-white narcissus, wedged into a bowl with pebbles, fill the room with their pungent fragrance when given just a bit of water at their bases.

Planted in the garden, most bulbs reward us with magnificent bloom the first year. Some, like lycoris and crinums, need to settle into their locations. It seems to take them one to three years before they will flower after planting. But in general, the challenge is to encourage repeat performances from those bulbs that bloom enthusiastically the first year.

Dr. A. A. De Hertogh, head of the Department of Horticultural Science at North Carolina State University, defines a successful bulb as one that blooms generously for at least three years. To have perennial bulbs in your garden, De Hertogh, who is a world-renowned expert on bulbs, emphasizes the importance of soil preparation, good drainage, proper feeding, and cultivar selection. He feels that in the past, Dutch bulb growers have done their consumers and ultimately themselves a disservice by claiming that the bulb has everything it needs. Plant it and it will bloom! This is an oversimplification. It is basically true for one year, but not for many seasons of flowering.

Bulb planting begins with soil preparation. If you are adding bulbs to an established bed, probably you have a good, friable soil. Spade in some additional compost and then plant your bulbs. But if you are a novice bulb grower, put your back into it, spade up that new bed, and add generous amounts of compost. "There's no substitute for good, old-fashioned spade gardening," says De Hertogh.

Thorough spading loosens the soil and allows the developing roots to spread quickly and establish themselves. Ideally, you will dig the bed 2 inches deeper than you will plant the bulbs. As a general rule, plant each bulb three times its diameter. For example, if you have 2-inch tulip bulbs, set them 6 to 8 inches into the ground, and therefore, prepare the garden at least 8 to 10 inches deep. Adapt this rule to your soil conditions. In sandy soils, bulbs should be planted a bit deeper; in heavy clay soils, not as deep.

Placing some bone meal underneath each bulb used to be the standard recommendation. However, through modern processing methods, most of the nutritional value of bone meal is lost. Today, the American Daffodil Society tells its members not to bother using this product. It recommends adding some superphosphate beneath daffodils at planting time.

Certainly some food is important to good bulb culture. Since 10 to 20 percent of the nutrients are lost from the soil each year, even bulbs need regular applications of fertilizer.

To produce those magnificent acres of bulbs at Keukenhof, the famous Dutch bulb center, the growers use 250 tons of well-rotted manure and 300 tons of compost each year. In lieu of manure, feed your bulbs twice a year with a balanced fertilizer like 8-8-8 or 10-10-10. Spring-flowering bulbs should be fed in the late fall and again when the leaves first show in the spring.

An alternative is to use Holland Bulb Booster, a slow-release 9-9-6 fertilizer that needs to be applied just once a year. Its formula was based on research done by Dr. P. V. Nelson at North Carolina State University. While slightly more expensive, it is a time-saving product for the busy gardener.

In the parts of my garden where I have many bulbs planted among azaleas, primroses, phloxes, and other shrubs and perennials, I do not want to feed in late fall and promote soft growth on those plants during our winter mild spells, so I wait and feed those bulbs only when the leaves appear in early spring. In this sort of mixed planting, it is difficult to give ideal care to any one plant. I compromise.

Gardening is often a matter of compromise. Consider planting the bulbs, for example. It's easy to dig holes with a trowel or a round, bulb-planting tool when planting bulbs in a well-prepared garden bed. However, if you're planting in the woods, it's almost impossible. Don't try to dig a neat hole among the roots and rocks with a trowel or even a spade: bring in your heavy equipment—a crowbar or a mattock. If you have a strong teenage son, now's the time to enlist his services. And if you are doing a large mass planting in an open meadow area, take a tip from landscape professionals and do the preliminary work with a rototiller.

When my husband and I are planting daffodils along woodland trails, we are pleased to get a bulb approximately deep enough in the ground, among the rampant tree roots and numerous rocks. We certainly do not prepare the ground underneath the bulbs. While we may not get the most perfect results or the highest possible yield, daffodils, crocus, muscari, and many other bulbs are resilient enough that they establish and bloom every year, even under our less than ideal treatment. Compromise.

Where you plant your bulbs (as well as the design you choose) depends on the style of your garden. In a formal situation, bulbs are usually precisely placed in neat geometric patterns. By the mid-1980s, I had seen several attractive mass plantings of bulbs arranged in Art Deco–type waves. Any formal planting is labor and cost intensive. Fresh, healthy bulbs of uniform size must be planted each year in vast numbers—by the hundreds or the thousands, depending on the size of the garden. While this type of formal planting is usually best left to the professional gardeners in public gardens, like Tryon Palace, Bellingrath Gardens, or the Colonial Williamsburg Gardens, some home gardeners may choose to garden intensively on a small, formal patio, at a driveway entrance, or in beds by the front door. Bulbs will be followed by annuals that will be replaced by mums in the fall. When the mums are pulled, the next crop of bulbs will be planted, perhaps with a cover of pansies for the winter months.

If yours is a more casual garden, bulbs will be attractive if used informally, in splashes and drifts. If you buy twenty-five tulips, don't scatter them one by one throughout the garden but group them close to one another. Let them give a mini-mass effect.

One English use of bulbs that is just beginning to gain wide acceptance in the United States is the planting of bulbs in lawns or meadows. Early species crocus are very attractive when sprinkled close to one another in the lawn edges beside the path. Daffodils, particularly the smaller types, are lovely in meadows. Perhaps the most captivating of all is the species *Narcissus Bulbicodium var. conspicuus*, commonly known as the petticoat daffodil. This tiny daffodil with its round yellow cup and spiky perianth is a charmer as a single flower. Massed by the thousands, as on the sloping meadows at Wisley in England, it's breathtakingly beautiful.

Whether you plant bulbs in a lawn or in a meadow area, remember that *the grass must not be mowed until the foliage of the bulbs is fully matured and going brown*. If it is a lawn area, you have to be willing to trade off the slightly scruffy, overgrown look of the grass for the beauty of the flowers.

Naturalizing bulbs in a woodsy wild flower garden is perhaps the most beautiful usage of all. Here you want to avoid orderly placement. One method is to gently toss a group of bulbs into the air and then plant them where they land. How close you plant them is again a matter of compro-

Tulip 'Golden Parade' massed for a formal effect

mise. For instant effect, put your bulbs close to one another. To postpone the day when you need to dig and divide the group of bulbs, place them several inches apart so that it will take some time for the area to be filled as the bulbs multiply.

Wherever you use bulbs, whether in a garden, woodland, or meadow, do not plant them in a spotty fashion. Groups of bulbs will be much more effective than one placed here and one there. I can think of two exceptions. If you are using an extremely large bulb in a modest garden, one may be enough. For example, a single *Allium giganteum*, surrounded by daffodils and low perennials, will be majestic in a small garden bed. Three might overwhelm that garden. To use a drift of these flowers that spike 3 to 4 feet high, you need to place them in a large garden where they will be in scale with all the other plantings.

The other exception is the collector's garden. There, the gardener will happily plant one choice bulb by itself. He may have paid fifty to seventy-five dollars for just one bulb of the newest hybrid daffodil. There are no aesthetically pleasing drifts of plants in this sort of garden. This gardener wants one of each.

Which bulbs you plant is very much a matter of personal taste. The major bulbs, sold by the millions, are daffodils, tulips, and hyacinths. However, a

A small garden intensively planted with tall *Fritillaria imperialis*
bulbs and daffodils

host of other interesting and sometimes exotic minor bulbs are also on the
market and becoming more readily available. For example, several years ago,
the charming oxalis from Chile, *O. adenophylla*, with its fan-pleated, gray-
blue leaves and clear pink flowers, was only available from nurseries that
specialized in plants for rock gardens. Today it is found in most garden
centers.

North Carolina State University recently completed a four-year study, largely funded by the Dutch Bulb Exporters Association, that provides southern gardeners with reliable information about bulb needs and desirable cultivars of the major bulbs. Eight hyacinths, 40 daffodils, and 133 different tulips were grown in test beds at Castle Hayne near Wilmington (zone 9), at the NCSU Arboretum in Raleigh (zone 8), and in the mountains at Fletcher, just south of Asheville (zone 7). The results of this study are shown in the table at the end of this chapter.

If you study the chart, you will notice that almost any bulb will do well in sandy soil. In our heavy Piedmont clay, fewer varieties give good results. *Drainage, drainage, drainage*—it's the constant refrain in southern gardening.

While I am trying to flood our woods with daffodils, adding some species tulips to the rock garden, and admiring hyacinths in others' gardens, I'm also planting a number of other bulb varieties each year. I use the term "bulb" in its broadest interpretation, referring not only to true bulbs, but also including tubers, rhizomes, tuberous roots, and corms.

One of my goals in my southern garden is to develop a twelve-month garden, with something in flower at every season of the year. For those gardeners farther south, year-round gardening is easy. Here, it is a challenge. Bulbs are my best tool, particularly the genus *Cyclamen*.

When we first moved south, garden writer William Lanier Hunt said, "You must raise some cyclamen on your hill." Then we hiked over his steep acres where he has thousands of cyclamen flourishing—blooming, self-hybridizing, and seeding themselves around. I became an instant enthusiast, if not an addict.

Different species of hardy cyclamen bloom in different seasons of the year. By careful selection of species, you can have some cyclamen in flower in your garden twelve months of the year. The easiest of all these Mediterranean tubers is *Cyclamen hederifolium* (formerly *C. neapolitanum*). In my garden, *C. h.* begins to produce its charming, 3/4-inch, pink flowers with reflexed petals in June and blooms well into December. Gradually, beautiful foliage appears and carpets the ground until late spring. The *C. h.* foliage is extremely variable. The leaves may be heart shaped or cut like ivy; long and thin, or full and broad—and all are handsomely patterned in shades of green, from a rich dark hue to a pale, almost white tone. If you raise 100 seedlings, no two will be exactly alike. This flowering plant is worth growing for the foliage alone.

The next easiest, both in terms of availability and culture, is *C. coum*. This dainty cyclamen comes into bloom right after *C. hederifolium*. Colorful buds show at the ground level in mid-November. Then the plant seems to sus-

Cyclamen coum flowering in January

pend activity until it is ready to flower in January. I check the garden every few days, expecting to see the small, crimson, pink, or magenta flowers appearing above the round foliage. *Cyclamen coum* takes its own time to go from bud to bloom. Both flowers and foliage are smaller than *C. hederifolium*. These two species also have white forms which I find very attractive.

Cyclamen graecum survives in my garden. Its large, patterned, velvety leaves are attractive, but it is a reluctant bloomer for me. Others that do flower nicely and are hardy here are *C. mirabile* (fall), *C. purpurescens* (summer), *C. creticum* (spring) and *C. cyprium* (fall).

Finding these plants is a problem. Some of our catalogs offer the most common varieties for sale as tubers. There are several reasons not to buy these bulbs. Unless the catalog states that all material is nursery-propagated, the tubers were probably dug in the wild. The conservation-minded among us object to this practice—and to be practical, by the time you get the dried-out tuber, your chances of reviving it are poor.

I have raised most of my cyclamen from seed. They germinate readily and bloom fifteen to thirty-six months from sowing, depending on the species. *Cyclamen hederifolium*, *C.coum*, and *C.purpurescens* have bloomed for me in fifteen months. The only propagation trick is to keep the seed pot in the dark until germination takes place. I simply cover the cyclamen pots with a piece of cardboard and begin checking the pots every few days after three weeks have passed.

Obtaining seed is another problem. Mine has come from the seed lists of the Alpine Garden Society and the American Rock Garden Society, and from friends. True aficionados also join the Cyclamen Society. Seed that has been donated to the societies may or may not be accurately labeled.

Once you have a plant or two, save your own seed to grow or share with friends. Unlike most plants that flower and set seed quickly, cyclamen seed is ripe and ready for collecting months later. For example, once a flower of *C. hederifolium* is pollinated, its stem coils down to ground level, like a bronzed spring. The hard seed capsule is in the center of the coil. Approximately six months later, the coil begins to relax and the seed pod softens. I check my plants frequently, beginning in the middle of May, because the gardener is in a race with the ants. Like bloodroot seeds, the cyclamen seed capsule attracts ants, and they quickly pounce on ripe seeds and carry them about the garden.

According to cyclamen expert Nancy Goodwin, *C. rohlfsianum* takes about ten months to produce its seed, and *C. purpurescens* can go as long as fifteen months from pollination to ripe seed. Winter-blooming *C. coum*, however, will set its seed in three to four months. Oddly enough, no matter when the cyclamen plants bloom, all seed is ripe in May or June.

Since these bulbs are so rewarding for our southern gardens, I was delighted when Nancy Goodwin opened her Montrose Nursery in 1984. While marketing a number of unusual perennials, she specializes in cyclamen, raises all of her own cyclamen from seed, and is careful about botanical accuracy. As far as I know, she is the only person in the United States who is so deeply involved with this intriguing genus.

While growing cyclamen alone can provide flowers throughout the year, there are more beautiful bulbs to plant, many more.

A small species crocus from Greece, *C. sieberi*, is usually the first to bloom in my garden, typically during the third week in January. Early in February, it is followed by *C. biflorus*, *C. chrysanthus*, and several of its cultivars, like 'Gypsy Girl' and 'Cream Beauty'. (The bloom schedule depends on the winter, of course. One year, *C. chrysanthus* opened its cheerful yellow flowers on January 8.) Along with *C. sieberi*, snowdrops (galanthus) and snowflakes (leucojum) produce their white bells in January. As you might guess from

Crocus sieberi, the first to bloom in
my garden each spring

An early snowdrop

their names, these bulbs will often poke through snow in colder climates.
Several species or cultivars of each are on the market.

In late February or early March, the large, hybrid crocus begin to flower,
along with the daffodils. 'February Gold' happens to be the earliest daffodil
I grow. At the same time, little purple drifts of *Iris reticulata* appear. Since
purple is a receding color, you need a close-up view of these small flowers,
but they are so charming that I plant several dozen bulbs each year. 'Har-
mony' is a lovely blue cultivar of this iris. If you prefer yellow, plant *I.
Danfordiae*.

While *I. reticulata* is subtle in the landscape, white, yellow, pink, and bi-
colored daffodils are splashy, particularly the large varieties like 'Mount
Hood', 'Actaea', or 'Ice Follies'. All daffodils I have planted have been reliable in my woods. They rebloom. They multiply. They come in a myriad of
sizes. I have had no insect or disease problems with daffodils and even the
voles ignore them. Wonderfully rewarding bulbs.

Gardeners in our area are particularly fortunate, because the only official
American Daffodil Society show in North Carolina is held at the North
Carolina Botanical Garden in Chapel Hill each March. Attending a specialty
show, whether it displays roses, daffodils, or lilies, is a wonderful way of seeing what is available in that plant group. New cultivars are displayed. Old
varieties compete. Strange new forms, like split corollas on daffodils, gradually gain acceptance.

Along with the daffodils comes a host of other bulbs flowering in March.
Cyclamen coum is still blooming. Muscari species add rich blues and purples
to contrast with the white and yellow daffodils. I began with *M. armenia-*

Iris reticulata

A species daffodil, *N. cananicularis*, best treated as an annual

American Daffodil Society Shows in the South

Arkansas
Hendrix College, **Conway**

Kentucky
Oxmoor Center, **Louisville**

Mississippi
Mississippi College, **Clinton**
National Guard Armory, **Hernando**

North Carolina
North Carolina Botanical Garden, **Chapel Hill**

Tennessee
Goldsmith's Civic Garden Center, **Memphis**
Cheekwood Botanical Garden, **Nashville**

Texas
Dallas Civic Garden Center, **Dallas**

Virginia
Gloucester Intermediate School, **Gloucester**
Tyson's Corner Mall, **McLean**
Christopher Newport College, **Newport News**

A massed display of *Erythronium tuolumnense* glowing in the sunlight

cum and have added other species as I could locate them in the trade. I'm
particularly fond of *M. comosum*, with its fluffy tassel top. However, southern garden writer Elizabeth Lawrence, writing about this bulb, states flatly,
"It is not pretty."

Native dogtooth violets (*Erythronium americanum*) appear, their charming little yellow heads nodding above their mottled, strappy foliage. The
larger, more showy hybrids of western species, like 'Pagoda', flower later in
the month. Years ago, the late George Lee, a plantsman with a beautiful
woodland garden in Connecticut, taught me to place a small stone beneath
erythronium bulbs. Otherwise, these bulbs tend to pull themselves deeper
and deeper into the ground each year and do not bloom well.

Previous owners had planted a large patch of blue and pink *Scilla campa-
nulata* (the woodland hyacinth) at the edge of the woods. More appear
annually.

Like muscari, alliums, and some of the other bulbs, scillas will seed themselves around, once they are established. They are easy to weed out, should
they pop up where you don't want them, and it will take many years before
I have too many.

Recently I have added *S. bifolia* to the rock garden. This small scilla from central and eastern Europe has the truest, clearest sky-blue color of any plant I know. It's charming.

A friend has just sent me a bag full of *S. autumnalis*, which he describes as "no great wonder but it *does* bloom pinkie-lavender in the fall, and is easy and self-sowing, so watch out." I'm delighted to add any fall or winter blooming plants to the garden.

Clumps of *Ipheion uniflorum* (*Tritelia uniflora*) were also scattered around the yard, and I've added more of these pale blue starflowers year by year. Again, a cultivar, 'Wisley Blue', is even better than the species. It is a richer light blue and the flowers last longer. Chionodoxas are smaller charmers of similar style, ideal for rock gardens or trough plantings.

While winter aconites (*Eranthus hyemalis* and *E. cilicia*) are reputed to be early bloomers, pushing through the January snow in northern gardens, here they bloom in mid-March. The golden yellow flowers, collared by a fringe of green leafy bracts, poke up on their short stems at the edge of the day lily bed. They grow best in a sunny location. I've found the return on investment in purchased aconites has been disappointing. Perhaps 20 to 30 percent of the dried tubers—whether presoaked or not—have broken dormancy and grown successfully for me. Perhaps you will be fortunate enough to have a friend who will share a flourishing colony of aconites with you.

Our native blue *Iris cristata* is another small springtime iris that edges paths nicely. The first spring we gardened here, a neighbor gave me some of the rhizomes, and I planted them on the driveway edge, in front of some daffodils and azaleas. I had brought a 4-inch pot of *I. cristata alba*, the white form, with me on our move from Michigan, and I divided those rhizomes and planted them around *Hydrangea quercifolia* (the oak-leaf hydrangea). Interestingly enough, the dwarf white iris is much more vigorous than the blue. If a rhizome of the blue species will send out two growths, one of the white ones will produce five or six new growths.

While the ideal time to divide the *I. c.* rhizomes is in the fall, after the foliage has ripened and gone down, this iris is resilient enough to be transplanted even while in flower—one of my favorite plants.

Another favorite group of bulbs is the anemones. Large or small, their flowers have great appeal. For spots where I want a dainty, ground-hugging effect, the finely-cut foliage and small, single, daisy-like flowers of *Anemone blanda* please me. I like to order and plant *A. blanda* in separate batches of pink, white, or blue, rather than in mixed colors as these bulbs are so often marketed. If you can locate named cultivars of these tubers, so much the better. For example, *A. b.* 'Charmer' is an improved *A. b. rosea*.

Woodland gardeners may also like the modest charms of *A. nemorosa*, the European woodland anemone. It produces its pale rose or white flowers on fragile six-to-ten-inch stems that blow in the slightest breeze. Other colors and even a double form are on the market.

With apologies for the flamboyance, I plant a large drift of *Anemone* de Caen at the edge of the woods facing the house. These large, sturdy anemones with their vivid scarlet, red, white, blue, and lavender flowers really belong in a perennial bed, not a woodland garden. However, we don't have a perennial garden at this home, and I must grow these plants, both for their beauty and as cut flowers.

Unlike daffodils, the anemones are not permanent in our woods. If I plant twenty-five that grow and flower the first year, perhaps half that number will appear the second year. I suspect they are a choice dish on our voles' menu. Since the tubers are so inexpensive and easy to plant, I now simply add a new group of anemones to the old, each fall. Because the tubers are so dried out by the time I receive them, I have followed the practice of soaking them overnight in warm water before planting. I note, however, that Roy Genders in *Bulbs, a Complete Handbook* says "this is not necessary and is a dangerous practise if the soil is heavy and badly drained."

Corydalis and fritillaria are two genera of bulbs with which I have little experience. European gardeners have been growing a number of them for many years. Some species have been appearing in our American catalogs during the past few years. While I have raise fibrous-rooted *Corydalis lutea* from seed, I have not grown the rarer, bright blue *C. cashmeriana*, a tuberous Asian variety, which I first admired in Jack Drake's nursery in Scotland. Since it thrived in his harsh northern climate, where his garden might be visited by frost every month of the year, it may well be a plant that is totally unsuited for our climate. Or perhaps it is one of the flexible marvels of the world's plant community and will do well here. I don't give up on any plant until I have killed it three times.

Fritillaria assyriaca blooms, lives, and returns in Nancy Goodwin's rock garden. *Fritillaria meleagris* is available from a number of sources, both in its wine-colored, checkerboard-patterned bells and in the white form. It grows 12 to 15 inches high and is another good subject for the rock garden. The genus *Fritillaria* is a large one—*Hortus III* mentions 100 species—and only a few of these species are available from specialist firms. The most extensive offering I have seen is in the catalog of Paul Christian in Wales.

When addressing a winter study weekend of the American Rock Garden Society, Christian urged everyone to raise frits and other bulbs from seed— sometimes the only way to obtain a rare variety. Propagating fritillarias from seed, however, is a project for the patient and serious gardener. Typically, they take seven years from seed to flower. As Christian pointed out, however, if one starts some seed each year, then after seven years, an interesting

One of the more unusual frits, *Fritillaria persicum*, adding its interesting form and subtle color to a southern garden

parade of blooming fritillarias will continue to flow out of the propagating area. (I'm in the fifth year of this project for optimists.)

While I enjoy a certain number of gardening challenges, I'm very appreciative of easy plants, easy methods. A number of the summer-flowering bulbs fall into this category—tuberous begonias, for example. No, not the typical tuberous begonias that flourish in the cool California mists at Antonelli's in Capitola, but the relatively new 'Non Stop' tuberous begonias, bred and introduced by the Ernst Benary Seed Company of Germany. These plants that were bred for heat-resistance have smaller flowers than regular tuberous begonias, but they are prolific, and they thrive in our summer heat and humidity. They are excellent plants for hanging baskets and other containers. 'Non Stop' begonias can be purchased as tubers or raised easily from seed.

Gladioli are another group of summer bulbs that are reliable and easy—plant healthy corms in full sun and they will bloom. Glads will grow in sandy or clay soils, but they must be well drained. Plant them 4–6 inches deep. They are less apt to need staking if grown in heavy soil or planted a little deeper in sandy soil. It is difficult to plant them too deep. On Crete, I noticed that while tourists admired the carmine spikes of *G. segetum* decorating every cultivated field, this species glad is a terrible pest to the farmers, because it pulls its corms 12 inches or more into the ground, below the blades of the plows. In the *Encyclopedia of Horticulture*, Thomas Everett notes that some of the Mediterranean species are hardy as far north as New York, if given a little mulch or other protection. Otherwise, we must dig and store both glads and tuberous begonias in the South.

Plants advertised as "hardy gladioli," actually acidanthera, look much like glads and the corms can winter in the ground. They need the same culture.

Gloriosa lilies (*Gloriosa Rothschildiana*) are wonderfully exotic additions to our southern landscape. The tubers can be grown successfully in containers, but in zone 8, the plants are fully hardy in the ground. Several readers who have old, reliable plants grow them in full sun on the south side of their homes. If you choose to grow gloriosas in pots, treat them much like amaryllis bulbs. Water and feed all summer and then let them dry off in the fall. Restart the tubers in the early spring.

Perhaps you want some 12-to-15-inch, knock-em-dead flowers atop 6-foot foliage for your large perennial garden or a border of foot-high, shrubby plants covered with 2-inch flowers from late summer until frost. Whatever the size and scale of your garden, there's a dahlia for you.

When I gardened in colder climes, I always thought of dahlias as labor-intensive plants, because they had to be dug each fall, stored carefully, and re-

In mid-summer, exotic gloriosa lilies enhance any garden. Grow the vines on a fence or on tall stakes.

Two of the many forms of dahlia flowers available today

planted the following spring. Not so in the South. Here dahlias need only a winter coat of mulch to survive our chilly days and nights.

Dr. De Hertogh is extremely high on these tuberous-rooted plants. "I feel the dahlia is one of the underutilized plants in the mid-South landscape," he says.

He recommends planting the dahlia tubers after all chance of frost is past. Enjoy the weeks of bloom in early summer and then, when those horrendously hot nights sock in and the dahlias begin to look miserable, cut them back drastically. Leave only two to three nodes on the largest ones and just 3 inches on the dwarfs. Regrowth will occur rapidly and they will produce exuberant bloom again in the early fall, lasting until frost.

Perhaps we all ought to take a fresh look at these plants that offer so much variety in color, shape, and size. They come in white and pink, rose, red, yellow, orange, lavender, purple, blends, and bicolors—almost every conceivable tint and hue except a true blue. For form, one gardener will be particularly attracted to the spiky cactus shape of some dahlia flowers, while another may prefer the soft, rounded petals of those classified as decorative.

Culture for dahlias is relatively simple. Enrich the bed with liberal amounts of compost, peat moss, or well-rotted manure and provide plenty of drainage. Plant the tubers with the crowns 2–3 inches below the surface of the soil. Stake the tall ones when you plant the tubers.

Locate your dahlia planting where it will receive some midday protection from the glaring sun. I remember visiting a Connecticut dahlia hobbyist who was growing 900 varieties in full sun, out in an open field. Here in the South, however, dahlias will do better with a small amount of shade.

You might call dahlias greedy plants on two counts; they like a lot of water and a lot of food. It's almost impossible to overfeed a dahlia, so plan on providing a balanced fertilizer at least once a month and preferably twice.

De Hertogh recommends heavy, frequent waterings, but notes that soaking the ground rather than watering overhead minimizes mildew problems. He also urges using a mulch around dahlia plantings to help keep the garden moist.

All experts seem to agree that an early pinch produces a more compact, attractive dahlia. Whether you have the large types or dwarfs, when the plants have two or three sets of true leaves, pinch out the center to stimulate all the lateral buds into growth. My Connecticut friend gave all her large dahlias a second pinch when the side shoots produced three sets of leaves.

Soon you will notice buds forming at the ends of the growing shoots—typically, a terminal bud and a couple of side buds. While these buds are small, you have a choice. If you leave all buds alone, you will have a generous display of relatively small flowers, which produces a fine mass effect in the garden. However, if you choose to disbud by removing all the side buds and allowing only the terminal flower to develop, you will produce fewer but larger flowers on longer stems, flowers suitable for show competition or for excellent cut flowers for your home. Never be reluctant to cut your dahlias; trimming simply spurs the plants into renewed growth and more flower production.

Dahlias are relatively pest-free. Aphids can be a problem, and Japanese beetles always munch on dahlias during their yearly invasion. If you have just a few plants, picking the beetles off by hand is effective, but in a large garden, you will probably choose to use an insecticide. Sevin works against both Japanese beetles and aphids, but must be repeated often.

In addition to purchasing named tuber cultivars, which are available in garden centers, in general seed catalogs, and from specialist nurseries, you can also raise dahlias from seed. It's fun to raise seedlings, of course, and if you want a large number of plants, it is also the most economical way to begin. The named tubers are varieties that have been carefully selected for their qualities of vigor, color, habit, and form; they are propagated vegetatively. When you raise a batch of seedlings, most of the plants will be acceptable, but perhaps only one or two will produce tubers worthy of saving for another year.

Whether you are raising the dwarf types from seed or tubers, keep in mind that they will perform as well in containers as in the garden. Three plants of a bright pink, cactus-flowered, dwarf dahlia planted in a redwood tub would be eye-catching on any patio.

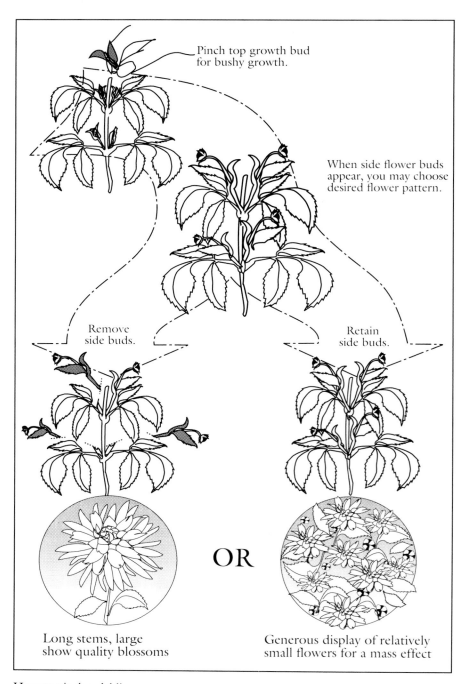

Pinch top growth bud for bushy growth.

When side flower buds appear, you may choose desired flower pattern.

Remove side buds.

Retain side buds.

OR

Long stems, large show quality blossoms

Generous display of relatively small flowers for a mass effect

How to pinch a dahlia

Agapanthus and lilies are two other summer-blooming, bulbous plants that will do well in containers or in the garden. I first encountered the lovely, airy umbels of *Agapanthus africanus* held high above strappy foliage when we moved to California from New England. The large, evergreen plants with blue or white flowers were fully hardy on the Monterey Peninsula, and there I also grew a miniature named 'Peter Pan'.

When we moved here, I wondered if agapanthus would do well in our garden, because the climates are similar. The Piedmont is just slightly colder. The first few gardeners I asked told me that agapanthus would not succeed here, but then a neighbor who had been growing a blue form for several years shared her plants with me, and they have thrived. They have survived the rigorous winters of 1983–84 and 1984–85. They endure our summer drought and muggy days and flower reliably every year.

My neighbor ordered these plants, sold as *A. africanus* 'Peter Pan', from the old Wayside Gardens in 1971. They are deciduous, not evergreen, although all my references agree that *A. africanus* is evergreen. In her recent book on perennials, Pamela Harper says that *A. africanus* is suitable for frost-free regions. These plants, sold as *A. africanus*, survived −9° easily.

Nomenclature for this genus of plants is confusing. You may find the same plant marketed as *A. orientalis*, *A. africanus*, or perhaps *A. umbellatus*. Since a number of our nurseries are beginning to carry agapanthus, I'd urge you to give these plants a try, no matter what name they carry.

I would like to collect some of the Headbourne hybrids that Pam Harper is growing in her garden. She describes them as fully hardy, deciduous, vigorous, drought resistant, growing in a low-fertility soil. "There is no reason why agapanthus should not become as common in Southeastern gardens as they are in California," she says.

In the ongoing point-counterpoint game of plant preferences, I noticed that California gardener Robert Cowden, writing in the spring 1987 issue of *Pacific Horticulture*, while talking about the ravages of deer in gardens, says, "We should welcome anything that will stop this blue rash [of agapanthus] from spreading."

In ground or in pots, these are not fussy plants. The ideal soil for them is a rich, loose loam, but they will tolerate clay nicely. They are labeled drought resistant. Water them frequently the first year, while they are getting established, and then they will be quite undemanding.

Mine are planted in a part of the garden where they get one feeding of a balanced fertilizer when the foliage appears in the spring and only sporadic watering. Some southern gardeners grow agapanthus in full sun. Mine are flowering nicely in partial shade—desirable, adaptable plants.

As with all flowering plants, it is a good idea to cut off the dead flower heads, unless you want to save the seeds. However, the dry agapanthus flower heads and stems are wonderful for dried arrangements in the fall, so I leave mine on the plants for that purpose. You can use them in their natural beige color or spray them any fanciful hue you choose. I've painted them bright orange for a competitive flower arrangement and white with a dusting of crystal glitter for a holiday bouquet.

I'm fond of multiple-purpose plants, particularly in a yard where gardening space is limited. Agapanthus are in this category: lovely plants in the garden, fine cut flowers, and interesting dried material.

Lilies can be somewhat more difficult in the South. Most of the great lily gardens are in the Northeast, the Northwest, and Canada, where the summer nights are cool and winter frosts help to control pathogens. However, there are a number of determined lily hobbyists in the South. One of the country's best lily growers lives in Chapel Hill. Retired chemistry professor George Doak is a judge for the North American Lily Society, and he has been growing and showing lilies since he was a young boy.

In addition to losing a number of lilies to disease problems here, Doak also used to have considerable trouble with voles. Evidently, like the man desperate for a cigarette, voles will scramble a mile for a lily bulb. After losing a number of lilies to these varmints, Doak tried planting lilies in wire baskets, only to discover that zinc was leaching from the wire baskets into the soil and stunting lily growth.

Finally another gardener suggested mixing quantities of gravel with the garden soil. Voles evidently find it most unpleasant and not worth the effort to dig their way through a gravel bed. Following this advice, Doak added 1 ton of gravel to each of two 10-by-15-foot beds, mixed the gravel with the soil to a depth of 12 inches, and has not been bothered by voles since.

Each fall, Doak adds some new lily bulbs to his prepared beds. "To me, one of the most important things in growing lilies is to buy from a reputable dealer—someone specializing in lilies," says Doak. He points out that unlike tulips, daffodils, and other hardy bulbs, lilies have only a short rest period. They are never truly dormant, so it is most important that the bulbs and their roots do not dry out. Specialists pay careful attention to the demands of lily bulb care, storage, and shipment; other firms usually do not.

When he sees the first growth in the spring, Doak feeds the lily garden with 2-10-10. "If I get around to it, I also use a little superphosphate in the fall," he added.

Standard care includes watering, weeding, mulching, and spraying. He likes to use a relatively thick cover of pine straw after his springtime weeding sessions. Spraying against aphids is a constant chore. "Aphids love the broad-leaved Orientals. They also spread virus problems. Since the Orientals

Lilium pumilum, an Asian species that thrives in the South

are readily susceptible to virus, I try to keep the aphids under control," says Doak. He routinely uses Malathion to combat aphids and, when necessary, sprays with Benlate to control botrytis.

While the beds of Asiatic lilies, like 'Enchantment', are in full sun, the Orientals receive some shade. "Orientals even prefer some dappled shade," says Doak. Take note, shade gardeners; there are some lilies you can grow successfully. There are also a number of species lilies for cultivation in sun or shade.

One advantage lilies bring to a garden is a long blooming sequence. By proper selection of bulb varieties, you can have lilies flowering in your yard over several months. Here, the Asiatics bloom in May and June, followed by the more spectacular Orientals during July and August.

To learn more about lily culture, read "Let's Grow Lilies," by Virginia Howie. This publication is available from the North American Lily Society for three dollars.

Along with Oriental lilies, caladiums are bulbous plants suitable for light shade or even relatively heavy shade. After all danger of frost is past, plant the tubers in containers or in the ground, water thoroughly, and watch them quickly sprout and unfurl those exotic heart-shaped or lanceolate leaves. The only care they will need is regular watering and an occasional feeding with a balanced fertilizer.

The first year I raised caladiums, I tried them in every possible location. Potted tubers grew in the house, on the shady screen porch, and in my sunniest outdoor location. In the first two places, the plants did develop some foliage, but they were too leggy. The potted caladiums in considerable sunlight were still attractive and compact on October 1. They produced their decorative foliage throughout the garden season. They also flowered, putting forth rather insignificant, arum-shaped flowers that matched the foliage. Cultivars do vary slightly in their light requirements.

Those caladium tubers I planted at the edge of the woods also thrived, but they looked terrible. Caladium foliage is so exotic that it looks totally out of place in a deciduous woodland. I quickly pulled them out.

However, their color range of white and green, rose-red and green, and pink and green was compatible with annual vinca 'Pink Panther'. In a formal bed, I planted some tubers between day lilies and filled the bed with this vinca. After the June day lily explosion, the vinca and caladiums made an attractive combination for the rest of the season.

These tubers are suitable for any sort of organized, formal planting, whether it be a raised bed, a foundation planting, a circle around a tree, or a container garden. Mass plantings of the same variety—such as 'White Queen', which has large white, heart-shaped leaves edged with green and veined in red—are particularly effective.

In October, caladium foliage begins to yellow and droop. Then dig the tubers, let them dry for a few days, allow the foliage to drop off naturally, and store them at room temperature in dry peat moss or sand until it is time to start the cycle again in the spring.

Indoors or out, my caladiums were bothered by neither pest nor disease. I consider them one of those wonderfully foolproof plants we all can grow with ease. Even if you are an extremely sophisticated gardener who loves a horticultural challenge, isn't it nice to have a few "reliables" in the yard?

For sunny locations, the large genus of alliums offers flowers in many sizes and colors. All are easy to grow. Perhaps you are already raising chives, leeks, garlic, or onions in your garden—all alliums. Of the more than 400 different allium species, only a handful are now on the market. If you have a sizable perennial garden, you might like the large violet balls of *A. giganteum*. For a large rock garden, try *A. karataviense*. Its broad, colorful leaves hug the ground and small spheres of white flowers tinged with lilac bloom on short stems. *Allium moly* produces bright yellow, airy flower heads on stems 12 to 18 inches high. You will find these and a few other allium varieties in catalogs today.

Lycoris are other summer- and fall-blooming bulbs that are reliable once established. However, they resent transplanting and may take two or three years to start blooming again after a move.

Lycoris squamigera, the South's 'Naked Ladies,' put up their strappy foliage in the spring. Then the foliage dies down and in midsummer tall stalks appear, carrying several large, pink flowers.

My favorite member of this genus is the red spider lily (*L. radiata*), which blooms in late September in my garden. Those airy flowers with their long, curved stamens seem to fulfill philosopher Mortimer Adler's two-pronged definition of beauty. Subjectively, they bring me great pleasure. I stop and look and smile. Objectively, the spider lily has inherent beauty, a perfection of form that makes it admirable in and of itself.

In *A Southern Garden*, Elizabeth Lawrence writes that the first red spider lilies were brought to North Carolina from Japan before the Civil War by Captain William Roberts, who accompanied Commodore Perry. They have multiplied and spread across the state. These lycoris are not hardy in Asheville or north of Baltimore but are a southern delight. More species are now available from some bulb specialists, providing white, yellow, purple, and orange lycoris for our gardens.

Other bulbs we all might add to our gardens for fall color, in addition to the lycoris and cyclamen previously mentioned, include the vivid yellow *Sternbergia lutea*, autumn crocus species, and a number of colchicum species and cultivars. *Colchicum* 'Lilac Wonder' is a large-flowered beauty with a lovely luminous quality to its flowers that I find particularly attractive.

The beauty of bulbs can reward you throughout the year. Often they work well if double-planted. For example, I have *Lycoris radiata* coming up through a ground cover of a spring-flowering phlox; my neighbor raises hers in a large bed covered with *Vinca minor*. Daffodils are aggressive enough to poke through ivy or vinca. Many combinations are attractive and double the use of the same garden space.

Since we order spring-flowering bulbs in the fall and autumn-flowering

Lycoris squamigera, the "Naked Ladies" of the South, blooming on bare stems late in the summer

ones in the summer, we often forget where we want new bulbs to be planted and where we already have some underground. I find it useful to make a few notes and take some photographs each season, as I stroll around the garden. When the daffodils and tulips are in bloom, look critically at your garden and jot down where you would like to add some more the following year. Note where you have a bare spot, a place to try something new. Be sure to add some new bulbs to your garden every year.

Red spider lilies (*Lycoris radiata*), more refined and elegant than
L. squamigera

Best Tulip, Daffodil, and Hyacinth Cultivars for the South

Flower	Zone 7	Zone 8	Zone 9
Tulips			
Very early bloom			Demeter
			Showwinner
			Stresa
Early	Dillenberg	White Emperor	Christmas Marvel
	Orange Emperor	(Purissima)	Toronto
			Queen of Sheba
			Beauty of Apeldoorn
			White Emperor
			(Purissima)
			Yokohama
Mid-season	High Society	Orange Emperor	Oranjezon
	Juan	Diplomate	Apeldoorn
	Demeter	Holland's Glorie	Margaret Herbst
	Negrita	Oxford	Oxford
	Diplomate	Merry Widow	Spring Song
	Frankfurt	Spring Song	Parade
	Ile de France	Beauty of Apeldoorn	Don Quichotte
	Oscar	Lucky Strike	Bellona
	Oxford	Parade	Candela
	Toronto	Candela	Yellow Dover
	Leen van der Mark	Golden Apeldoorn	Golden Oxford
	Merry Widow	Golden Parade	Striped Apeldoorn
	Princess Victoria	Monte Carlo	
	Spring Song	Yellow Dover	
	Beauty of Apeldoorn	Golden Oxford	
	Los Angeles	Jewel of Spring	
	Thule	Gudoshnik	
	Blenda	Striped Apeldoorn	
	Preludium		
	Kierzerskroon		
	Kansas		
	Candela		
	Golden Apeldoorn		
	Golden Parade		
	Hoangho		
	Yellow Dover		
	Yokohama		
	Golden Oxford		
	Jewel of Spring		
	Gudoshnik		
	Striped Apeldoorn		

Flower	Zone 7	Zone 8	Zone 9
Tulips			
Late	Oranjezon	Orange Bouquet	Angelique
	Bing Crosby	Rosy Wings	Balalaika
	Dyanito	Red Matador	Renown
	Holland's Glorie	Kees Nelis	
	Oriental Beauty	Don Quichotte	
	Kees Nelis	Jimmy	
	Ballade	Gordon Cooper	
	Ad Rem	Duke of Wellington	
	Karel Doorman	Maureen	
	Parade	West Point	
	Don Quichotte		
	Jimmy		
	Gordon Cooper		
	Prince Charles		
	Arabian Mystery		
	Dreaming Maid		
	Make Up		
	Delmonte		
	Douglas Baader		
	West Point		
Very late		Orange Favourite	Orange Favourite
		Burgundy Lace	
		Sorbet	
		Smiling Queen	
Daffodils			
Very early bloom	Ice Follies	Ice Follies	Ice Follies
	Fortune	Fortune	Tête a Tête
	Jumblie	February Gold	February Gold
	Brighton	Gigantic Star	Gigantic Star
	February Gold	Unsurpassable	
	Gigantic Star		
	Golden Harvest		
	Unsurpassable		
	Yellow Sun		
Early	Barrett Browning	Flower Record	Flower Record
	Estella de Mol	Barrett Browning	Barrett Browning
	Magnet	Magnet	Goblet
	Sugarbush	Jumblie	Carbineer
	Van Sion	Tête a Tête	Fortune
		Trevithian	Jumblie
			Brighton

Flower	Zone 7	Zone 8	Zone 9
Daffodils			
Mid-season	Flower Record	Professor Einstein	Mount Hood
	Professor Einstein	Mount Hood	Thalia Triandrus
	Mount Hood	Duke of Windsor	Tresamble
	Jack Snipe	Estella de Mol	Estella de Mol
	Minnow	Goblet	Sugarbush
	Birma	Jack Snipe	Birma
	Carbineer	Minnow	Inglescombe
	Tahiti	Sugarbush	Peeping Tom
	Peeping Tom	Birma	Standard Value
	Standard Value	Carbineer	Trevithian
	Trevithian	Peeping Tom	Yellow Hope Petticoat
		Standard Value	
Late	Flower Drift	Mary Copeland	Geranium
	Mrs. R. O. Backhouse	Salome	Mary Copeland
	Salome	Thalia Triandrus	Mrs. R. O. Backhouse
	Thalia Triandrus	Tresamble	Bridal Crown
	Tresamble	Bridal Crown	Suzy
	Bridal Crown	Suzy	Baby Moon
	Suzy	Hawera	Hawera
Very late	Geranium	Geranium	Salome
		Mrs. R. O. Backhouse	Yellow Cheerfulness
		Cheerfulness	
Hyacinths			
	Delft Blue	Blue Jacket	Blue Jacket
	Ostara	Delft Blue	Delft Blue
	City of Haarlem	Ostara	Ostara
		Lady Derby	Lady Derby
		Jan Bos	Pink Pearl
		City of Haarlem	Carnegie

These recommendations are based on a four-year study directed by Dr. Paul V. Nelson of North Carolina State University. The 250 bulb cultivars tested were rated on a scale of 0 to 5. The cultivars shown here are those that rated 3 or above. The test beds in Fletcher (zone 7) and Raleigh (zone 8) were of typical southern clay. The tests at the coast in Wilmington (zone 9) were in a sandy soil. The complete results of the study are available, at $2.00 per copy, from the Department of Agricultural Communications, Box 7630, North Carolina State University, Raleigh, NC 27695.

9

Roses

Poets wax rhapsodic about the ethereal beauty of roses. Even today's most liberated ladies are charmed by the gift of a dozen long-stemmed red roses. Each year, more than 625 million cut roses are grown and sold in the United States. And by the thousands, Americans want to raise roses in their gardens. Roses are romantic, rewarding, demanding, richly colored or pale and subtle of hue, often fragrant, always beautiful. No wonder the rose was selected as our national flower in 1986. Whether you want to grow a miniature rose in a 3-inch pot on your windowsill or enjoy a floriferous climbing "Peace" rose romping 30 feet or more along a balcony railing; whether you choose to raise the latest introduction in hybrid teas, vivid and multipetaled, or seek the charm of an ancient, single, five-petaled rose from China, there is a rose for you and your garden.

If you are an absolute beginner wondering which roses to select for your yard, there are several ways to go about your search. Visit your community rose garden, walk the paths, and jot down the names of the plants you most admire. Almost every town has a public rose garden, such is the popularity of these beautiful flowers. For example, here in the Research Triangle, Raleigh has a large municipal rose garden which includes a display of All-America Rose Selections, Duke University has a lovely rose garden in Durham at the Sarah P. Duke Gardens, Chapel Hill offers a richesse of roses in front of the Morehead Planatarium, and there are a number of other, smaller display gardens around our area. Certainly, if you are ever near Shreveport, Louisiana, be sure to visit the American Rose Society garden where more than 15,000 rose bushes are on display.

Attend the nearest rose show. Rosarians love to share their expertise with one another and with interested newcomers. There will be informative educational exhibits, and flowers, a wonderful abundance of flowers. If you spend some time at the show tables, admiring blooms and reading labels, you can see which roses make the best show roses and which varieties appeal to you. Catalog photographs are often deceptive. As one local rose grower said, "Give me an ordinary rose, some water to sprinkle on its petals and a camera with a close-up lens, and I will give you a magnificent rose picture." It's better to see the real flower, in order to appreciate its size and fragrance and substance. In the average rose show, you will see 200 or more different varieties, including hybrid teas, grandifloras, floribundas, polyanthas, climbers, shrubs, old roses, and miniatures. In a public garden, you would have the advantage of seeing the growth habits of the different varieties, but the number of varieties would usually be limited to a few dozen.

Visit private gardens. In our area, each May several of the members of the local rose society open their gardens to the public on a Sunday afternoon. Each garden is interesting, and they differ widely. In one city yard, the owners raise more than 1000 varieties for show competition and garden beauty. At another home, the gentleman is growing rows of understock and has selected a number of reliable parents for his sizable hybridizing project. In all the gardens, the host gardeners willingly chat about their joys and problems in rose growing. Check your newspaper in the spring. Probably some similar event is going on in your town. Also, in many cities, I know that the local rosarians offer rose-pruning clinics in early spring, and these clinics are a fine way to learn about rose care in your locale.

The American Rose Society also has organized a large group of Consulting Rosarians. Throughout the country, these experienced growers are ready

All-America Rose Selections Gardens for the South

Test Gardens
Thomasville Nurseries, Thomasville, Georgia

University of Southwestern Louisiana, Lafayette, Louisiana

Missouri Botanical Gardens, St. Louis, Missouri

Tulsa, Oklahoma

Orangeburg, South Carolina

Tyler Rose Garden, Tyler, Texas

Demonstration Garden
Fernbank Science Center, Atlanta, Georgia

---

and willing to share their knowledge with novice growers. For a list of the Consulting Rosarians, write to the American Rose Society.

The society also publishes an annual *Handbook for Selecting Roses*, which lists all the roses commercially available in the United States, from miniatures to climbers, states their color classes, and rates them as to how well they grow. To order the handbook, send one dollar and a self-addressed, stamped envelope to the American Rose Society.

Let's assume you decide to raise modern hybrids. Pick your site in a sunny spot and prepare the soil. As with so many of our plantings in the South, good drainage is one of the answers to successful rose cultivation here. For some gardens, raised beds are the best solution. If you will be growing in a bed at ground level, spade in a lot of organic material to create a friable soil.

How do you want to grow roses? Do you want to have beds of neatly mulched rose bushes lined up in precise patterns? Do you want rose beds edged with some low plant like thyme, dwarf yaupon holly, or Mondo grass? Or do you want your roses incorporated into perennial beds? Rose growing is a high-maintenance sport. From the first leaf break in the spring until the last leaf fall at frost, rose growers need to maintain a constant spray program to produce perfect roses. Because of this attention roses demand, it is easiest to raise them in rose beds, rather than in combination with other plants that don't need that continuous maintenance. However, if you think of combining a luscious, clear pink 'Queen Elizabeth' grandiflora rose with spikes of blue veronica or salvia and airy white baby's breath, or some orange-red 'Spartan' floribundas beside pale blue *Linum perennis* blowing in each breeze, with some white petunias in the foreground, you can envision roses adding great richness and beauty to any perennial garden or bedding plant display.

If you intend to grow most of your roses for competition, and you want only show-quality plants in your yard, I suggest creating rose beds. Otherwise, grow them in combination with other plants if you choose.

Where do you purchase your first roses? Many people begin by picking up one of those tempting bundles at the grocery store. These plants are generally inexpensive, but they are not of the best quality and only a few varieties are available. Since today all roses are graded and the top grade is #1, I would urge buyers to pay a little more and begin with a top quality plant. Number 1 roses are sturdy plants that must have three or four healthy canes, and once planted, they will take off quickly to become floriferous, vigorous plants.

But perhaps the grocery store purchase lived and bloomed, and you are then tempted to buy more varieties. Check out your local garden center.

Frequently nurseries and garden centers bring in some of the more reliable cultivars and offer 'Fragrant Cloud', 'Tropicana', 'Electron', or 'Chicago Peace'. Even better, perhaps you live somewhere near a firm that specializes in roses and brings in 100 or more varieties during the winter, pots them up, and offers well-established container plants that are growing vigorously by the time for early spring planting.

If you do not have access to any good, container-grown roses, don't despair. It is perfectly easy to order dormant, bare-root roses from specialist firms like Jackson and Perkins. Plant them carefully, and they will flourish. (One local rosarian is particularly pleased with the roses shipped to him by a Canadian firm, Hortico.) If you are not ready to plant your roses when the shipment arrives, hold them in a trench. Bury the roots, water them well, and they will wait until you are ready to work in the garden.

Since roses have relatively large root systems, dig a generous hole for each rose. We usually follow the old directions of making a small mound in the center of the hole and spreading the roots out over that mound. Placement of the rose in the ground is important. The crown (that spot where the graft was budded onto the understock) should be just above ground level, here in the South. After the rose is in place, my husband fills the hole about two-thirds full of soil and then sticks a gently flowing hose down into the hole and soaks it thoroughly. He then fills in the rest of the hole and waters again.

With the roses all planted, your maintenance begins. They need regular watering, feeding, and spraying. Here in the heat and humidity of the South, our worst rose problems seem to be diseases like black spot and mildew. Rain is inevitable, but otherwise, to minimize fungal problems, do not water overhead. Soak the ground. Of the methods we have tried, I have been most satisfied with a Chapin-type irrigation system. We buried the large, black plastic hose under mulch and ran individual spaghetti tubes tipped with small emitters to each rose. At the hose bib, we installed an inexpensive timer that I could turn on easily to water the rose garden for an hour or for two hours, as needed. In our periods of drought, the roses should be watered thoroughly once a week.

An inch of mulch will help to retain the moisture, as well as minimizing weeding and making the bed more attractive. Which mulch you use is a matter of taste and cost. Many materials are suitable. Here in the Piedmont, bark or pine needles are the most available mulches. Perhaps shredded sugar cane or buckwheat hulls are the mulch of choice in your area.

How heavily you feed will depend on whether you are a competitive rosarian, trying to produce the largest flowers on the best-looking, dark green, leathery foliage or just enjoying a few roses in your yard. The casual grower will probably toss some complete fertilizer on the roses early in the springtime, along with all the perennials and shrubs, and feed them again later in the spring and once again late in the summer. The serious grower feeds monthly and may use a foliar feed a week or two before a show. One of our competitive growers has decided that feeding smaller amounts every two weeks produces the most winning flowers, and considering the trophies he wins each year, I cannot argue with him.

To produce perfect, show-stopping flowers on damage-free foliage, many rosarians spray once a week with a combined fungicide and insecticide. At this time, the most effective complete spray is Orthenex, although older, reliable products like Phaltan, Benlate, or Daconil can give good results as fungicides. Since new products are being developed and older chemicals frequently being withdrawn from the market, it is difficult to give specific recommendations. I suggest following the advice of your county extension agent who should be informed about all of the latest research and recommendations.

To minimize fungal problems, try planting the rose varieties that are most resistant. Chapel Hill's leading rosarian, Gene Strowd, has found that the 'Portrait', 'White Masterpiece', 'Electron', 'Tropicana', 'Tiffany', 'Peace', 'Lady X', 'Queen Elizabeth', 'Gold Medal', 'Pristine', and 'Pink Parfait' have fewer fungus problems than the others. You will note that there are no red varieties on his list.

'Gold Medal', an outstanding rose for southern gardens

To prevent noticeable insect damage, inspect your plants daily, identify any problems early, and use the appropriate treatment. Aphids are probably the most common pest on the succulent tips of rose shrubs, but Japanese beetles head for rose, clematis, crape myrtle, and hibiscus plants as moths to a flame, and roses can also be bothered by scale, thrips, mites, and some other pests.

The homeowner who is simply enjoying some roses in his perennial garden will be much more relaxed about foliar damage than the competitive rosarian in the weeks before a show. The gardener who chooses to use no chemicals at all in his garden also accepts some damage. Like my grandmother who threw the dishpan full of soapy water on her roses to wash away the aphids, today's organic gardener may use Safer Insecticidal Soap. And that same gardener may handpick the Japanese beetles and drop them in a can of kerosene rather than spray or dust the plants. How you treat your roses—your entire garden—is both a practical and a philosophical matter.

So far I have discussed all the work involved in raising roses. Let's not forget the great rewards. You can decorate your home throughout the garden season with beautiful cut roses. 'Betty Prior' shrubs, covered with single pink-and-white flowers, can be used en masse as a low hedge, or two or three bushes might make a pleasant planting by the kitchen steps. A climbing 'Cecile Brunner' will both decorate the pole or trellis where it is planted and provide miniature pink flowers for tiny arrangements. You can share bouquets with friends and family. Some prostrate roses can serve as ground covers. Dried petals make wonderful potpourri to enjoy during the winter months. The flowers themselves can be dried in silica gel for use in dried flower arrangements. Tree rose bushes make wonderful container plants for your patio. If competition is part of the fun of gardening for you, you can work and dream and hope one day to win the Queen of the Show at your local springtime rose show. Roses are extremely beautiful, and there are many different ways to enjoy them. Sharing them is one of the great joys of growing roses.

Expect that your rose garden will have one magnificent burst of bloom in the late springtime, the plants will continue to bear occasional flowers throughout the heat of the summer, and with the cooler days of fall, they will produce another generous flush.

With the first frost, it is time to put your rose bushes to bed for the winter. That is an easier task here in the South than it is for northern gardeners. I have a friend in Minneapolis who loves roses, and to grow them successfully there, he goes through an onerous process called the Minnesota Tip. For each of his thirty-five tea roses, he digs a trench. He loosens the root ball and tips the entire plant on its side in the trench. He then covers the plant with soil and adds a layer of leaves for the winter months. We don't have to go to such extremes.

However, as you know, our winters can be tricky. The hardest weather for roses and all our other trees and shrubs to endure occurs during those winters when we have warm, mild weather for weeks. Nothing has hardened off. Then we get zapped with below zero temperatures. Tender, lush growth is badly damaged or killed. During the worst winter I have experienced here, I was out in my shirtsleeves on New Year's Day. The temperature was in the 70s. Two weeks later, we were shocked by record-breaking cold that killed many plants and put old established camellias and crape myrtles to the ground. Rosarians lost quite a few roses that year.

There are a number of ways to protect roses during the winter. Several regional experts seem to agree that covering the base of each plant with a generous mound of mulch offers adequate protection here. Gene Strowd says, "The best thing anyone can do is to make collars out of 3-foot building paper, staple the ends together, place the collars around the roses and fill them with a mulch that drains well." He also prunes each shrub back to about 3 feet to avoid stress from vigorous winter winds. If a tall shrub is buffeted back and forth, it tends to become loosened and perhaps to crack open the ground, leaving roots vulnerable to cold and damage.

Later in the winter season, Strowd applies a dormant spray of lime and sulphur. He uses this spray once after the third hard frost, and he repeats it again about the middle of February. This spray eliminates any lingering red spider mites and helps to control fungal problems. If you are a relative newcomer to the South, having gardened in northern climes, and have never used a dormant spray on your roses, remember that this spray can be a useful addition to your rose maintenance program in this part of the country.

When the buds begin to break in early springtime, it is time to prune your roses for the coming season. Be sure to have sharp loppers and hand pruners available. As in all pruning, you first want to prevent or eliminate a wild tangle of criss-crossing branches. Then you shape the shrub. When pruning your hybrid teas, grandifloras, and floribundas, you are trying to encourage a symmetrical, open form for each shrub. You do this by cutting to specific buds and directing the new growth outward.

Remove any buds that are breaking where you do not want a new branch to grow by simply rubbing the small bud off the stem with your finger. Frequently three tiny shoots are forming at one node. One will grow slightly to the right, one in the center, and one slightly to the left. Select the one that will be most desirable for the shape of your plant and rub off the others. This fingertip pruning is fast and easy.

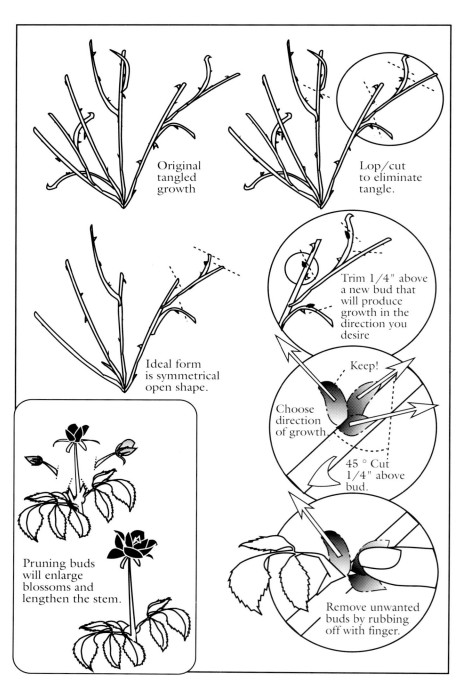

Original
tangled
growth

Lop/cut
to eliminate
tangle.

Ideal form
is symmetrical
open shape.

Trim 1/4" above
a new bud that
will produce
growth in the
direction you
desire

Keep!

Choose
direction
of growth.

45 ° Cut
1/4" above
bud.

Pruning buds
will enlarge
blossoms and
lengthen the stem.

Remove unwanted
buds by rubbing
off with finger.

Pruning a rose

Pruning a climber depends on which variety you plant. Ones that grow slowly may just need damaged tips or branches removed. Rampant ones should receive vigorous pruning to keep them attractive. If you are growing one of the latter types, remove some of the oldest canes each year after the first flush of spring bloom.

One reader wrote to ask me what to do after a rose blooms and the blossom fades. Should she clip off the remains? Absolutely! With roses, as with our other garden flowers, the practice of dead-heading is desirable. If you remove the spent flowers, you are preventing that plant from setting seeds, and the plant's energy will go into producing more flowers.

When you remove a spent rose, however, don't just snip off the top. Each time you cut a rose for the house or dead-head a garden flower, you should thoughtfully prune your shrub. Cutting, after all, is pruning, whether good or bad pruning. When you want to cut a stem, let your eye roam down that stem to the next outward-growing bud. Prune that stem just above that bud and make your cut at an angle. A good rule of thumb is to cut just above the second five-segment leaf from the top.

There's an exception to every rule, of course, and there are some old-fashioned roses like the rugosas that are grown as much for the beauty of their hips as for their flowers. *Rosa carolina* keeps its shiny red hips until late winter, and *R. virginiana*'s fruits are lovely until late fall. These old roses should not be dead-headed but allowed to form those large, decorative, red or orange hips. Remember, too, that rose hips are an excellent source of vitamin C, and they can be made into syrup or jelly.

Whether it is nostalgia, a yearning for the rich fragrances bred out of so many of the modern roses, or the practical search for disease-resistant roses, many gardeners today are growing and appreciating old roses. An old rose garden is full of romantic names like 'Zephirine Drouhin', 'Souvenir de la Malmaison', 'Rose de Rescht', all antique hybrids, and ancient species like *Rosa damascena bifera*, extolled for its intense perfume since Greek and Roman days. This damask rose is the source for attar of roses, still used in many of today's perfumes.

Many of the ancient species roses and their hybrid offspring bloom only once, in the springtime. However, during the late 1700s, species roses from China were introduced to Europe and used in breeding new and lovely roses. The China roses brought with them the characteristic of blooming more than once a year, so today we have many desirable old roses—early hybrids—that put on a magnificent show in the late spring and then bloom sporadically the rest of the year. The China roses also contributed a less desirable genetic characteristic: they are slightly more tender and more susceptible to mildew than other lines of old roses.

'Old Blush', a semidouble, clear pink China rose that dates from before

1750, is one of the old roses that performs wonderfully well in southern gardens. It blooms throughout the gardening season. Gene Strowd recommends 'Belinda', a hybrid musk rose from 1936. It is never bothered by black spot. One catalog describes it as "a great rose with a strong constitution." Two old roses that resist our summer heat and keep blooming through the hottest days are 'B. R. Kant' and 'Aloha'. 'B. R. Kant' is a repeat bloomer with double pink flowers. It has excellent foliage. 'Aloha' is one of the older modern roses, a climbing hybrid tea introduced in 1949. It is typically covered with peachy pink flowers.

There are a vast number of old roses in cultivation, and each gardener develops favorites. At Chatwood in Hillsborough, North Carolina, Mrs. Ralph Watkins has developed an enchanting garden that contains more than 400 varieties of old roses, plus another 100–125 modern hybrid teas, floribundas, and grandifloras, and she delights in them all. According to garden historians, hers is the most complete collection of old roses in the South. Mrs. Watkins's involvement in the Hillsborough Historical Society was responsible for the beginnings of this garden. She and other members decided to produce a booklet about the old gardens in their community, so the committee sought out as many pre–Civil War gardens as they could discover, and they wrote short descriptions of each. Most of the gardens contained old roses, unnamed and unidentified. Mrs. Watkins found these plants particularly beautiful, so she slipped as many as possible, rooted those cuttings, and began what is now an extensive collection.

Gradually she began to identify some of her finds and learn their histories. Studying the background of historic roses leads the researching gardener all over the world. Mrs. Watkins began to learn about European species like *R. gallica* and *R. damascena*, *R. rugosa* and *R. Wichuriana* from Asia, our own *R. carolina*, and many others. These and all the other rose species are the ancestors of our modern roses. She continues to be fascinated with the history of the roses; she has developed a wonderful library on the subject.

Culture for the old roses is much the same as that for modern roses. Select the proper location and plant them in good, friable soil, enriched with compost, leaf mold, or similar organic materials. For example, the native soil in the rose beds at the Watkins garden, double-dug, is amended with chicken manure and sawdust. Nutrients are added, based on soil samples of the local earth. While most books or articles about old roses say that one should feed them regularly, Mrs. Watkins's chief gardener, Doug Ruhren, feels that most gardeners feed too much. "If the soil is well prepared, you just need to keep adding organic materials," he says. "Certainly the once-blooming roses need no more food than a forsythia. The repeat-blooming ones need consistent moisture more than food."

The welcoming gateway at Mrs. Watkins's rose garden, with climbing
roses overhead and old roses massed on each side

Chance seedling

Rosa virginiana

Rosa rugosa

R. 'Carolina Morn'

R. 'Alice Vind'
Old roses

R. 'Silver Moon'

Ruhren and other growers of historic roses spray any varieties that show signs of mildew or black spot. Many of the old roses will need no fungicidal sprays, some will require such spraying, and one old rose—*Rosa hugonis* and its offspring—will completely defoliate if sprayed.

When choosing a site, remember that while the modern hybrids demand at least a full halfday of sunlight, antique roses tolerate more shade. Three varieties that were planted in a driveway bed when we bought this house are covered with flowers each spring, and that bed gets almost no direct sunlight. One collector grows her old roses in the dappled shade provided by tall deciduous trees, carefully thinned.

Pruning is the one aspect of rose care that differs from standard treatment. While the old roses that offer continual bloom should be pruned in late winter like the modern roses, the ones that bloom only in spring should be treated like forsythia and other spring-blooming shrubs and pruned only after they flower, late in the spring. Like raspberries or blackberries, all the old wood should be gradually pruned out of those shrubs each year.

With the current interest in old roses, you will probably find a few varieties, like *R. Banksiae lutea* (the Lady Banks rose) in your local garden centers. However, for an extensive choice, you will have to order from distant specialist nurseries. Beverly Dobson, 215 Harriman Road, Irvington, NY 10533, issues the *Combined Rose List*, which she updates annually. It lists all roses commercially available in the United States and which specialist nurseries carry them. You can order the booklet directly from Ms. Dobson for five dollars.

As with the modern roses, one of the best ways to familiarize yourself with old roses is to visit an historical garden with a collection of old roses. For example, the National Arboretum in Washington, D.C., has a collection of old roses as part of its magnificent herb garden. Along with our interest in heritage seeds and plants of antique origin, today many of us are interested in garden restoration. Almost every community has at least one lovely old building with a garden carefully and authentically restored, and the restoration usually includes some old roses. You can also learn more about old roses by joining the Heritage Roses Group, a national fellowship of gardeners who cherish the old roses. This group puts out an informative quarterly newsletter.

In addition to the old roses and the modern types many of us grow, there is another whole group of roses to enjoy. Miniature roses have great appeal. They come in as wide a color range as their large cousins, the hybrid teas, and these tiny gems duplicate the form, fragrance, and perfection of regular roses, in a diminutive size. Whether you want a tree rose, a climber, or a tea rose, there is a miniature to suit your taste. They can be used in a number of different ways. Some rosarians edge their beds of full-sized roses with the miniatures. Some gardeners grow them in window boxes. Others have tiny patio gardens or townhouse yards most appropriately filled with small plants, including miniature roses. I have grown miniatures around the base of a containerized standard rose, on my windowsill, and in my fluorescent light garden. I've even raised a tiny species, *R. rehderiana* (baby rose) from seed offered by the Park Seed Company.

These little plants are tough and reliable. They take the same management as the larger roses—water, food, and regular spraying. One local grower does feed the miniatures more often than his regular roses, using a dilute solution. He has also discovered that they tend to get more frequent infestations of spider mites, since the plants are growing so close to the ground, so his miniatures get a monthly spraying with a miticide.

If I could raise just one miniature, it would be 'Toy Clown', in its bright blend of yellow and red. But there is a miniature rose to everyone's taste— white, red, yellow, pink, blends, and bicolors.

These and all other roses are easily propagated by cuttings. Rosarians differ on the pros and cons of having roses on their own roots as opposed to ones that are grafted onto a rootstock. When we lived in Connecticut, I found that roses I had propagated seemed to be more winter hardy than the commercial, grafted varieties. In any case, it is fun to root your own plants, and it is often the best way to obtain one of the old roses that you cannot find on the market. Most rosarians are generous people. It they know you are looking for a certain variety, they will gladly share a cutting or two.

Like our other garden plants, species roses will come true from seed. They germinate readily and will bloom in a matter of weeks. If, on the other hand, you decide to raise a batch of seedlings from your 'Peace' rose, pollinated by some passing bee, expect to produce a wildly diverse group of seedlings. Most, if not all, of these seedlings will be worthless. Breeders who study all the parentage and carefully cross selected roses have to grow thousands of seedlings before they produce one that is worth saving. If you have the field space to grow a large number of seedlings, making your own crosses and growing the seedlings can become a fascinating avocation. Although it is unusual, an amateur rosarian can produce an All-America rose. Californian Anthony Perry did it with 'Broadway' in 1986.

Most homeowners will gladly leave sophisticated propagation to experts like Bill Warriner, an award-winning rose breeder at Jackson and Perkins, and simply enjoy the results of their work. We will visit the garden centers, read the catalogs, and buy roses that are ready to grow and flower for us. Rose cultivation is far from the easiest type of gardening, but the rewards are magnificent!

10

Perennials

Perennial fever has infected all gardeners during the 1980s. Just as hemlines cycle up and down, and men's ties are broad, then slim, then broad again, so do plant groups cycle in popularity. In the 1960s, gardeners were most concerned with "low-maintenance landscaping." Busy people wanted their grounds plain and simple.

A decade later, a house plant craze swept America. Plants were "in." Formerly bare living rooms were filled with pittosporums, aglaeonemas, and Boston ferns. Every window displayed a hanging basket. Homeowners who had never raised anything but a philodendron were suddenly talking knowledgeably about streptocarpus, phalaenopsis, and dracaenas.

Today we take house plants for granted. That ardor has cooled. In the 1980s, the hot, new gardening mania is for perennial gardening. Suddenly a Perennial Plant Association has formed, all the great garden centers like Longwood and Callaway are offering perennial symposia, articles about perennials are appearing in every magazine, and a host of new perennial nurseries are springing up around the country. Everyone wants to garden with perennials.

What is a perennial, anyway? According to most gardening books, it is a plant that grows, flowers, dies back to its roots, crown, rhizomes, etc., each year and then reappears the following gardening season. You may see the phrase "herbaceous perennial," which simply means that that plant has no woody material.

Some perennials, like the trilliums, dodocatheons, and our native spring beauties (*Claytonia virginica*) disappear as soon as they are through their flower and seed production. This disappearing act is disconcerting to the novice gardener, who thinks that the plant has died when it is simply an ephemeral. Each year, that plant makes a fleeting appearance. Some other perennials, like the dentarias, always go dormant in summer, and yet others

Primula veris, easy to raise from seed and reliable in the South

will go dormant if they get too dry. Pamela Harper commented to me that her asphodeline disappeared one year, and she thought it had died, but it reappeared the following spring. I find that polyanthus primroses tend to do that in my garden. Healthy little green rosettes reappear after the first generous fall rains.

Other perennials such as hostas disappear completely in the fall after the first frost. Yet others do not disappear at all. *Primula veris*, *P. vulgaris*, *P. polyanthus*, our native *Phlox divaricata*, and a number of other perennials mark their places throughout the southern winter looking somewhat ratty but evergreen.

Yet other genera of perennials contain both evergreen and herbaceous species and hybrids. The Christmas-rose (*Helleborus niger*) and the Lenten-rose (*Helleborus orientalis*), for example, keep their leathery, divided leaves throughout the winter. Rarer hellebores like *H. purpurascens* and *H. viridis* are deciduous.

And some perennials that are totally deciduous in northern gardens become partially or totally evergreen, depending on how far south they are being cultivated. *Tiarella cordifolia* (the foam flower) is one example of this type of plant. It goes to the ground in cold climates. In the Carolina Piedmont, it maintains a straggly appearance during the winter. Farther south, in Alabama, it is fully evergreen.

There are short-lived perennials like columbines that may persist in your garden for only three to five years. Peonies, however, just get bigger and better each year with normal care, and they may be their most magnificent after they are twenty to thirty years old.

Peonies are sturdy and reliable when left in one place. Like some other perennials, particularly those with deep tap roots, they resent transplanting. Day lilies, primroses, and hostas, on the other hand, can be dug and moved even when in flower. Water them in thoroughly and they will continue to grow and bloom as if they had not been disturbed.

While certain perennials have specific needs for lime or location or water that must be met, many are flexible and will adapt to a number of different situations with a reasonable amount of general care. For each plant that we grow, an absolutely ideal set of circumstances exists. For example, day lilies will have the most vigorous foliage and be the most floriferous if they are grown in full sun and watered regularly. However, they are also rewarding, if not so perfect, when grown on a dry roadside bank or in considerable shade. The unwatered roadside plants are floriferous but smaller. The foliage is stressed. The shade-grown day lilies are not as floriferous and the plants are more lax. The deeper the shade, the fewer the flowers. If one is living on a shady lot, even a few flowers may be very rewarding. I enjoy

The airy froth of our native foam flower

some mat campanulas that sprawl loosely and bloom in our shady woods. In a sunny wall, the same plant would be tight, compact, and covered with flowers. But we don't have a sunny wall here, so I appreciate the 50 percent return on investment the campanulas provide in less than ideal conditions.

Perennials can be used in a number of ways. In addition to developing a traditional perennial bed, gardeners can combine many shade-tolerant perennials with azaleas and rhododendrons in a naturalized woodland setting. An informal blend of small trees, shrubs, and perennials works well around a pool. There are even perennial water plants like water lilies, sarracenias and colorful *Iris laevigata* for planting directly into the pool. In Lake George, the small garden pool behind our house, the lilies are planted in wire cages on the bottom of the 18-inch deep pool and the other plants are in pots, supported by rocks so that the surface of each pot is just below the water's surface.

Some perennials are suitable for our sun-baked, dry roadsides, and others thrive in boggy marshes. A number of perennials can be grown effectively in containers. With creative gardeners experimenting today, the uses of perennials are almost limitless.

Somewhere in the depths of my files, I have a long piece of graph paper with an intricate pattern for a 300-foot perennial bed designed on it. We moved away from Connecticut before I could implement that plan, and since then I have never lived on land where such a garden would be appropriate. However, I learned a lot during the hours I researched perennials and then arranged and rearranged little colored circles on that graph paper to represent iris, peonies, day lilies, salvia, Oriental poppies, gypsophila, and all the other perennials I wanted in my garden.

I was inspired by visiting Elda and Walter Haring in their Greenwich, Connecticut, garden. There, along with their indoor light garden, greenhouse, vegetable beds, and cutting garden, they had a glorious and extensive perennial border. In the tradition of great English gardens like Hidcote and Savill, the perennial bed was a long, relatively narrow strip, placed in front of a hemlock hedge.

Few American gardens have the tall, weathered, brick walls or ancient hedges of English gardens that provide such attractive backdrops for perennials. One gardening friend was fortunate enough to purchase a home with a 100-year-old boxwood hedge in place, and she has designed an interesting, 300-foot perennial garden in front of the boxwood—a garden of varying depth, with a front edge of flowing, gentle curves.

However, many of us are in new homes, starting from scratch. We don't want to spend the money for tall brick walls. Perhaps an attractive fence or a quick-growing hedge of Leyland cypress or holly may be the answer, if we

Iris laevigata sitting in a pool, with *Rhododendron* 'Roseum Elegans' in the background

want a background for a traditional perennial bed. Any hedge demands routine pruning and shaping. The more vigorous the plant, the more frequent the maintenance required.

Most of our ideas about perennial gardening come from England. We listen to English lecturers like Beth Chatto, who spoke on dry gardening to an audience here in the Piedmont a few years ago. We delight in tours of England and Scotland that take us into historic gardens of Bodnant, Chatsworth, or Sissinghurst. And we read English books, old and new.

Enjoy them all, but don't try to take English gardening ideas literally. In her windswept and dry, but relatively cool, corner of England, Beth Chatto doesn't really know what dry gardening is like in our Southeast, where we may have to endure an eight-to-twelve-week drought with the thermometer in the 90s. Her concept of a dry garden does not match the reality of what we gardeners have to deal with here.

When you are traveling in the British Isles, absorb all of the attractive and interesting gardening ideas possible. Don't try to replicate an English perennial garden here, but be inspired by all that you see. I first noticed skillful double-planting in an English garden where alstroemerias were coming up through kochias. Note attractive combinations of plants and see how skillfully and enthusiastically the English use a number of our native plants, like echinacea, stokesia, and goldenrods, in their perennial beds.

I'm sure all gardeners read—most read gardening books omnivorously. We haunt used book stores in the hopes of finding a copy of Dorretta Klaber's book on gentians or Louise Beebe Wilder's *Pleasures and Problems of a Rock Garden*. We browse through the shelves of gardening books in every bookstore and check the offerings of the Garden Book Club.

In recent years, we have been blessed with a number of desirable reprints of books we have been unable to obtain in the original. For southern gardeners, the most valuable reprints have been the books of Elizabeth Lawrence. *A Southern Garden* was reissued by the University of North Carolina Press, and Duke Press brought out *The Little Bulbs*. You may be able to find an old copy of her *Gardens in Winter*, inspiring to all of us who are working to achieve a twelve-month garden.

Many wonderful, informative, opinionated English gardening books have also been reprinted. Probably the Gertrude Jekyll books have been the most influential during the last decade. Every American perennial grower should read her *Colour Schemes for the Flower Garden*.

New books that have had an important impact on the way we garden with perennials are *Perennials in Your Garden* from Alan Bloom in England, *Perennials* by Pamela Harper and Frederick McGourty, and Emily Brown's *Landscaping with Perennials*.

Bloom is famous for moving perennials out of that traditional long, rectangular bed in front of a wall or hedge. He designs perennial islands of varying sizes and attractively curved shapes, islands that are intended to be in the lawn, not delineating its perimeter. More and more American gardeners are experimenting with Bloom's ideas. Like homeowners choosing wallpaper, some are wildly successful; others create tasteless melanges.

The book by Harper and McGourty is a reasonably priced, large-format, softcover book published by HPBooks. While the authors provide practical information about selecting, siting, planting, and propagating perennials, 115 of 155 pages are devoted to a gallery of perennials, all photographed magnificently by Pamela Harper. Cultural information about each plant accompanies the photograph. This book is a valuable reference. I particularly like it for southern gardeners, because, while McGourty gardens in Connecticut, Harper grows her plants in Tidewater Virginia, and so she brings southern experience to her information about perennial gardening.

The many design ideas presented in *Landscaping with Perennials* are wonderfully useful and stimulating. It is an excellent book to read before you begin to design your perennial garden. The plant information has a decidedly Californian flavor, which is understandable, since Mrs. Brown is gardening in the San Francisco area.

Perhaps you have drawn inspiration from all or any of these books I've mentioned. Now you are ready to garden with perennials. Before you turn over the first clod of earth, give the matter considerable thought. Decide on both the site and the style of your new garden. While many books suggest that you place it near the house, where you will enjoy it daily (perhaps beside the patio, near a doorway, or along the driveway) remember that unless you incorporate a number of dwarf conifers and evergreen perennials into your design, it could look quite bare in winter when the herbaceous perennials have gone to the ground. Select the location of your perennial garden carefully.

Decide if you want to follow the English tradition of long rectangular beds or if you prefer the more contemporary look of asymmetrical, flowing, island beds.

Then plan the flow of color, blooming sequences, textures, and patterns of your garden. While it is not necessary to create your garden on graph paper, doing so can help to avoid mistakes. It can clarify your thinking.

Like much of our gardening, perennial gardening begins with good soil preparation, as covered in the chapter on soils. Most perennials do not like wet feet, so pay attention to the southern gardener's first commandment—drainage, drainage, drainage. Raised beds may be your answer. However, remember that because raised beds do provide good drainage, they also demand more frequent watering.

With your garden bed prepared, it is time to go ahead and place your perennials. In the traditional beds set against a fence or wall, tall plants like thermopsis, phlomis, or liatris logically go at the back, medium height plants are in the middle, and the shortest ones go in the front. To make the pattern more interesting, vary it occasionally by bringing a tall plant forward or moving a shorter one back. Create an interesting skyline.

In the island type of planting, the tallest plants create a central spine for the garden and the others are arranged accordingly.

Beginners often ask how much space should be allowed for perennials. While each perennial has an ultimate height, there is no ultimate width for perennial plants. Typically, each clump gets larger each year, until it is divided. The larger the mature plant, the more space you should give it initially. Primroses in the front of the border might be planted 10–12 inches apart, while McKana giant columbines in the middle of the bed deserve 18–20 inches of space, and the tallest perennials like liatris, ligularias, and phlox may need 2 to 3 feet each. Be sure to allow generous space between plants that don't like to be moved, like peonies, poppies, and dictamnus, and fill in between them with more portable plants.

Typically, perennials are arranged in groups of three or five. Of course it

The late summer exuberance of grasses, rudbeckias, and black-eyed susans in a large perennial garden

all depends on the scale of the garden. In a vast planting, you might use nine or more in a drift. As in flower arranging, uneven numbers generally are the most pleasing, although, like every other rule, this one is made to be broken.

Also, any garden should have an occasional, spectacular single specimen like a wonderful tree peony or *Hosta tokudama aureo-nebulosa.*

Depending on the size of your original plants, it will take from one to three years for the plants in the perennial bed to fill in and grow together. The Harings grew all of their perennials from seed, producing sturdy, small plants the first year. Some perennials will bloom the first year from seed, but most flower during the second gardening season. A few take three or more years to produce flowers.

Many perennials are easy to raise from seed, which is a cost-effective way to produce plants in numbers. It also allows you to raise many plants that are unobtainable any other way. For example, in 1985, I raised twenty different species of campanulas from seed, none of which was available from any nursery. Seed propagation is simple, and it's fun. It also is a project for the patient gardener.

Of course seed propagation is useful only when you want to raise a species. Many of our best perennials are cultivars and can be duplicated only by vegetative propagation.

The impatient gardener with few budget restrictions will visit local nurseries and order mature plants from mail-order, specialist nurseries. His is an expensive way to garden, but it creates an instant effect.

For the gardener who does not want to do his own propagating but wants to buy a number of small plants at reasonable prices, at the time of this book's publication, Bluestone Perennials of Madison, Ohio, is doing an outstanding job of producing quality seedlings and rooted cuttings. For the price of one mature perennial at a nursery, you can obtain three small, healthy starts of that salvia, coreopsis, or chrysanthemum. One warning: a perennial expert mentioned that sometimes the plants are not true to name. This problem is not Bluestone's alone, but common to a number of nurseries and bulb houses.

Trading divisions with fellow gardeners and shopping for perennials at your local garden club sales are other ways to increase your perennial collection gradually.

For small propagations or new purchases, it is helpful to have a nursery bed or two. Like a cold frame, a behind-the-scenes nursery bed is a valuable part of a garden's support system. Even in an established perennial garden, some plants will need replacement occasionally, and a nursery bed allows you to have new plants ready at all times.

The airy seed heads of a pulsatilla, *left*, and a clematis, *right*, decorate the garden long after flowering is past

In addition to replacing an unattractive or dead plant, gardeners also need to remove spent flower stalks, and to weed, stake, feed, and divide perennials. As Kipling said, "Gardens are not made by singing 'Oh, how beautiful' and sitting in the shade." But the hours spent in a flowering garden are not work but joy to most gardeners. One friend gets truly irate when visitors tour her lovely garden and their only comment is "What a lot of work!" To her and her husband, their garden is beauty, pleasure—a delightful and rewarding way of life.

As this gardener moves around her garden in the spring, she snaps off the head of any daffodil that is through blooming. Dead-heading is just that—simply removing the flower head after it has passed its prime. You prevent the plant from setting seed and so the energy that would have gone into that reproductive act goes into building a stronger plant. In some cases, dead-heading may encourage the perennial to rebloom.

There are two reasons to allow any plant to go to seed. First, you may want to save the seed of a special plant for another season. It does not pay to save hybrid seed, as the progeny will be extremely diverse and often undesirable. However, many of our garden perennials, like *Stachys lanata*, *Delphinium tricorne*, and *Tradescantia virginiana*, are species that will come true from seed.

And secondly, some seed heads, like those of clematis and pulsatillas, are extremely decorative. These fluffy whorls or round heads of seeds that will eventually blow away on the wind are a beautiful bonus after flowering.

Weeding is more of a chore in the early years of a newly developed garden. The need for weeding will lessen as the plants mature and grow together, allowing fewer weed seeds to germinate and grow. Roundup is the gardener's best friend. Used with care, it helps gardeners maintain extensive gardens without hours of back-killing weeding. If you are a purist about using no chemicals in your yard, then put on your Walkman and enjoy some Mozart or Dave Brubeck while you are on your hands and knees pulling the weeds. If you wait until after a soaking rainfall and then give each weed a gentle wiggle back and forth, most of these undesirable plants will come out easily.

Staking is one of the more controversial garden activities. With some plants, it can be avoided by pinching them back to keep them compact. If one must stake, the staking materials and techniques should be subtle. Staking is necessary or desirable for those plants, like dahlias, that grow tall and will topple over without support. The curator at Savill Garden in England believes in using only natural material. One April, we saw a gardener there staking delphiniums with tall brush. Here in America, we use a lot of wooden or bamboo stakes, with plastic tape, green twine or plastic-covered wire twists. For many of the plants that require staking, like the floppy balloon flower (platycodon), I like the plant supports recently introduced from England. They are round frames on three legs with a mesh top through which the plant grows—much like old-fashioned peony supports. The mature plant then hides the frame and is held attractively above the ground. The most common mistake we gardeners make is to wait until the plant is fairly tall and then try to make it adapt to the staking. Stake early and discreetly, when the plants first show themselves above ground.

Early spring is also the time to fertilize the perennial garden. After the leaves and other winter debris are raked off, I broadcast a balanced fertilizer, like 10-10-10, over all the garden surface. Follow the directions on the package, as they will vary slightly, depending on the formula of the fertilizer you have purchased.

If yours is a new garden bed into which you have incorporated some fertilizer, you probably will not need to provide additional fertilizer during the first year. In established gardens, I like to add a balanced fertilizer and a fresh layer of compost to the bed each year. Gradually, the soil improves.

All plants receive that one feeding, and then I spot feed voracious perennials like gentians and dahlias throughout the season. In the woodland garden, I toss the balanced fertilizer with considerable abandon. It is hard to overfeed there, because all of the perennial plants are receiving so much competition from the tree roots. I've never burned a perennial in the woods unless I accidentally dropped some of the 10-10-10 into the crown of the plant rather than on the ground around it. Do watch your plants for signs of fertilizer burn or other problems. As you work in the garden, notice whether a plant is flagging in the morning hours and water thoroughly. Many perennials will droop a little during one of our hot afternoons. That's normal. (To confuse matters, sometimes our perennials, like our house plants, flag because of overwatering that has caused root rot.) Observe when foliage begins to get pale, indicating lack of nitrogen. And be sure to catch and identify insect and disease problems early.

For example, I know that the first whiff of mild spring weather will bring out the slugs and snails. I watch my primroses and hostas, which always seem to be the first targets. With the first sign of these slimy pests, I scatter slug bait around vulnerable areas—particularly in the cold frames and the nursery.

I also have learned that the day lilies attract a fluffy white mealybug here in the South, so I look for the first signs of that pest in June and spray accordingly. We also watch for the first Japanese beetles on the clematis and roses. As you garden in the South, you will gradually learn to anticipate problems and thereby minimize them.

By becoming very familiar with your plants, you will also know when to divide them. Some perennials, like poppies and the aforementioned peonies, resent digging and never require division. You would only disturb one if it had to be transplanted, or if you needed another plant of the same variety.

Other plants, like Shasta daisies and other members of the chrysanthemum clan, will tell you that they need division by dying off in the center of the clump. Restart those perennials by taking vigorous sections of the outer growth and discard the center. Some perennials, including day lilies and irises, are so vigorous that they require division every two or three years. If bloom diminishes, that's a clear signal that the perennial needs division.

Early spring or midfall is the best time to do most dividing, just as those are the best times to plant perennials—emphasis on fall. With today's containerized plants, it is quite possible to plant perennials year-round. The one caveat is water, water, water the first year of planting, particularly if you put any plant in the ground during the summer here in the South. It is easier on both the plant and the gardener if planting is done in the fall, and the new plant can establish a good root system in its new location before it has to survive a hot and muggy summer.

Beginning gardeners ask which perennials to plant. If I could choose just two, they would be day lilies for sun and hostas for shade. John Elsley, procurement specialist for Wayside Gardens, Greenwood, South Carolina, says flatly, "Day lilies are the most important and valuable perennials in the United States!" That is a broad statement, but I understand why he feels that way. I have grown day lilies north, south, east, and west in these United States, and have found them to be reliable, tough, beautiful, and easy to grow in all types of soil and in all climates.

Although day lilies (Hemerocallis) are always described as plants for sunny locations—and indeed, they will grow in an open field here in the South—they are flexible enough to grow and bloom in partial shade.

Like boxwood and some other plants from colonial days, day lilies were brought to this country by early settlers. In many areas, the old-fashioned varieties have escaped from gardens and naturalized on the roadsides. We take their orange and gold splashes of color for granted.

Modern hybrids, however, are far removed from those ordinary roadside lilies. Today we can purchase day lilies that vary from 1 to 6 feet in height. The dwarf ones are becoming very popular for small gardens or container growing. Breeders have developed a wide range of colors from the palest moonbeam yellow to a rich purple. Some day lilies are bicolors; others have green throats. Flower forms range from broad and chunky to open and spidery. Blossoms may be sleek or ruffled.

I won't begin to discuss cultivars. Hundreds are on the market today and more are being introduced each year. If you are interested in exceptional day lilies, beyond those available at your local garden center, seek out a specialist near you and visit during blooming season when you can select your plants in flower. If that is not possible, order from a specialist like Iron Gate Gardens. Note that catalogs offer dormant, semidormant, and evergreen day lilies. Evergreen varieties do not have foliage twelve months of the year. Here the term "evergreen" means that the buds and the leaf tips are at soil level during the winter. The leaves will probably be nipped by frost. Nonetheless, the evergreen varieties are worth growing. Some of the most spectacular day lilies are in that category. Just trim off the leaf tip damage in the spring and enjoy the bloom.

The one cultivar I will mention is H. 'Stella D'Oro', because this golden hybrid, developed by Walter Jablonski, was the first everblooming day lily. It is a beautiful plant itself, but it is particularly exciting because of the great promise it offers to future day lily breeding programs. We will see generations of everblooming day lilies in the years ahead. These plants will be a great boon to gardeners with limited space.

There's always the contrary opinion, of course. One gardening friend says, "I don't want everblooming day lilies any more than I want strawberries in January. I love the succession of bloom. I'd get tired of day lilies if they bloomed all season."

Day lilies can be used in a number of ways. They are impressive in mass plantings, or a few can be incorporated into a perennial garden. Elsley recommends a combined bed of daffodils and day lilies for a long season of beauty. The developing day lily foliage covers the dying daffodil leaves. I have added some bulbs of *Lycoris squamigera* for late summer flowering in our day lily bed, and I edge this garden with a ground cover of sweet woodruff (*Galium odoratum*, frequently sold under its old name, *Asperula odorata*).

Although the drought-resistant roadside day lilies survive, bloom, and reappear each year with no care at all, your garden day lilies and hostas will perform best for you if you give them generous amounts of water during our dry periods.

Hostas, sometimes called funkia or plaintain lilies, are perennial imports from the Orient that have adapted nicely to American gardens. While twenty-five or thirty years ago only a few hostas like the common *H. plantaginea*, with its large, heart-shaped, green leaves, and a green and white form

One of the Sieboldii group of hostas, with *Lycoris squamigera* blooms, in front of a boxwood hedge

of *H. fortunei* were on the market, today hundreds of different ones are available and more are coming each season.

As with day lilies, hybridizers are busily at work creating large hostas and miniature ones; hostas with thin, strappy leaves or large, fat ones, foliage in a wide range of colors, from the rich blues through all hues of green to gold and yellow, plus a number of interesting variegations.

Commercial growers are also importing many interesting hostas from Japan, where the current passion for this valuable group of plants is even higher than here in America.

Hostas are easy to cultivate. For ideal conditions, plant them in moist, humusy soil in an area that provides light shade. However, they are extremely adaptable. They will grow well in almost any soil and will tolerate a good deal of sunlight and even drought.

For example, in our very hot and dry Piedmont summer of 1983, our family was on vacation during the last two weeks of August when the thermometer frequently recorded 95–100°. We had had no rain for weeks. The woodland trail gardens went unwatered in our absence, and we lost a number of plants. However, I was delighted to find that along with a few campanulas and other tough plants, all of the hostas survived.

They are equally flexible in their light requirements. While all hostas survive and some even flower in considerable shade, they will flourish in partial shade and some even survive full southern sunshine.

A University of North Carolina botany professor, James Massey, who also owns a day lily nursery, has been experimenting with a few hostas in his open, sunny field beds. He has found that while the blue varieties like *H.* 'Krossa's Regal' do not do well in the sun because they lose their blue coloration, several other hostas are successful. Two that he particularly recommends are *H.* 'Honeybells', a tall hosta with fragrant flowers, and a variegated form of *H. undulata*.

Once planted, hostas need only minimal maintenance. Each spring I give them one feeding. Left in one location, most hostas form attractive, ever-increasing clumps. They do not need to be dug and divided every two or three years as day lilies and irises do, but they don't resent division. In fact, that is the most common way of propagation.

If you want to increase your hosta population, dig up the clump in either midfall or early spring. Shake the soil off the root mass and then gently tease apart the individual crowns and replant them. Some hostas, like *H. tokudama* and its relatives, are extremely slow to reproduce and then do it sparingly, which is reflected in the price you will pay at the nursery. Many varieties that multiply readily are available for from three to five dollars,

Sedum spectabile

while ones like *H. tokudama* will cost several times that amount.

While division is the only way to maintain the genetic characteristics of many of the unique hybrids, it's also easy to raise hostas from seed. Finding seed to raise is not so easy, however. A few seed companies offer a limited selection of hosta seeds, but if you really become interested in hostas and want to raise a number of different ones from seed, I suggest joining the American Hosta Society, which has an extensive seed list.

I also value hostas in my garden because they are almost pest free. I say "almost" because hostas are like caviar to snails and slugs. Other than these voracious, slimy nibblers, I never see a pest on the hostas. In the past, I would have called them disease free, but I understand that fungus rots are becoming quite a problem with some of the expensive hosta cultivars.

Hostas do flower, of course, but, with one exception, I find the flowers generally insignificant. I know a number of hosta enthusiasts will disagree with me, but I raise hostas for their beautiful foliage, not their flowers. That one exception is the large-leaved *H. plantaginea*, which produces spikes of relatively large, wonderfully fragrant white flowers in mid-August. A bowl of these blooms is long lasting and will perfume the entire house.

Flower arrangers love hostas, however, for the foliage, not the flowers. All the leaves condition well, are quite malleable, and last a long time in an arrangement.

Beyond hostas and day lilies, there is a host of interesting and lovely perennials for your consideration. Hundreds of species and cultivars are on the market and more are added to the list each year. However, we may have some problems in finding the quality plants we want for our gardens. In 1986, Elsley said that we will have a real shortage of good perennials for about a decade. While a number of perennial growers had hoped that propagation by tissue culture would provide the thousands of quality clones that the perennial market demanded, they have found that operating such sophisticated laboratories is extremely expensive, and—even worse—tissue culture does not work in a number of cases. Professionals have mostly returned to the slower methods of seeds, divisions, and cuttings.

While nurserymen will continue to produce the reliable old favorites, like *Phlox* 'Miss Lingard', *Sedum spectabile*, and McKana columbines, creative growers are looking in Europe and Asia for new and interesting perennials to introduce to the American market. In the last decade, we have seen new plants like *Disporum flavum* and *Tricyrtis hirta* introduced here, as well as improved versions of old favorites, like the pale and lovely *Coreopsis* 'Moonbeam'.

There has also been a burst of enthusiasm for ornamental grasses to be

One of the relatively recent introductions from Japan, *Disporum flavum*, adds its modest charm to the spring garden

used in the perennial garden or in naturalized sites. Pampas grass (*Cortaderia selloana*) and blue fescue (*Festuca glauca*) have been in cultivation for many years, but the different miscanthus species, fountain grass (*Pennisetum setaceum*), plume grass (*Erianthus ravennae*), and quaking grass (*Briza media*) are just a few of the varieties on the market today. I'm particularly fond of a decorative sedge, *Carex Morrowii* 'Variegata', which makes a neat 12-inch clump of attractively variegated grassy foliage.

I think this search for unusual introductions and improved cultivars will continue. Wayside Gardens and White Flower Farm are two leaders in this field. Both catalogs are colorfully illustrated and packed with cultural information. Many of the smaller perennial nurseries indicate which plants are new to their lists each year. Our perennial gardens will be as new as this year's introductions—and as old-fashioned as grandmother's border.

Perennials for the Southern Garden

Name	Color	Height	Season of Bloom	Comment
For the Sunny Border				
Achillea	white, red, or yellow	2–3'	summer	dry nicely
Agapanthus	white or blue	3–4'	summer	try 'Peter Pan' or Headbourne hybrids
Amsonia	light blue	2–3'	early summer	
Anemone pulsatilla	purple, red, or white	12"	spring	decorative seed heads
Aquilegia	wide range of color	tiny to 3'	spring	McKana hybrids, fine and large
Armeria maritima	pink or white	6"	spring	drought tolerant
Asclepias tuberosa	yellow, or-ange, or red	2–3'	summer	cuts well, also drought tolerant
Aster x Frikartii	lavender-blue	2–3'	summer to frost	the best aster, say most gardeners
Baptisia australis	purple-blue	4'	early summer	
Boltonia asteroides 'Snowbank'	white	4–5'	early fall	spectacular bouquet of white daisies
Campanula	violet hues blue or white	low mat to 4' spikes	late spring	a huge genus
Chrysanthemum	wide range	6" to 3'	fall	many compact varieties for border
C. x superbum	white	1–3'	summer	shasta daisy
Coreopsis	yellows	1–3'	summer	'Moonbeam' is a choice, pale yellow
Dictamnus	white or pink	3'	early summer	
Echinacea	purple or white	3'	summer	coneflower, long period of bloom
Eupatorium coelestinum	lavender-blue	2'	late summer, early fall	

Name	Color	Height	Season of Bloom	Comment
Euphorbia	white	prostrate to 4′	early summer	a large genus, mostly grown for foliage, form
Gaillardia	red and yellow	dwarf to 3′	summer–frost	good cut flower
Gaura lindheimeri	white	4 + ′	summer–frost	
Gerbera	many, vivid	12–18″	early summer; again, fall	hardy most years in my zone 7 garden
Gypsophila paniculata	white, pink	3–4′	summer	airy touch to bouquets
Hemerocallis	wide range	12″ to 3′	early summer	'Stella D'Oro' first everblooming day lily
Heuchera	pink, red, or white	18″	late spring, early summer	
Hibiscus x moscheutos	pink, red, or white	3–6′	summer	huge, 12″ flowers
Iris	every color	a few inches to 4′	spring	borers are a major problem; large genus, many useful ones
Kniphofia	reds, yellows, cream, blends	2–4′	late summer	red hot poker, showy
Liatris	purple or white	2–6′	late summer	nice spikes
Monarda didyma hybrids	red or pink	3′	summer	'Cambridge Scarlet' or 'Croftway Pink'
Paeonia	wide range	2–4′	late spring	best in sun, some bloom in light shade
Papaver orientale	orange, pink, red, white	3–4′	late spring, early summer	oriental poppy
Phlox paniculata	no blue, no yellow	3–4′	summer	mildew a problem
Platycodon grandiflorus	blue, pink, or white	3′	summer	balloon flower, needs staking
Rudbeckia 'Goldsturm'	golden	2 + ′	late summer, early fall	long bloom

Name	Color	Height	Season of Bloom	Comment
Salvia	blue, purple, white, red	1½–5'	summer	large genus
Sedum 'Autumn Joy'	pink, aging to red	18" to 2'	summer to fall	choice clump
Solidago	yellows	12" to 3'	early fall	huge genus
Stokesia laevis	blue	12–24"	early summer	great with day lilies
Veronica	blue or white	mat to 3'	late spring	large genus
Yucca	white	3–5'	summer to fall	appropriate only in desert or beach garden

Best in Light Shade

Name	Color	Height	Season of Bloom	Comment
Aegopodium podograria 'Variegatum'	green with white foliage	6–12"	unimportant	rampant and beautiful as ground cover
Arum italicum 'Pictum'	variegated leaves, orange-red berries	15"	unimportant	grown for leaves and berries
Asperula odorata	white	6"	May	ground cover, flavoring for May wine
Astilbe	white, red, or pink	6" to 4'	early summer	ferny foliage, plumy blooms
Begonia grandis (*Evansiana*)	pink or white	2'	fall	only hardy begonia
Bergenia	white, pink, or red	12"	late spring	leathery leaves
Cimicifuga racemosa	white	to 6'	summer	black cohosh
Corydalis lutea	yellow	6"	summer	ferny foliage, seeds nicely
Dicentra spectabilis	pink or white	3'	spring	old-fashioned charm
Disporum flavum	yellow bells	15"	spring	recent arrival from Japan

Name	Color	Height	Season of Bloom	Comment
Epimedium	yellow, white, red blend, orange	8–12"	spring	prune off old foliage before early bloom
Hellebore	white, greenish, wine	12–36"	late winter	several desirable species
Hosta	white, lavender	6" to 3–4'	summer	hundreds of varieties, grown for foliage
Kirengeshoma palmata	yellow	3'	late summer	Japanese treasure
Lamium maculatum 'Beacon Silver' 'White Nancy'	pink white	6"	late spring	good, herbaceous ground cover, variegated foliage
Ligularia species	yellow	3–6'	summer to early fall	foliage wilts in heat
L. 'The Rocket'				choice cultivar
Lysimachia clethroides	white	3'	midsummer	curved flower spikes
Polygonatum odoratum Thunbergii 'Variegatum'	white	2–3'	spring	very choice, arching branches
Primula	many colors	3" to 3–4'	spring	many species and hybrids thrive in southern shade
Pulmonaria 'Mrs. Moon'	pink-blue	12"	spring	variegated leaves
P. angustifolia	clear blue			green leaves
Thalictrum	lavender, white, or yellow	3 + '	spring or summer	airy
Trycirtis hirta	lavender	2–3'	fall	newcomer from Japan
T. bakeri	yellow		summer	
Tradescantia	blue, purple, white	2'	summer	rebloom if cut back after flowering
T. 'Iris Pritchard'	white, flushed with violet			

11

Annuals

Each September our North Carolina roadsides are covered with golden bouquets when *Bidens polylepsis*, the beautiful, exuberant ditch daisies, are in bloom. The several bidens species that flourish in the South are annuals, members of that large group of plants that germinate, grow, bloom, set seed, and die, all in one year.

Some ardent wild flower enthusiasts seed the roadsides. I had a friend in California who threw pounds of California poppy (*Eschscholzia californica*) seed on the roadsides along route 68 between Salinas and Monterey. Single-handedly, he created a wonderful floral display during the several years he devoted to this project.

Most of us simply appreciate nature's abundance when the roadside annuals are blooming, but we all raise a number of cultivated annuals in our gardens. In this chapter, I'm using the word "annual" in a broad sense, to include all those half-hardy perennials like geraniums, snapdragons, or the tender *Salvia leucantha* that we treat as annuals in our gardens.

Purchasing bedding plants is the easy, quick, and expensive way to obtain flowers for your garden. A flat of bedding plants picked up at the local grocery store or garden center adds instant magic to a perennial garden, a display bed of annuals, a container garden, or a hanging basket.

Most annuals are easily raised from seed, a time-consuming but thrifty way of gardening. Because I find propagation the most interesting and rewarding part of gardening, I raise most of my plants myself. It's fun.

Bedding plant growers are becoming more innovative each year, and you will probably find some interesting plants for sale each spring. For example, in the early 1980s, ornamental cabbages and kales were popular, and by the middle of the decade, the beautiful and long-lasting flowers of lisianthus (*Eustoma grandiflorum*) were beginning to find their share of the market. However, the bedding plant industry is business, big business, and the

A southern roadside bank flooded with *Bidens polylepis*

growers tend to grow millions and millions of a limited number of plants. If you want something unusual, like tithonia or hunnemannia, you will probably have to raise it from seed.

Since bedding plants are timed to reach the market just as the roots fill the cell packs and the small plants are ready to go into the ground, it pays you, the gardener, to be ready too. If you intend to put the plants in the garden, refresh the soil by spading in some compost, peat moss, or other organic material and a complete fertilizer like 5-10-5. If you plan to grow your plants in containers, have clean pots or baskets ready, along with a supply of potting soil.

Then off you go to pick out your plants. Select them carefully. It's been my experience that garden centers take good care of their containerized material, large and small. Other outlets may or may not have someone who is experienced in plant care watering and selling their bedding plants. Be a very selective customer. Reject spindly petunias that have been reaching for the light, wilted marigolds drooping over the edge of the flat, or impatiens with brown edges on the leaves. Look for vigorous, healthy plants in full, uninterrupted growth. Avoid any plants that have been too long in the flat and are root-bound. (If in doubt, push gently on the bottom of the cell and check the condition of the root ball.)

Unless you are already familiar with the plants you are purchasing, read the labels attentively. Bedding plant growers are providing a lot of information on labels today. You will be able to learn the ultimate size of the plant, whether it is a 4-foot cleome or a miniature snapdragon; the color, if the plants are not already in flower; and the preferred location, whether in sun or shade.

After you have purchased your plants, treat them kindly. I always think of bedding plants as ice cream. On a hot day, they should not be in the trunk of my car any longer than it would take that frozen dessert to begin to soften. Make your plants your last purchase before you head home.

Put the flats of plants in the shade and water well if you are not ready to plant them right away. Be sure that the plants never dry out. Neglect can leave you with dead or damaged plants.

Most bedding plants are sold in the plastic cell packs in which each seedling has its own cell or small, individual pot. When you are ready to remove the plants from the pack, don't tug on the leaves. Squeeze the slanted sides of a cell, give a gentle push on the bottom and the plant will pop out, intact. If it is at all root-bound, I gently cut the surface of the root mass in several places with the edge of my trowel. This type of root pruning encourages the production of new, fine feeder roots.

Occasionally you may still find plants sold in common flats. If you buy a large flat of sweet alyssum, for example, you can either take a sharp knife and cut the flat into squares, as if you were cutting a pan of brownies, or turn the flat out onto your hand, flip it rightside up and then gently tease the plants' root systems apart.

Of course the sooner you whisk the seedlings into the garden, the better. Ideally you would transplant on a gray, misty day, but since gardening, like much of life, is seldom managed under ideal conditions, you'll wind up doing it when convenient—perhaps on a hot, sunny day. Water the new plants in thoroughly, preferably with a dilute fertilizer solution. Several brands of water-soluble fertilizers with a high middle number, like 5-10-5 or 15-30-15, are on the market today. These plant foods work well to get the new transplants off to a strong start. Then mist the foliage and shade the new plants with inverted strawberry baskets, folded cardboard, a flat or board raised on bricks—anything to protect the plants for the first few days.

All gardeners are accustomed to listening to weather reports. We want to know if it will rain. We want to know how hot or cold our days and nights will be. In the fall, we want to pay attention to the first frost warnings. And in the beautiful, variable days of spring, we need to know when our last frost will occur.

In our area, the average last day of frost is April 15. I tend to rush the season. I time my tomatoes, impatiens, and other tender plants so that they go outdoors in a cold frame about March 15. They harden off for a couple of weeks, and then I put them in the ground April 1. I realize I'm taking a risk, so I listen carefully to the temperature predictions during the weeks of April and I stand by to cover the beds with old sheets, plastic, or newspapers. If you want to stay in close touch with weather forecasts, buy a weather radio. These little battery radios are set to broadcast the National Weather Service information in your area, twenty-four hours a day. A gardening friend gave me one of these gadgets recently, and now I wouldn't be without it.

If you are a conservative gardener, you will put your tender plants in the garden after the average last recorded frost in your area, recognizing the fact that an average last day of frost is just that—an average. On more than one spring, our southern gardens have been hit by a late frost. The most conservative of gardeners waits until the last recorded date of frost, which is May 10 in the area where I live and then plants his garden in total safety. Of course most years I am harvesting tomatoes and enjoying flowers on my impatiens several weeks before that gardener.

Gardening with annuals is labor intensive; you have to replant the annuals each year. How much each of us utilizes annuals is a matter of individual choice. And any annual garden you develop may have a theme or simply be a collection of flowers you enjoy in combination with one another. Perhaps you have a large circle in your driveway that you want to flood with color each summer, so one year you plant hundreds of marigolds, geraniums, ageratum, and dusty miller. Perhaps the next spring, you use tall cleome, blue salvia, airy cosmos, and two sizes of zinnias. During the national Bicentennial Celebration in 1976, many American gardeners created red, white, and blue gardens, using combinations like red salvia, blue ageratum, and white petunias. I still see some of those plantings around.

Personally, I find monochromatic gardens very effective. One local gardener loves red. Her front yard is ablaze with red salvia, geraniums, and zinnias. At the Ball Company test garden outside Chicago, one year a grower had designed a charming annual garden in apricot-orange, using plumed celosia 'Apricot Brandy', marigold 'Orange Boy', marigold 'Janie', salvia 'Carabiniere Orange', and an experimental zinnia. Rather than using the traditional low-medium-tall method of planting, the heights in this bed undulated, and the effect was very pleasing. If serenity suits you, you might like to develop a small, peaceful, all-white annual garden near your patio where

A creative and attractive use of two colors in a mass planting of mums used as annuals

Perennials enhanced by the thoughtful placement of annuals (photograph by Pamela Harper)

you can enjoy the evening fragrance of *Nicotiana* 'Nicki White', planted in combination with white petunias, snapdragons, cleomes, and caladiums.

A perennial enthusiast may choose to enhance his carefully planned perennial border by adding long-lasting color from some selected annuals. Flower arrangers will have rows of annuals like celosias, larkspurs, stocks, snapdragons, asters, and marigolds lined up for cutting purposes. Annual herbs, like basil and dill, add a gourmet touch to family meals. And for container gardening, annuals are wonderful. It's impossible to beat the season's bloom provided by pots of geraniums or baskets of impatiens.

However you choose to use annuals, begin with a plan, a design. It can be as simple as a list or as detailed as a garden portrait drawn on graph paper. What better way to spend a winter evening than paging through the wonderful wish books from several seed companies and jotting down ideas. As you plan, keep a number of factors in mind. The first thing to consider is whether your garden will be in sun or shade. Most annuals are sun-loving plants, but there are a number that will thrive and flower in shade. Then, when selecting flowers for your site, consider color, height, form, textures,

Zinnia 'Yellow Marvel'

Helichrysum 'Hot Bikini'

New in 1988 bedding plant trials, a subtle verbena, 'Blush Coral', with buds of deep coral and open florets of soft peach

and also foliage color and texture. Think about combinations that please you. Pick some old favorites, and then try something new—particularly any plants described as heat and drought tolerant.

If you are anywhere near an All-America Selections display or trial garden, visit the garden in midsummer. Stroll the paths and take notes about your likes and dislikes. While bedding plant trials are geared to providing information for the academic and professional observers, they are open to all amateur gardeners. In these trials, we can see the old favorites like the single grandiflora petunia 'White Cascade' compared with newer varieties like 'Supermagic White' or 'Crockett's Victory White'.

The comparisons of old and new varieties are always interesting. Sometimes the old reliable cultivar is best. In other comparison tests, the newest hybrid is obviously more compact, uniform, vigorous, and floriferous. Catalog descriptions are enticing—sometimes accurate and sometimes excessive. I like to see the plants in cultivation. When I visited the Park Seed Company trials one July day, and our group of garden writers stood near the beds of marigolds at noon, in full sun, when the temperature was 105°, I felt sure that any plant that survived those conditions was tough enough for southern gardening.

At the North Carolina State University trial grounds, new varieties are on display each year. As you know, new is not always better (for example, breeders have a way to go to surpass that exciting, reliable, floriferous impatiens 'Blitz', an All-America Selection winner in 1981) but new is usually interesting and occasionally extraordinarily impressive.

In the mid-1980s, lisianthus was an outstanding new introduction to the horticultural scene. Japanese breeders had taken an American prairie gentian (*Eustoma grandiflorum*) and developed attractive heat- and drought-tolerant plants with blue-gray foliage and large, long-lasting single and double flowers in white and hues of pink and purple. Growers are still learning how to master the idiosyncracies of these plants, but I'm sure we will see more of them. Lisianthus hybrids are lovely in the garden, make long-lasting cut flowers, and will be in bloom as long as five months when grown as house plants. Because they take several months from seed to flower, I suggest you buy plants rather than start lisianthus seedlings, unless you have a home greenhouse. You may find them called either eustoma or lisianthus.

I mentioned the ornamental cabbages and kales. Keep these plants in mind for fall and winter decoration. I have seen their colorful heads holding up well in December and January here, long after all other annuals have been frozen.

Southern gardeners can grow most annuals. However, some annuals, like portulaca and verbena, do extremely well in our muggy summer heat. A few

Alabama
Birmingham Botanical Gardens, 2612 Lane Park Road, Birmingham
Bellingrath Gardens, Route 1, Theodore

Georgia
University of Georgia Botanical Garden, 2450 S. Milledge Avenue, Athens
City of Atlanta, Buckhead Park, Atlanta
City of Atlanta, Grant Park, Atlanta
City of Atlanta, International Boulevard, Atlanta
Georgia Institute of Technology, North Avenue, Atlanta
Georgia Experiment Station, Experiment Street, Experiment
Oak Hills Gardens, Berry College, Mount Berry

Kentucky
Kentucky Fair and Expo Center, Louisville

Louisiana
Hodges Gardens, Many

Mississippi
Jackson State University, Botanical Garden, Jackson
Mynelle Gardens, Jackson Botanical Garden, Jackson

Missouri
Southeast Missouri State University, Cape Girardeau
Charleston High School, Charleston

North Carolina
Blue Ridge Technical College, Flatrock
Western Piedmont Community College Formal Gardens, Morganton
North Carolina State University, Raleigh
Reynolda Gardens, Winston-Salem

Oklahoma
Oklahoma State University Technical Institute, Oklahoma City
Cherokee Gardens, Tahlequah

South Carolina
Clemson University, Clemson

Tennessee
University of Tennessee, Knoxville (gardens at branch campuses)
Memphis Botanic Garden, Memphis

Texas
Dallas Arboretum and Botanical Garden, Dallas
Dallas Civic Garden Center, Dallas
Fort Worth Botanic Garden, Fort Worth

San Antonio Botanical Center, San Antonio
Porter & Son, Stephenville

Virginia
American Horticultural Society, Alexandria
Virginia Polytechnic Institute and State University, Blacksburg
J. Sargeant Reynolds Community College, Goochland
Kings Dominion, Doswell
Norfolk Botanical Gardens, Norfolk
Virginia Western Community College, Roanoke
Virginia Truck and Ornamental Research Station, Virginia Beach
Busch Gardens, Williamsburg

---

others, like sweet peas, that I associate with cool Maine coastal gardens, I have not even tried to grow in the South. It well may be that with careful protection and early planting, some years I could produce an early crop of those wonderfully fragrant flowers. Maybe next year . . .

Whichever annuals you are choosing to grow, you are growing them for the color—exuberant, continuous color. Too often I see six lonely, straggly petunias planted around a mailbox, as if the homeowner bought one six-cell pack, stuck the plants in the ground and never watered them. If you want a planting of annuals near the mailbox, fine. Design it. Incorporate plants of different heights, plants of compatible colors. Make the bed interesting— perhaps a teardrop shape, or a large L. And if it is in an area that will seldom be watered, don't chose petunias, but look to the drought-resistant annuals like gaillardias and gazanias or perennials such as euphorbias, coreopsis species and cultivars, rudbeckias, and santolinas.

For shade gardening, the top two annuals are impatiens and fibrous-rooted begonias. Both can be planted for spectacular, massed effect, used as garden borders, or grown in containers, and they are both reliable, easy plants to cultivate. No pests have ever bothered either one in our gardens. Impatiens come in varieties like the 'Shady Lady' series that will grow 12 to 15 inches high, ultradwarf ones like 6-inch 'Mini Cherry', and all heights in between. Both single and double flowers are available in white, orange, lavender, rose, pink, and related colors. I've already mentioned 'Blitz', which is one of the outstanding hybrids of this decade, a most desirable plant. The original prizewinning 'Blitz' was the orange-scarlet color, but today 'Blitz' comes in a series of several colors. The rich red 'Blitz' is particularly attractive. If you don't want vivid color, then a quiet carpet of neutral white impatiens in the shade lends a cooling effect on one of our hot summer days. Pick one color and plant a mass of it.

The New Guinea varieties are exciting additions to the list of impatiens we can grow. These plants, developed from species collected in New Guinea, are larger than other impatiens and have larger flowers. Many varieties have variegated foliage. They will tolerate shade but bloom better and have more pronounced variegation if given some sun. For several years, these plants were available only as bedding plants, propagated vegetatively. However, we are now beginning to see some New Guinea impatiens seed offered. Spectacular beds of these annuals are included in the 70,000-square-foot atrium garden at the Opryland Hotel in Nashville.

If you think of fibrous-rooted begonias as small-flowered plants your grandmother raised, take another look. In recent trials at North Carolina State University, thirty-two different varieties were on display— double and single flowers; small, medium, and large flowers; pinks, whites, reds, and bicolors; on green, chocolate-colored, or green-with-a-red-edge foliage. I thought *B*. 'Coco Ducolor', bearing large white flowers trimmed with a deep pink edge, was particularly handsome. If, one year, you find a begonia you particularly like, it is easy to pot up a plant or two in the fall, raise them

The huge flowers of *Begonia* 'Coco Ducolor'

as house plants during the winter, and take cuttings for your springtime garden about the first of the year. These begonias will flower all winter. The only drawback is the fact that they shed flowers every day, so the area beneath the pots tends to be messy.

Annual vincas are other flowering plants for shade gardens. Truly flexible, they also flourish in full sun, and for our southern gardens, note that they are also heat and drought tolerant. They have not yet gained the popularity of impatiens and begonias, but they have much to offer. Bush types, like 'Pink Panther', have been around for a while, but the newer carpeting vincas are growing in popularity. Look for 'Rose Carpet', 'Pink Carpet', and 'Dawn Carpet'. These floriferous plants grow just 3 inches high but will cover 24 inches of ground. One warning. Scientists at North Carolina State have learned that if you are gardening on land that was formerly a tobacco field, annual vinca may well develop Black Shank. This annual is very susceptible to soil-borne fungus problems.

Plants don't always need flowers for vivid color. Coleus varieties are grown for the lively foliage. In fact, most gardeners cut off the insignificant flower spikes when they appear. Open any seed catalog to the coleus page, and you will see lemon yellow, white with green edge, red with green edge, red with yellow edge, deep wine, and many other color combinations on flat, or ruffled, or finely cut leaves—wonderful annuals for the shade.

I'd almost forgotten about the touch-me-nots, the balsams. These relatives of impatiens are lovely, floriferous plants that we don't often see in gardens today. They bloom up the stem, rather than on top of the plants, and they are available in both standard 20-to-24-inch plants and dwarf 10-inch varieties. Balsams are old-fashioned plants I grew twenty-five years ago. I think I'll bring them back into our shade garden next year. They are easy from seed sown directly in the garden.

While it is perfectly feasible and sometimes desirable to have a bed of annuals (covering a spring-flowering bulb garden, for example), one of the best uses for annuals is to add color to a perennial planting. No matter how expert the gardener, it is difficult, if not impossible, to design a perennial garden that will be beautiful in all seasons. At Sissinghurst, Vita Sackville-West didn't try to have one perfect garden. Rather, she designed a series of garden rooms, separated by walls or hedges. One part of the garden might peak in May and then be relatively uninteresting the rest of the year. Another section of the garden would be at its best in July. Since most of us are gardening on a much more modest scale and have but one or two "garden rooms," colorful annuals are one way to enliven our perennial gardens and give them continuous interest.

One bed in our yard evolves from peony bloom through day lilies to a carpet of impatiens that flowers until frost. I've added 'Floral Carpet' snapdragons and a small species marigold, *Tagetes filifolia*, to the rock garden for summer color. In a bed near the driveway, I've planted tall 'Madame Butterfly' hybrid snaps and dwarf 'Janie' French marigolds in a perennial bed that contains day lilies, shasta daisies, *Sedum spectabile*, spikes of blue veronica, McKana hybrid columbines, and other perennials. White begonias or impatiens can enhance a planting of white and green variegated hosta in the shady part of a garden. Combinations of annuals with your perennials are limited only by your imagination, your creativity. There are no rights and wrongs. Plant whatever pleases you.

Pansies are old-fashioned plants that have a new look. The multiflora pansies, like the 'Universal' series, are both heat resistant and cold tolerant. They have performed extremely well in Georgia and in trials at the Park Seed Company in South Carolina.

Snapdragons, by the way, are usually described as half-hardy perennials, although most gardeners treat them as annuals. I left the large ones in the bed last year, and just about half of them returned. Probably if I had mulched them well or if our garden were a bit farther south, they would be fully perennial.

I mentioned the butterfly type. I find the open, ruffled florets beautiful, but my traditionalist husband wants snapdragons that snap. Next year, next year . . . So many of our gardening choices are simply a matter of personal taste.

Many gardeners like to have their perennial beds edged with low plants. A narrow border of liriope, Mondo grass, low boxwood, petunias, or sweet alyssum helps to unify a large perennial garden filled with many diverse elements. For more than fifty years, my mother has edged her rather eclectic beds of bulbs, annuals, perennials, and roses with annual sweet alyssum (*Lobularia maritima*). This low border of clear white, mildly fragrant flowers, in bloom from Memorial Day until the first frost, not only ties the garden all together, but it provides a crisp separation between garden and lawn.

When she began planting sweet alyssum, she probably was using the original species, a rather straggly plant that would grow to 10 inches or more. Over the years, that border has evolved into a lower, more compact, floriferous, and attractive planting as breeders developed varieties like 'Carpet of Snow' and 'Snowcloth Improved'.

While a white edging provides a certain neutrality for a colorful garden, occasionally you might like to use either the pink or purple forms of sweet alyssum that have been developed from sports. 'Royal Carpet', a rich violet-purple, earned the All-America Selections award in 1953 and 'Rosie o'Day', the first rose-colored alyssum, won the same award in 1961. I can imagine a handsome, all-white garden edged with 'Royal Carpet', for example.

If you are growing flowers for cutting, you won't bother with aesthetic

Pansy 'Coronation Gold'

considerations like garden design or borders. Find a sunny place behind a fence or at the far end of the vegetable garden and plant trim rows of annuals and perennials. You can even use a black plastic or newspaper mulch. This garden is not for public viewing. The flowers are for arrangements to enjoy inside your home or to share with friends.

If you only have space for two types of flowers, make them zinnias and snapdragons. Their colors of white, red, pink, yellow, and orange are the same and their forms contrast well. Arrangers are always looking for round and linear shapes to work with. Zinnias and snaps both last well as cut flowers, and they will continue to flower until frost.

If you have plenty of space for cut flower production, then you have many options. Consider your color scheme. If you want vivid reds, yellows, and oranges for your home, grow nasturtiums, marigolds, geraniums, plumed celosia, red salvia, cosmos, gaillardia, gladioli, salpiglossis. Remember to plant dwarf forms for tiny dressing table or tray bouquets as well as large varieties for dramatic foyer or buffet designs.

One friend who decorates her home in pinks and blues plants larkspur, pink poppies, stock, asters, dianthus, veronicas, and blue salvia, in addition to pink and white zinnias and snaps, in her cutting garden.

If you are gardening in an area that will not be plowed each year, then you can also plant some perennials like columbines, gerberas, lavender, yarrows, butterfly weed, dahlias, and roses in your neatly organized cutting garden. Poppies, both annual and perennial, add lovely style and substance to an arrangement. They are long-lasting if you remember to sear the stem ends when you cut the flowers. It may look ridiculous to go into the garden carrying a lighted candle on a sunny day, but any flower arranger will understand. Burn the ends of any materials, like poppies or euphorbias, that ooze milky sap. Remember that it is best to cut all material early in the morning, when the stems and flowers are at their best.

I like to grow some baby's breath or dill for filler material. They add a light and airy touch to any flower arrangement. Both the annual and the perennial types of baby's breath are attractive, and dill gives you an additional bonus, because it can provide tangy flavor to your cool summer soups or salads.

And don't forget the everlastings when you are planting your cutting garden. Strawflowers, globe amaranth, Bells of Ireland—attractive line material fresh or dried—nigella, scabiosa, statice, or the biennial money plant (*Lunaria annua*) all dry easily for colorful winter arrangements.

Gardeners don't usually raise petunias for cutting, but they are excellent annuals for sunny garden beds or for container growing. While the emphasis has shifted away from petunias during the past decade, they are still important to the bedding plant industry. We gardeners buy a lot of petunias each year, and breeders continue to develop new and improved varieties. As you shop for petunias, remember that those labeled "grandiflora" have fewer, larger flowers, while the "multiflora" varieties carry a large number of smaller flowers. The multifloras also are more weather resistant and botrytis tolerant. Petunias come with single or double flowers, in solid white, pink, purple, or picotee and star patterns. Yellow petunias are relatively new and still have a long way to go to equal the floriferousness and vigor of the other colors. I have yet to see a yellow petunia to which I would give garden space.

If you are going to be gone a week or two for a summer holiday, cut your petunias back vigorously and fertilize the plants before you go, and they will perform with renewed vigor later in the summer.

For bedding plants, patio containers, window boxes, and hanging baskets, geraniums are produced by the millions throughout the country. The bedding plant nurseries are growing two types: seedling geraniums and geraniums grown from cuttings. As consumers, we really don't care how the plants are produced. We want healthy, vigorous plants with lots of flowers—geraniums that will perform well in our plantings throughout the season. With both the seed companies and the producers of geraniums from cuttings vying to bring a better product to the greenhouse growers, we will

Small alpine poppies, suitable for a rock garden

Often found in old southern gardens, the opium poppy, *Papaver somniferum*, is beautiful in bud, flower, and seed pod

surely benefit. In local nurseries, I notice that they are growing a number of named geranium cultivars, rather than just offering red, pink, salmon, and white, as in the past. Progress.

If you like to raise your own plants from seed, geraniums are among the easiest. The seed germinates in about three days and the plants bloom in four months or less. Although the hybrid seed is very expensive, raising your own geraniums is cost-effective. When I added up the expenses of potting soil, seeds, fertilizer, electricity, and pots, I found that twenty-four geraniums, grown under fluorescent lights for four months, cost about one-third what the same sized plants would have cost at the garden center. Of course I propagate most of my plants from seed just for the sheer fun of it—and to raise varieties unavailable as bedding plants in our growing area.

Both petunias and geraniums, like many other standard bedding plants, are outstanding in containers. Many of us use redwood tubs, half barrels, plastic olive barrels, large plastic pots, hanging baskets, clay pots, strawberry jars, and even glazed pottery pots filled with annuals to decorate our decks, patios, or porches. To enjoy the flexibility of container gardening, all you need is the container, the plants, and the potting soil.

For any container that will sit on the ground, I like to cover the drainage holes with a fine mesh screening, to keep out slugs and other pests. Then I fill the container two-thirds with a porous potting soil mix, place the plants in the container, and fill in with additional potting soil. We used to think that it was necessary to crock the pots generously to provide drainage, but recent studies have shown that no crocks or gravel is necessary. Simply provide a very open soil mix and water it well.

The good news/bad news about a porous mix is that it drains very quickly. The roots will have a generous supply of oxygen all around them. But, in our hot summers, we probably will have to water our container plants every day and, on the hottest days, twice a day.

Watering is a challenge, particularly when it comes to hanging baskets. They dry out very quickly in our heat. I keep hoping to build a lath house where I can raise a crop of hanging baskets and have them all on an automatic watering system. Then it would be easy to rotate baskets to the front porch, enjoy the *Abutilon* 'Moonchimes', or the 'Non-stop' begonia, or the vining geranium at its peak and then return it to the lath house for additional tender, loving care.

With that sort of a setup, it would be easy to provide a constant weak solution of water-soluble fertilizer to the baskets, just as professional nurserymen do.

Since I don't yet have that lath house, and most of us don't, I am aware that my hanging baskets will need daily and perhaps twice-daily waterings. The smaller the container, the more frequent the demand for water. Plastic

Annual *Kochia Childsii* (burning bush or summer cypress) makes a handsome foil for geraniums

pots will retain water better than clay or wire baskets. The location of the hanging basket also affects its need for water. If it is in a breezy spot, it will dry out more quickly than if it is in a more protected place.

You can grow almost any plant in a container if you choose to do so. Perhaps you live in a town house with a tiny back courtyard, but you would like to raise a few vegetables. Check any seed catalog today and you will see that it offers a number of miniature vegetables, including corn, that are ideal for container gardening. Radishes and carrots are easy candidates for pot culture, as are determinate tomatoes. For hanging baskets, select tomato varieties like 'Minibel', intended to cascade over the edge of the pot.

Strawberries are decorative and delicious when grown in strawberry jars, but the same many-pocketed containers can be attractive filled with herbs or flowering annuals.

Standards, those lollypop plants on tall stems, look wonderful in redwood boxes. Buy tree roses, or create your own standard lantana or geranium by selecting one stem to grow straight up. As the plant grows, keep removing the lowest foliage. When it is as tall as you desire, pinch out the tip of the stem and allow it to branch and create the head of the standard. Around the base of the standard, plant appropriate annuals. Keeping your standard plants through the winter is a challenge, unless you have a greenhouse or precisely the right window, sunny and cool.

Everybody has a favorite way of planting geraniums in patio containers. Some like to combine them with asparagus fern or dusty miller. Others like the trailing appearance of plain or variegated *Vinca major*, or one of the fine ivies, like 'Needlepoint', around the edge of the pot. You probably have seen some wonderfully creative container plantings and some hideous ones. When you see something you really find attractive, make a note of the combination. California garden centers seem to be ahead of East Coast ones in offering lovely, imaginative containers and baskets, but that trend is developing throughout the South. I'm sure we will be seeing more creative container plantings and better designed baskets in the years ahead. We are being inspired by people like Tony Avent, the young man responsible for the landscaping at the North Carolina Fair Grounds, who decorates the roadways with wondrous containers of New Guinea impatiens, regular impatiens (the best, he says!), 'Non Stop' begonias, lantana, allamanda, tibouchina, and many other plants. We learn from the baskets and standards displayed at Callaway, and we are tempted to try azaleas in hanging baskets when we see the beautiful springtime displays of them at the Missouri Botanical Garden or at Bellingrath Gardens in Mobile. A lot of professionals in all our southern states are producing beautiful, enticing containers that we can emulate.

There are basically two ways to plant flowering hanging baskets. Either you fill the container with only one variety, or you create a combination planting. If you are using the standard plastic hanging pots or other containers planted only at the top, select viny material—plants that want to hang down. Even within one group of plants, like impatiens, there is often a variety that lends itself to basket culture. For example, as I write this book, the 'Futura' impatiens series seems to be the impatiens variety of choice for baskets. 'Futura' plants want to droop, to hang down. One trick to creating a full, floriferous basket that looks like a professional impatiens planting is to let the plant get slightly dry and wilty. Then hang a light weight on each of the long stems, let them be pulled down over the sides of the basket, and then water thoroughly. The impatiens stems will stay in place after they are watered. I use small fishing weights on soft plastic ties to manipulate a number of plants, including impatiens and abutilons. Applying this training technique to hanging basket plants is just an adaptation of methods long in use by fruit tree growers.

The most magnificent baskets are those that are created in large wire frames. To make one of these plantings, line the wire frame with damp sphagnum moss, fill the basket with potting soil and then poke your fingers through the moss and insert small plants through scattered spaces in the wire. Finally, plant the top of the basket. You don't need to fill every gap, but place your starter plants about 3 inches apart. After the basket is planted, water it thoroughly and never let it dry out. (One easy way to water any basket that will be hanging above eye level is to take a small clay pot, seal the hole in the bottom with a cork or chewing gum, place that pot at the top center of your basket and keep it continuously full of water.) With this method of inserting small root balls through the moss into the potting soil, the plants quickly take root in the basket and produce one of those spectacular, huge balls of flowers. Your choice of plants, again, is a matter of taste. Almost any small annuals will work well in this sort of planting. One of the most handsome baskets I have seen blended blue and yellow pansies with white sweet alyssum. You can create your basket of dwarf marigolds, impatiens, petunias, lobelia, sweet alyssum, browallia, morning glories, or many, many other annuals, perennials, and shrubs.

Some of the most effective baskets I have ever seen are at Walt Disney World. The horticulturists there have developed permanent plantings of hanging junipers in large baskets, with a place for a 6-inch pot in the center. The center pot of floriferous annuals is changed several times a year; the junipers go on forever.

Just as professional gardeners use annuals in many ways, so can we amateurs. We are limited only by our own gardening time, our budgets, and our imaginations.

12

Native Plants and Meadow Gardens

What is a native plant, anyway? It can be a mountain azalea, kalmia, or trillium; a woodland fern; a tough, drought-resistant roadside butterfly weed or yarrow; a sand verbena or marsh pink from the coast; or a beautiful bog orchid or carnivorous plant from one of the region's swampy areas. It is indigenous, a plant belonging to a particular locale. Some plants, like *Polygonum vivaparum*, *Lychnis apetala*, and *Potentilla hyparctica* are circumpolar. They are native plants around the world. Others are endemic plants, plants native only to Greece, or California, or Nepal, or Alabama. Many endemics are rare. For example, *Shortia galacifolia* occurs in colonies in only ten counties in North and South Carolina and Georgia. A few, like the three small clumps of elusive *Iliamna coreyi* in Virginia, are so rare that they are found in only one colony, in one corner of one county, in one country. The diversity of native plants is enormous.

We have an abundance of interesting, attractive, and useful native plants here in the South. Until fairly recently, these wild flowers, these weeds, were appreciated only by a minority of gardeners who brought them into their gardens and treasured them as much as or more than the most exotic modern hybrids.

Several factors have contributed to the current enthusiasm for native plants. For example, since World War II, thousands of Americans have visited England, Germany, and other parts of Europe where they have seen many of our rare and ordinary wild flowers flourishing in perennial beds. A large mass of double bloodroot decorates the wild garden at Kew; erythroniums sparkle in the sun at the Oxford Botanic Garden; trilliums are found in almost every public and private garden; selected forms of different gold-

One of our rare and treasured southeastern natives, *Shortia galacifolia*

enrods bring late summer gleams to sunny English perennial gardens. The Europeans grow our native plants and grow them very well.

Another reason for the current interest in natives is the growing awareness that the world's plant collection is finite. We cannot continue to allow professional collectors to dig thousands of cyclamen tubers in Turkey. Commercial orchid growers must not be allowed to pillage the jungles of South America. Wild flower nurseries should no longer go into the mountains to collect thousands of trilliums, ferns, and orchids but rather, should propagate their plants from seed, cuttings, division, or even tissue culture.

Groups like the Nature Conservancy are buying parcels of land that are rich in native flora and fauna to manage and preserve these areas for future generations of Americans to appreciate and enjoy. Rescue parties go to building sites and save wild orchids, ferns, native azaleas, and shortia as well as desirable common native plants from the ravages of the bulldozers.

At the Mount Cuba Center in Pennsylvania, Mrs. Lammot duPont Copeland has established a center for research into the garden uses of mid-Atlantic and southeastern Piedmont natives, along with an emphasis on the conservation of these natives. This program is directed by Richard Lighty, who sums it up neatly by saying, "The Piedmont covers nine states, from New Jersey to central Alabama. We estimate that the area contains about 1500

Native Plants and Meadow Gardens · 197

species that have ornamental potential. We are already growing about 1000 of them at Mount Cuba for evaluation. We intend both to promote garden usage and to encourage protection of these Piedmont natives."

Country-wide enthusiasm for native plants has been increased by the National Wildflower Research Center in Austin, Texas. This center was founded in 1982 by Lady Bird Johnson, with the able assistance of Carlton B. Lees, retired senior vice-president of the New York Botanical Garden. She donated 60 acres and $125,000 to start the project. The stated purposes of this center are to learn about the nation's wild flowers and to serve as a nationwide clearinghouse for scientific information and developments in policies of land use. The center is concerned with saving endangered species and encouraging the use of appropriate wild flowers in public and private landscapes.

A third reason many people are turning to the use of native plants in the landscape is the plants' perfect adaptation to their own native habitats. I've seen this pattern throughout the country. California gardeners have come to appreciate their native manzanitas, ceonothuses, and poppies. Drought-taxed gardens in the Southwest are now often beautifully designed with cacti and succulents. And here, few plants grow better in the southeastern United States than our southeastern natives.

Some introduced plants do thrive in our part of the country. If you didn't know better, you would think that the honeysuckle romping over roadside banks, up signposts, and through untamed woodlands is a native plant. Not so. *Lonicera japonica*, as the name suggests, came from Asia. Beautiful if controlled, it is a fragrant pest throughout our part of the country. Kudzu (*Pueraria lobata*) is another introduced Asian vine that has taken over the South.

But although you will see these and other introduced plants in our region, for the most part, those plants that are found in the fields, woodlands, bogs, mountain wilderness areas, or coastal marshes are native to their locales. (We are apt to find more introduced wildlings near ports where seeds from other parts of the world were dumped ashore with the ship's ballast in years past.)

If you are just beginning to get acquainted with native plants, there are a number of ways to familiarize yourself with them. Open your eyes to the roadside beauty of dogwood and redbud trees in the springtime, followed by perennials like the Stokes' aster, yarrows, and the butterfly weed in June. Enjoy the fragrance of the fringe tree when it perfumes an entire yard in the springtime. Appreciate the rich patterns of the golden ditch daisies late in the summer. Delight in the exuberance of wild azalea bloom. Notice the exotic flowers on the native passion flower vine near a neighbor's mailbox.

The butterfly weed thrives in carefully tended perennial beds or on neglected, unwatered roadsides

When we moved to our country acres, I discovered that our driveway was wonderfully rich with wild flowers. Small clumps of bluets dot the roadside edges; pussytoes and green-and-gold provide interest for weeks; blue-eyed grass and some daisies vie for sunny space with grasses, orange butterfly weed, and its more common relative, the white-headed milkweed. Violets are everywhere. The yellow evening primroses are followed by the lavender-blue *Ruellia caroliniensis* flowers, which look like small petunia blossoms on a vertical stem. Their passing signals the time to cut the green growth in our ditches.

We are particularly fortunate in living near the North Carolina Botanical Garden. In one brief visit, I can tour the mountain habitat, the Piedmont garden, and the coastal plains. I can see what plants thrive in the various locales and I can also follow the succession of bloom. This center, started in 1966, has a narrow focus. On its limited budget, it very wisely does not attempt to be a botanical garden like Kew, New York, or Edinburgh. Its mandate is to study and preserve the flora of the Southeast, to research propagation methods, and to encourage use of native plants in both public and private locations. The garden emphasizes conservation through propagation.

Take advantage of opportunities in your local community. Even the tiniest of towns often has a nature trail or a wild flower garden. Seek out a hobbyist who has a native plant garden. Join your regional chapter of the Native Plant Society. Participate in local hikes offered by various preservation groups.

Perhaps even take one of the many tours offered by your garden club, botanical garden, or other group. One of the highlights of our first spring in North Carolina was a trek into the Cataloochie Valley of the Smoky Mountains National Park, led by Ritchie Bell, then director of the North Carolina Botanical Garden. As we hiked the Mount Sterling trail, on the way to the peak we saw *Trillium grandiflorum* by the thousands; near the top, we strolled through a mixed meadow of daisies, erythroniums, red trilliums, spring beauties, and a number of other species; coming down the trail, we saw a dutchman's pipe hanging from a tree limb; we saw a saxifrage, ferns by a brook, and one boulder-strewn hillside covered with *Sedum ternatum* in snowy-white flower; and lower down, there were lovely clumps of the showy orchis. Seeing these and many other species in their native habitats made this trip one of the special treats of North Carolina living.

Stimulate your growing interest in native plants by buying the best popular book about wild flowers in your region. Here in North Carolina, the reference book to begin with is *Wild Flowers of North Carolina*, by William S. Justice and C. Ritchie Bell. (I like to mark each plant description with a comment in the margin about the location and the date I first saw that particular wild flower.) Almost every state or area has such a book. If you become more serious about your wild flower observations, you will want to own the definitive book about the flora of your state or region. Ours is the *Manual of the Vascular Flora of the Carolinas*. This sort of technical botanical book will assist you in plant identification, and you may find that keying out an unknown plant is a challenge you enjoy.

Finally, the book every wild flower grower should own is *Growing and Propagating Wild Flowers* by Harry R. Phillips and the staff of the North Carolina Botanical Garden, published in 1985. All of the knowledge and expertise gained there during several years of experimentation and study has been neatly put together. The 300 pages are packed with information about culture, plant characteristics, propagation, uses for the various wild plants, seed collection and storage, and much, much more. It also contains chapters on ferns and carnivorous plants.

Enjoy and appreciate all of the wild flowers, and then decide just what place they should have in your garden.

The most formal use for native plants is to incorporate them into a perennial bed. Many of us are already growing some wildlings without realizing that they are indeed native to our part of the country. For example, the blue

Trillium grandiflorum

of the Stokes' aster (*Stokesia laevis*) is wonderful in combination with orange, peach, and yellow day lilies. Spikes of lavender *Liatris spicata* provide strong vertical accents for any perennial bed during the late summer. (Both of these species also are available in white forms.)

While a number of modern cultivars of rudbeckia are on the market (*Rudbeckia* 'Goldsturm' is particularly admired by many gardeners), another group of gardeners prizes the native species like *R. hirta* and *R. laciniata*, *R. triloba* and *R. fulgida*. These black-eyed susans and related cone flowers all work well in a sunny perennial bed or in more naturalistic settings.

Other bright native daisies that add yellows to a perennial garden are a number of coreopsis species, the white-with-a-yellow-center oxeye daisy (*Chrysanthemum leucanthemum*) and the annual *Gaillardia pulchella*.

For a large perennial garden, masses of *Monarda didyma* provide wonderful, rich color. This member of the mint family, which grows naturally in moist situations, is a lovely red. Hummingbirds love it. The species is a fine plant, but I must admit a weakness for a monarda cultivar, the clear pink *M. d.* 'Croftway Pink'. Note the species' native habitat and plant any bee balm in an area that will receive regular waterings during our dry periods.

The ferny foliage and flat heads of yarrow add other forms to the sunny perennial garden. The white species, *Achillea millefolium*, works as well in

Primula kisoana, a charming Japanese primrose with furry stems and leaves, suitable for the southern shade garden

the garden as some of the other horticultural color forms, like *A.* 'Cerise Queen', *A.* 'Coronation Gold' or *A.* 'Rose Beauty'. An added plus to the yarrows is that they dry so nicely for winter arrangements.

The cheerful butterfly weed (*Asclepias tuberosa*) produces its colorful flower clusters during the summer. In the wild, you will find it in many shadings, from yellow through orange to red. The butterfly weed is one of those wonderfully flexible plants that will thrive in a garden situation, tenderly cared for, and survive very nicely when growing totally neglected on the roadsides.

You may choose to use wild flowers in a neat perennial bed, in an English-type woodland garden, at a brook's edge, on a roadside bank, or in a man-made meadow or prairie. Each of us has a different vision of what a garden should be—thank heavens! How dull it would be if we all saw life through exactly the same eyes. This thought was underlined for me the spring of 1987, when I visited two gardens on the same day. One had been developed by a total neatnik. He had built small hexagonal beds of precisely cut logs, trim raised beds, and small, precise rock garden beds. Not a weed was in sight. His nursery area was filled with perfectly grown plants lined up as for parade march.

The other garden was a paradigm of horticultural confusion. The woman had been rescuing wild flowers from bulldozers at building sites and highway developments for more than thirty years and had planted all of her finds on her 3 acres. Yellow lady slipper orchids peeked up through ferns and tiarella foliage. Native azaleas were in flower, wild phlox and columbine had seeded themselves around. Her garden was wild and wonderful—yet this gardener is a purist in one way. She has allowed only native North Carolina plants to have space in her garden.

My own garden is somewhere in between these two extremes. The scree bed is neat and precise, weeded regularly and labeled accurately. The woodland, however, is on its way to a partially controlled state of casual displays. It will take a number of years for this garden to look like the floriferous wild garden I see in my mind's eye, but already the ants are cooperating by carrying seeds of bloodroot and cyclamen about, and the *Phlox divericata* and *Aquilegia canadensis* are seeding themselves attractively around the garden. I look forward to the day when a number of the plants intermingle, and I shall spot a columbine nesting at the base of a tree as if it had been planted there. After all, should any plant become a weed, growing where I do not want it to grow, all I need to do is pull it out and either discard it or pot it up to share with a friend.

It will be fun to observe the columbine population over the next decade or so. These airy beauties are notoriously promiscuous. Since I am presently growing more than twenty different species, from 3 inches to 3 feet tall and in a wide range of colors, including white, blue, red, pink, yellow, and blends, the future offspring should be interesting.

I am not at all a purist. For example, our woodland has not only some of the lovely deciduous native azaleas, but a number of cultivars of the introduced, evergreen types. I happily mix natives and cultivars from all parts of the globe—anything that pleases me and will survive in this location. For example, the blue of the Chinese *Iris tectorum* at the wood's edge echoes the blue of native *Phlox divaricata* 20 feet away on another trail.

Ours is a deciduous woodland, primarily oak, hickory, and tulip trees, with an understory of dogwoods and an occasional redbud. Naturally occurring shrubs include several species of viburnums, deciduous azaleas, evergreen and deciduous hollies, and native blueberries. At ground level, we found several attractive native plants already in situ—wild gingers, a bottle gentian, green-and-gold, violets, blue and white forms of ruellia, false solomon's seal, solomon's seal, bellwort, rattle-snake plantain, oxalis, pennywort, skullcap, and others. I leave them alone, unless I want to plant something more desirable in a particular location. We also had vigorous growths of a number of brambles and vines, which we continue to remove.

Year by year, we clear areas and add more lovely native plants, plus cyclamen, primroses, azaleas, rhododendrons, and other compatible plants from around the world.

The shade-tolerant native plants begin in early spring with the ephemerals. One of the earliest is the dog-tooth violet, *Erythronium americanum*. The narrow, dark green leaves are mottled with wine-brown irregular spots. From the center of the pair of leaves comes a stem bearing a single yellow flower with reflexed tepals (sepals and petals that combine to make one flower). One plant is something to admire on your hands and knees: several hundred carpeting a corner of a woodland garden are truly lovely—modest, but lovely. (For showier erythroniums, gardeners often add some of the larger Western natives and their cultivars, like *E. grandiflorum*, *E. californicum*, *E. tuolumnense*, or *E. revolutum* 'Pagoda'.)

Several dicentra species add airy flowers to the woodland garden. Squirrel corn (*D. canadensis*) and dutchman's breeches (*D. cucullaria*) are among the ephemerals that come and go quickly in the springtime. Both are relatively small and charming en masse. *D. eximia* is a larger perennial that will produce its bleeding hearts from late spring until fall if the garden area gets enough water. The wild pink form is attractive, but I find the white bleeding heart, *D. e.* 'Alba', even more useful.

The toothworts (dentaria species) are other ephemerals which decorate the springtime woods with attractively cut foliage and dainty white flowers. I particularly like *Dentaria diphylla*, one of the two species that are growing in our shade garden, because, although it does vanish after its springtime flowering period, the attractive, glossy, toothed foliage reappears in the fall and is evergreen during our winter. Anemones, too, come and go, offering their unique charms.

As a group, probably the most exciting ephemerals are the trilliums. Everyone should begin with the showiest, most reliable—the sparkling white, large *T. grandiflorum*. While some of the trilliums are said to be difficult in cultivation, *T. grandiflorum* is easy and flexible. I have seen it carpeting a flat Michigan woodland by the thousands, and I have also seen it covering the sides of Mount Sterling in the Smokies. It is hardy over an extensive range, and it tolerates our Piedmont conditions if humus is added to the soil and regular watering is maintained during our hot, dry summers.

Because all of the trilliums have been overcollected by nurseries supplying them to the trade by the thousands, the North Carolina Botanical Garden has made particular efforts to learn how to propagate these lovely, three-petaled flowers and to share this knowledge freely with amateur gardeners and nurserymen. Harry Phillips taught me how to check the seed pods several weeks after flowering and to gather the seed as it turns from white to reddish brown, even if the seed pod has not yet opened. One peeks. It's important to collect the mature seed immediately. Otherwise, ants will drag the seed down into underground tunnels where the arils on the seed coats serve as a food source.

He also showed me how to wound the rhizomes in order to encourage divisions to sprout. After the blossoms fade, he digs up the clump of trillium, washes off the soil and gently cuts a groove around the rhizome, just beneath the newest growth. He dusts the cut with a fungicide and replants. After it flowers the following year, he digs the plant again and removes the tiny, rooted bulblets that have formed at the cut. He plants the bulblets. It takes a year or two more to produce a flowering plant from each bulblet.

While *T. grandiflorum* is smashing in the woods or in a perennial bed, we can add a large number of other beautiful trilliums to our shade garden. They come with wine-colored flowers (*T. vaseyi, T. cuneatum,* or *T. erectum*); with yellow flowers (*T. viride var. luteum*); with erect flowers like *T. grandiflorum*; or with subtly nodding flowers found underneath the foliage (*T. cernuum* or *T. vaseyi*). There's even a white beauty splashed with red at the base of each petal, the painted trillium (*T. undulatum*). The painted trillium is the most difficult to cultivate and should be attempted only by very experienced gardeners. The list goes on, and each species has its own charm, its own beauty to contribute to the garden. For those who like double flowers, a double form of *T. grandiflorum* is on the market today, expensive, but available.

Like double bloodroot, *Sanquinaria canadensis* cv. 'Multiplex', the double form of *T. grandiflorum* is interesting, but I prefer the purity of the single. Each of us has his own idea about what is beautiful. My husband wants to plant a pink peony with a huge ball of petals; I yearn for the serenity of a single, white tree peony. The clash of a 'Copperman' azalea planted next to *Rhododendron* 'Roseum Elegans' makes my teeth ache but that color combination doesn't disturb my mate at all. Each gardener sees things differently—and I find I'm not consistent. Sometimes I like the simple and subtle; sometimes the loud and splashy.

Along with trilliums, bloodroot, and other spring-flowering plants, native hepaticas add their charms to woodland gardens. The small flowers are attractive, particularly in drifts, and the decorative, three-lobed foliage lasts throughout the year, much like tiarella foliage. Here in our corner of the Piedmont, the foam flower (*Tiarella cordifolia var. collina*) and its close relative *Heuchera americana* are almost evergreen. The foliage hangs on until well into the winter, but it looks progressively burnt and unattractive. Farther south, they are totally evergreen.

Although I generally plant only perennials in the woodland garden, the biennial phacelia is an exception. I welcome the airy foliage and blue flowers in late spring—nice in combination with yellow primroses. Since it reseeds itself readily, phacelia naturalizes in the woods gracefully after one planting.

The most challenging and perhaps the most beautiful
trillium, *T. undulatum*, the painted trillium

All gardeners treasure good blue plants, I think. There are relatively so
few of them. *Amsonia tabernaemontana* makes 2-to-3-foot clumps covered
with light blue, starry flowers. It flourishes in the woods or in a sunny perennial bed. One of the flexible natives.

Another adaptable blue native that I have grown and treasured wherever
we have gardened is *Iris cristata*. Like many of the plants that will tolerate a
fairly wide range of growing conditions, *I. c.* is more compact and more
floriferous the more light it is given, but it does flower consistently in shade.

Carpets of blue phlox are expanding and seedling trilliums and blood-
roots are appearing near their parent plants as we continue to clear paths,
eliminate brush and vines, and plant more and more wild flowers, both native and foreign, in our woods.

We are gardening on a dry hillside, but if you are fortunate enough to
have a moist streamside or boggy area, there are a number of lovely wild
flowers for that area too. Spring begins with the skunk cabbage with its
wine-red exotic flower and foliage that lasts well in flower arrangements.
Those who are not purists will plant the western *Lysichiton americanum*,
with its large, vivid yellow flowers—spectacular in lakeside displays at Savill
Gardens in England. Lacking a bog, you may want to have a small, boggy
garden in a container or develop one in the informal garden by lining a
small excavated area with plastic and filling it with moist peat moss.

Streamside planting of the western skunk cabbage, *Lysichiton americanum*

Iris pseudocorus, naturalized from Europe, does very well here in boggy areas. Then there are decorative sedges (like the white bracted sedge), arrowleafs, pickerel weed, the cardinal flower, and even intriguing carnivorous plants like droseras, sarracenias, and venus fly traps.

Gardening on the hot, dry roadside bank is another matter. On our roadside, we weed out pine seedlings, grasses, trumpet vine, and honeysuckle in spots where we add drought-resistant natives to those already naturalized there. That area receives no watering after the plants are first established, so only the stalwart survive—particularly in the years of ten to twelve weeks of drought. To establish new plantings, we water with a hose and a 50-gallon drum of water we bring to the roadside in the trunk of the car. Fortunately the driveway has a steep pitch just there, so gravity does the work. Obviously, watering is not an easy chore, and we do as little of it as possible. How much depends on the rainfall in any given summer.

Some daisies, butterfly weed, milkweed, ruellia, blue-eyed grass, and a few other hardy plants were thriving under these tough conditions. We have added more butterfly weed, some white and some wine-colored cone flowers, thermopsis, coreopsis, black-eyed susans, several oenotheras, and some goldenrods. Queen Anne's lace, an introduced species that behaves like a native weed all over the eastern United States, adds its white, lacy caps to the summer display.

We planted a few hardy, non-native shrubs on the bank also, and started a Carolina jessamine climbing a wire cage installed around the trunk of a tall pine tree at the edge of the woods. Since this roadside garden is underneath power lines, I am careful to keep all plantings low—clearly no threat to the lines. So far, the power companies involved have protected this garden when mowing.

The coral honeysuckle (*Lonicera sempervirens*) is another native that puts on a wonderful show if it is given a sunny site and a fence or a wire support to climb upon.

I intend to expand this wild garden more each year, adding more and more seedlings of those varieties already established at the roadside and additional drought-tolerant plants like chickory, yarrows, joe-pye-weed, other goldenrods, and fall asters. As you may guess from the description of weeding, propagating, planting, watering to establish new plantings, and more weeding, wild flower gardening is not a low-maintenance hobby.

I mentioned planting seedlings. While it sounds simple and fast to scatter wild flower seed around, research at the North Carolina Botanical Garden indicates little or no success with this method of wild flower gardening. With the exception of *Bidens* species, the lovely, annual ditch daisies, start seedlings as you would any other garden perennials and then transplant the sizable seedlings into their permanent, prepared locations. So I dust our roadside ditches with bidens seed each spring, and otherwise, I raise my wild flowers from seed, cuttings, or divisions.

Our roadside garden is closely related to meadow or prairie gardening, popularized in the mid-1980s. Every magazine seemed to have wonderful pictures of colorful meadows covered with poppies, buttercups, and silenes or Texas roadside banks covered with lupines; writers praised the ease and low maintenance when gardening with native plants; catalogs and garden shops offered enticing packages of wild flower seed. These promotions all seemed to suggest that all a gardener had to do was to throw some wild flower seed around and voilà, a beautiful meadow, a wild flower paradise.

Not true. Particularly not true here in the Southeast, where prairies and wild meadows are not native. If you notice the natural progression of plants in a cleared field here, you will see weeds like Queen Anne's lace, poke weed, and chicory appear the first year. They will vie with each other for space and the most vigorous will begin to take over. Vines and brambles will sneak into the sunlit opening. Birds will drop poison ivy seeds that will germinate. Pine seedlings pop up. If unmanaged, that field will revert to pine woodland in a matter of years.

In the prairie states, open grassland areas may stretch for miles without a tree in sight.

If we want to create something like a prairie or meadow, we must manage the land and its plants.

Although the concept of creating meadows and prairies is relatively new, both amateurs and professionals have been experimenting with the idea. All of those who have tried to create this sort of wild flower garden have learned that vigorous, noxious weeds are the main problem. Anytime we disturb the soil, weed seeds that have been dormant for years are brought to the surface and germinate. It takes a great deal of effort to make an area weed-free and to keep it that way. The American Horticultural Society has decided that the best method for its trial meadow is to spray the area with herbicides every three or four years, after which it totally replants the area.

Perhaps the experience of one southeastern amateur will illustrate the joys and the problems of attempting to create a meadow garden. By 1986, Muriel Easterling had spent six years on this project, and she continues to work on it. She has found it exhilarating, frustrating, and occasionally discouraging. In her approximately 30-by-150-foot meadow garden, she has survived a number of failures and now delights when the planned succession of bloom occurs. She is constantly maintaining a balance, so that the most vigorous plants do not completely take over the meadow. Pine and other tree seedlings must regularly be removed from the Easterling meadow. (Pines will not resprout when cut to the ground, but other tree seedlings too large to be pulled must be cut down and then treated with stump killer.)

As we parents all do while raising children, Mrs. Easterling has found herself eating many of her words on meadow gardening. Originally she said that each plant had to make it on its own—no water, except when transplanting, no weeding, and no soil improvement. To begin to match her mental picture of a carefree blend of wild flowers in the meadow behind her house, she has found herself intervening in all the above ways. Let it be fully understood—meadow gardening is *not* low-maintenance gardening.

It is also not neat or organized gardening, as most of us would define the term. The beauty of an artificial meadow or prairie comes in its wild splendor, where the Stokes' aster, butterfly weed, chicory, coreopsis, yarrow, joe-pye-weed and bee balm vie for space. "The fun thing about a meadow is the surprises," says Mrs. Easterling. "You never know what will appear—or what will die."

Because little had been published on this subject, Mrs. Easterling learned by doing. However, in 1986 *The Wildflower Meadow Book*, by Laura C. Martin, appeared—the first in what will probably be a long list of books on the subject. The author is a botanist, working as coordinator of native plant research at the Atlanta Botanical Gardens. Her book gives the interested gardener details about designing, planting, and maintaining a meadow. It then follows with information about suitable plants, region by region. It's a useful tool to go along with the Phillips book on propagation and cultivation of wild flowers.

If we garden at all, a number of native plants are inevitably a part of our garden scheme. If we get avidly interested in native plants, there is a world of beauty to explore.

Books on Native Plants of the South

Alabama

Flora: Mohr, Charles. *Plant Life of Alabama*. Montgomery: Brown Printing, 1901.

Arkansas

Flora: Smith, Edwin B. *An Atlas and Annotated List of the Vascular Plants of Arkansas*. Fayetteville: University of Arkansas, 1978.
Wild flowers: Hunter, Carl G. *Wildflowers of Arkansas*. Little Rock: Ozark Society Foundation, 1984.

Georgia

Flora: Duncan, Wilbur H., and John T. Kartesz, *Vascular Flora of Georgia*. Athens: University of Georgia Press, 1981.

Kentucky

Wild flowers: Wharton, Mary E., and Roger W. Barbour. *The Wildflowers & Ferns of Kentucky.* Lexington: University Press of Kentucky, 1971.

Louisiana

Flora: MacRoberts, D. T. *The Vascular Plants of Louisiana.* Shreveport: Louisiana State University in Shreveport, 1984.
Wild flowers: Brown, Clair A. *Wildflowers of Louisiana and Adjoining States.* Baton Rouge: Louisiana State University Press, 1972.

North Carolina

Flora: Radford, Albert E., Harry E. Ahles, and C. Ritchie Bell. *Manual of the Vascular Flora of the Carolinas.* Chapel Hill: University of North Carolina Press, 1968.
Wild flowers: Justice, William S., and C. Ritchie Bell. *Wild Flowers of North Carolina.* Chapel Hill: University of North Carolina Press, 1979.

Oklahoma

Flora: Stemen, Thomas R., and W. Stanley Myers. *Oklahoma Flora.* Oklahoma City: Harlow Publishing Corp., 1937.

South Carolina

Flora: Radford, Albert E., Harry E. Ahles, and C. Ritchie Bell. *Manual of the Vascular Flora of the Carolinas.* Chapel Hill: University of North Carolina Press, 1968.
Wild flowers: Batson, Wade T. *Wild Flowers in South Carolina.* Columbia: University of South Carolina Press, 1964.

Tennessee

Flora: Gattinger, Augustin. *The Flora of Tennessee.* Nashville: Gospel Advocate Publishing Co., 1901.

Texas

Flora: Lundell, Cyrus Longworth. *Flora of Texas.* Dallas: University Press, Southern Methodist University, 1955.
Wild flowers: Loughmiller, Campbell, and Lynn Loughmiller. *Texas Wildflowers.* Austin: University of Texas Press, 1984.

Virginia

Flora: Massey, A. B., compiler. *Virginia Flora.* Blacksburg: Virginia Experiment Station, 1961.
Wild flowers: Gupton, Oscar W., and Fred C. Swope. *Wildflowers of the Shenandoah Valley and Blue Ridge Mountains.* Charlottesville: University Press of Virginia, 1979.
Gupton, Oscar W., and Fred C. Swope. *Wildflowers of Tidewater Virginia.* Charlottesville: University Press of Virginia, 1982.

Also, a long-range project, the multivolume *Vascular Flora of the Southeastern United States,* is underway. The first volume came out in 1980. That volume was written by Arthur Cronquist, and the entire series will be published by the University of North Carolina Press.

13

Rock Gardening

If you see a rock gardener with a faraway look in his eye, he's not dreaming of snorkeling at Caneel Bay. He's yearning to clamber over rocks to see peachy pink *Lewisia Tweedii* blooms blowing in the breeze on an almost vertical rock slide in the Wenatchee Mountains of central Washington. Or he may be imagining a hike down the Sumarian Gorge on Crete in search of a rare white tulip, or fantasizing about an exotic blue poppy from Nepal.

It's the mountain plants that fascinate rock gardeners. Those sturdy small plants with extraordinarily deep roots and spectacular flowers come from the alpine meadows, bogs, or rocky outcrops high above the tree line on the mountains of the world.

Successful rock gardening began in the early 1900s when English gardener, writer, and plant collector Reginald Farrer discovered that alpines would grow, flower, and thrive in an impoverished soil mix, mostly gravel with a little loam or leaf mold. Excellent drainage was the secret.

When Farrer concocted his lean soil mix, he was imitating the mountain conditions where rock plants are found. A leaf blows into mountain debris and decays, thereby providing a small amount of humus and nourishment. A seed blows into the same crevice and germinates, sending forth roots that may extend several feet into the mountain. A tough alpine is born.

Rock gardeners talk about "scree" conditions, and that's simply doing it Farrer's way, gardening with a lot of pea-sized gravel and very little humus. I had read about screes and even tried to create a scree in part of our garden, but it wasn't until I was clambering up an almost vertical pile of detritus on Mount Parnes in Greece, trying to photograph *Aethionema saxatile*, that I really understood "scree."

I slipped and skidded on the loose rock—one step down for every two steps up. Finally, I crept up to the spot where that tough Persian candytuft was in bloom, its pink flowers completely covering the foliage. A gem!

Give aethionemas sun and ordinary garden soil, and they are one of the easiest genera to grow in a southern garden. I'm growing mine with very sharp drainage, but that is not necessary for this genus. Aethionemas are flexible plants. One particularly attractive cultivar is *A*. 'Warley Rose', available from a number of specialist nurseries.

Actually there's an enormous number of interesting alpines that are easy to grow, after you learn a few facts about them. Find out whether they will thrive in sun or shade, acid or lime, scree, bog, meadow, or woodland conditions. Adjust recommendations to your particular location. Southern gardeners should pay attention to the native sites of plants that interest them. For example, I have made three attempts at raising meconopsis. The seeds germinate readily, sturdy little plants grow during the spring—and each potful turns to mush during our summer muggs. While Scottish gardeners may have these beautiful blue Himalayan poppies thriving in their mist and chill, the Asian meconopsis really will not do well here. However, the yellow Welch poppy (*Meconopsis cambrica*), native to Western Europe, has survived in a friend's southern garden for at least three years.

On the other hand, hardy cyclamen from Greece and Turkey grow, bloom, and seed themselves about. Seek out Mediterranean plants—that was the first southern gardening lesson I remember learning from experienced southern gardener Bill Hunt, shortly after we moved to Chapel Hill.

As we have gardened here, we have also learned that a number of Asian plants thrive in the southeastern United States. Dr. Clifford Parks at the University of North Carolina has been studying some of the divericants— our native plants that have a close relative in only one other part of the world, Southeast Asia. Our tulip tree (*Liriodendron Tulipifera*) has a twin in China, *L. chinense*. The only two shortias in the world are found here (*S. galacifolia*) and in Japan (*S. soldanelloides*). We-Du Nurseries is specializing in these interesting Asian counterparts and lists a section of them in its catalog.

When I'm checking seed lists or ordering from catalogs, I do pay attention to the origin of the plant I am considering. I continue to experiment with plants from all over the world, but I expect the best results when gardening with southeastern natives of America and Asia and the wild flowers of the Mediterranean region.

Some plants are ubiquitous—seemingly totally flexible. Hostas, for example, grow in almost every climate and all types of soil. They are both cold hardy and heat tolerant. While I talk about hostas in the chapter on perennials, there are also some minihostas suitable for small rock gardens. Right now I'm raising a tiny, 6-inch-high species from Japan that has been distributed as #57. *Hosta venusta* is another charming, 6-inch pygmy.

Ellie Brinckerhoff Spingarn, a professional rock gardener in Connecticut, points out that there is a miniature alpine version of almost every large perennial in a formal garden. As an example, perhaps you are already growing *Campanula persicifolia*, the 3-foot-tall, peach-bells campanula. *Campanula Portenschlagiana* is one of many easy-to-grow, mat campanulas, delightful creeping over a rock or decorating a rock wall. It is covered with small, light blue-purple bells, which enliven the garden just after the early burst of spring bloom.

We tend to think of clematis as the soaring 20-to-30-foot floriferous vines of *C. Jackmanii* or *C. montana* 'Elizabeth', but *C. integrifolia* is perfect for the rock garden. It's a summer-blooming, herbaceous clematis, 1 to 2 feet high, bedecked with nodding violet-blue flowers.

Everyone is familiar with a number of goldenrods as native roadside plants. While Americans tend to ignore their beauty, English gardeners cultivate some goldenrods in the perennial beds. However, dwarf forms, such as the 6-inch *Solidago minutissima*, are suitable for a sunny rock garden. Primroses, too, come in miniature forms, such as *Primula Reidii, P. frondosa, P. farinosa,* or *P. minima.*

This herbaceous clematis, *C. integrifolia*, is covered with hanging blue-violet bells and decorative seed heads for many weeks

Even the garden pinks have tiny cousins. The small, floriferous *Dianthus* 'Tiny Rubies' is charming, but perhaps the most choice is *D. myrtinervius*, which forms a small mat of fine foliage topped with bright cerise flowers.

Many of the alpine plants that grow so well in English and New England rock gardens will thrive here in the South. Others won't. Enthusiasts still have a lot of experimenting to do.

Rock gardening is not new to the South. In 1934, Elizabeth Lawrence and William Lanier Hunt from North Carolina were founding members of the American Rock Garden Society. Bill Hunt reminisces about a plant display he put on in the late 1930s. He carted in ice and dug native plants, like pussy toes (*Antennaria solitaria*) and moss pink phloxes (*P. subulata*), that are found growing with rocks in the wild. He followed his observations of the natural ecology and selected plants for very hot places.

He also organized a garden week in the Blue Ridge Mountains that was attended by gardeners from all over the South. Experts like Dr. William C. Coker from the University of North Carolina, Dr. Orland White of the University of Virginia, and garden writer Montague Free were on the program. One day was devoted to rock gardening. There were a number of lively discussions on the subject. Bill remembers Dr. White saying, "Well, I don't think you'd want to put dahlias in a rock garden," and Free came right back with, "I just went through Mexico on a train and lots of the rocks were filled with dahlias!"

Even today, experts don't agree on which plants belong in a rock garden. Some gardeners grow any plants that please them in their rock gardens, even some small annuals for summer color. Purists, on the other hand, will scorn annuals—and the purest of the purists will have nothing to do with hybrids. They will grow only the native species from the mountains of the world. At the 1984 celebration of the fiftieth year of the American Rock Garden Society (ARGS), Tom Everett, expert horticulturist and author of the New York Botanical Garden's *Encyclopedia of Horticulture*, suggested to the large gathering of rock gardening enthusiasts that we should be growing all plants associated with rocks in nature, whether they come from the seashore, the prairie, or the mountain top.

At first, southern rock gardening was primarily devoted to southeastern native plants like those displayed by Bill Hunt. One important element of the society was the Nik-Nar Nursery, operated in the 1930s by Mr. and Mrs. Latte Clement near Asheville, and their emphasis was on southeastern natives. The Clements were enthusiastic and active rock gardeners in the early days of the society.

According to Bill Hunt, the finest rock garden in the South was Rose Hill's in Charlottesville, Virginia. But there were a number of enthusiasts during those years. Another Virginian, Elizabeth Rawlinson, was growing alpines and lecturing on the subject. Fine rock gardens were developed in the limestone areas near Nashville, Tennessee, and others in Birmingham, Alabama.

Elizabeth Lawrence was experimenting, growing rock plants and keeping records of her results. In her book *A Southern Garden*, Elizabeth Lawrence mentions that she sent a lengthy list of plants suitable for southern rock gardens to the American Rock Garden Society. The relatively new Piedmont Chapter of ARGS has started a long-range project of developing a list of reliable plants for southern rock gardens, a list we hope to share with all interested southern gardeners. The chapter has defined a successful plant as one that survives and returns at least three years.

When we formed our Piedmont Chapter in 1985, we learned that one of our gardeners has a rock garden that is probably 130 years old. Another member purchased a house and uncovered the remnants of a rock garden that is about thirty years old. A few very choice plants still survived beneath the ivy and the brush. In Chapel Hill, lily specialist George Doak has been giving rock plants the most severe test. For more than thirty years, he has been growing a number of tiny bulbs and tough plants in a sun-baked, south-facing bank that is seldom watered. Other members are creating new rock gardens. But from the number of existing old rock gardens in our one small corner of the South, it is clear that there is nothing new about southern rock gardening.

When I asked Bill Hunt why the initial enthusiasm for southern rock gardening didn't continue and mature, he said, "War and azaleas." World War II changed a number of aspects of our lives. Gardeners turned to Victory Gardens to provide food for their families and neighbors. Many hobbies, including gardening, were held in abeyance during those years. After the war, the azalea explosion occurred in the South. While azaleas had been around since the first ones were introduced into this country in 1840, during the 1950s "people really got interested in azaleas—so gaudy. Azaleas killed everything else," Hunt said.

Gradually the azalea craze passed. Today these shrubs are a standard, accepted feature of southern gardening. After the craving in the 1960s for low-maintenance landscaping, and then the wave of interest in house plants in the 1970s, in the 1980s many gardeners seem to have returned to an interest in challenging, sophisticated, high-maintenance gardening, with all its labor and rewards. We see renewed fascination with perennial plants and in the design of perennial gardens; in native plants and meadow gardening; and in the creation and maintenance of rock gardens filled with rare plants from all corners of the world.

Massive thirty-ton rocks have been artfully arranged to create this charming rock garden

There are two ways to create a rock garden. If you are fortunate enough to have a piece of property with a rocky ledge on it, just clean off the brambles and poison ivy—the bones of the garden are there. Fill the pockets with an appropriately lean soil mix, and your natural rock garden will be a wonderful haven for many different phloxes, aubretias, dwarf iris, mat campanulas, small bulbs, and a host of other plants.

Most of us have to create our rock gardens. This job demands the eye of an artist combined with the drudgery of a pyramid slave. All American rock gardeners should own *Rock Gardening*, by Linc (H. Lincoln) Foster. Along with offering a lengthy encyclopedia of rock plants, Linc discusses site selection and construction of raised beds, planted rock walls, various types of outcrops and ledges, alpine meadows, screes, and moraines.

Rock gardeners jokingly talk about one-man or two-men gardens, depending on the size of the rocks that have been moved about and placed carefully. With the help of small logs as rollers, a pulley and lever system, or a mover's cart, one man can move rocks of considerable size. If, however, you want to move 30-ton boulders about, it will take heavy equipment and be an expensive project.

Your rock garden can be as simple as a trough or a windowbox planting containing forty or fifty tiny, choice alpines, or it can cover acres. Your rock garden can be carefully designed, as was John Osborne's garden in Westport, Connecticut, or it can grow like Topsy. Norman Singer and Geoffrey Charlesworth have acres to play with in western Massachusetts, and each year they dump the garden debris in a large pile that decomposes and becomes the base for the new, mounded bed for the following year. Theirs is the epitome of a collector's garden. Design is not of major importance to them, but over the years, these two superb plantsmen have raised every plant on the ARGS seed list, and more. In his recent book, *The Opinionated Gardener*, Charlesworth contends that each of us has two gardeners at war within our soul. Gardener #1 wants a neat, formal garden of perfectly grown and artistically arranged plants. Gardener #2 wants to grow one of everything in joyous abandon, amid a proliferation of labels.

Since a rock garden tends to be a collector's garden, aesthetically it helps if you find some unifying factor when planning your garden. Repetition of form, such as the small mounds that unify the rock garden at the Missouri Botanical Garden, or the use of color can tie a collector's garden together. In California, Harland Hand uses a variety of gray plants to blend his artistic collector's garden together, and his technique is very effective.

To label or not to label is always a question. Most of us have fallible memories. It's easy to recall twenty or thirty plants, but rock gardeners are plant collectors and if you are raising 500 different species and cultivars, you must have some system of identification. Some gardeners label, others make charts or keep detailed notebooks, others do both. It's always nice to know just what plants you are growing and enjoying. You *must* have accurate botanical names of any plants you are studying, breeding, or exhibiting.

There is no perfect label. The ideal label would be legible from a standing position, yet totally unobtrusive and inexpensive, and it would last for twenty years. "The only permanent label is one chiseled into rock," one gardening friend said. Too many rock gardeners' gardens, mine included, look like graveyards for mice—all those little white markers scattered about. I write on plastic labels with a marking pencil. Plant names remain legible much longer than with the marking pens I have tried. Good quality plastic labels last several years, if they are not knocked out of place by pets, birds, or human visitors. I have tried the green and the brown labels, but they are not unobtrusive. The green is not a plant green and the brown is not the color of soil. A number of gardeners use aluminum or copper tags. Others like the etched zinc nameplates on long wire standards that poke deep into the ground.

One reasonably discreet label can be made by punching your information into 3/8-inch green Dymo tape. Double the length of tape, fold it back, and let it adhere to itself. If you then punch a hole in one end and put it on a wire to stick into the ground, it will last for a number of years. Whichever method you choose, somehow identify your plants. For our relatively small scree garden, I back up the labels with a notebook in which I keep a monthly review of that bed.

As I have visited different corners of our country during ARGS meetings, I have admired delightful, artistic rock gardens designed to fit the size and scale of a tiny city lot. I have seen rock walls built to hold the tumbling mat plants of the world—campanulas, aurinias, aubretias, arenarias, and many more. One Minnesota rock gardener spent thousands of dollars on the rock work involved in replicating a Swiss mountain stream. Many charming and inviting rock gardens have been developed by knowledgeable and enthusiastic gardeners with very limited budgets. Anything goes!

Several times during the past twenty years, I have been fortunate enough to visit the ultimate American rock garden of Linc and Timmy Foster in Falls Village, Connecticut. They had an entire mountainside to enhance, enriched by the music of a rushing mountain stream. At the Fosters', charming, sand-cast troughs containing tiny, rare treasures, like saxifrages, drabas, ramondas, and small gentians, edge the low patio wall by the house. Visitors stroll through an alpine meadow of interwoven phloxes, silenes, tiny daisies, irises, douglasias, androsaces, and many, many other plants, on the way to the bridge that leads them up higher and higher through rhododendron glens and past a spectacular large rock covered with floriferous lewisias, their pink and apricot flowers blowing in the breeze.

Each gardener has a different vision, a different dream for his garden. Perhaps, like Singer and Charlesworth, he wants to raise every rock plant of the world. Perhaps he wants to specialize in one genus, like *Primulaceae* or *Gentianaceae*. Perhaps, like ARGS president Lee Raden, he enjoys a genetic scramble of phloxes blooming and self-hybridizing all over a huge hummock.

There is no one right way to rock garden. But whether you raise alpines in a small trough, a rock wall, a raised bed, on a large mound, in an alpine meadow, or on a natural rock formation, the key word is DRAINAGE. How often do we hear that word, when we talk about southern gardening? It doesn't matter whether we are growing roses, rhododendrons, perennials, or alpines, they all benefit from good drainage.

Raised beds are a useful and attractive method of gardening in all parts of the country, but we make more extensive use of them here in the South. Frequently our soil is poor, and it is much easier to build a raised garden with a soil mix created to our specifications than to amend the soil.

Recently, my husband and I constructed and planted a scree garden across the front of the house. I wanted it beside the house, where I could enjoy it daily. When we bought the house, overgrown, mundane shrubs lined the side of the house, all the way to the front door. It called for fresh landscaping.

What we have done is not good landscape design. While I am aware of the principles of design, there is no space for drifts of the same material in such a limited area. It's a collector's garden.

Since we were going to create a mounded bed, rather than attempt to dig out the old bushes, we simply cut them to the ground and applied a stump killer. I stretched out a garden hose and designed the curved front edge of the bed. We killed the grass within the proposed garden. Then my husband put in a lot of hard work installing a good drainage system for this garden area. At the back edge of the garden-to-be, he dug a foot-deep trench, filled the bottom with 5/8-inch gravel, placed 4-inch, perforated plastic drainage pipe, surrounded the pipe with gravel, and tied the perforated pipe into solid drainage lines, which he ran under the front walk and into a trench that leads off into the woods. At the same time, he tied the two drain pipes into the system with solid pipe. What I can describe in one paragraph took weeks of gardening time. It was an arduous task.

The next step was to construct the bed itself—another tough job. First we put down about 6 inches of the large gravel and then began the mound. We wanted to mimic the lean soil of mountain detritus— mostly rock with a little humus.

Our mixture was approximately half small, 3/8-inch gravel, one-quarter bark, and one-quarter what is sold as topsoil in our area—largely sand. (I have since learned from Howard Pfeifer, a designer of rock gardens, that we should have added some superphosphate to promote flowering. Plants I expected to flower that first spring did not oblige. I did not intend to fertilize this bed at all, but after talking with Howard, I spot fertilized the plants of the garden early the next spring, using a fertilizer with a high middle number, and the garden was extremely floriferous that year.)

With the help of two hardy teenagers, we moved the many wheelbarrow loads to the garden, and it began to take shape. After debating the use of an automatic watering system, I decided to water this bed by hand. I linger with the hose near some of the plants and bypass others as I water. Since it is a small garden, this daily attention is not onerous, it is a pleasure. It helps me to look at everything every day. Plants that demand drought for part of the year are planted in the area beneath the eaves where no rain falls. Then I water as needed. In April I put more than 300 plants into this garden. I've

The snowflake flowers of *Phlox bifida* 'Alba' decorate a springtime
rock garden

lost some and added a number more. Some things have disappointed me;
many have delighted me. Let me share a few observations with you:

Phloxes are wonderful, floriferous mats for a rock garden. Which ones you
use depends on the size and scale of your garden. I do not use *P. divaricata*
in our small scree garden, but it is charming and effective in Nancy Goodwin's larger rock garden. If you think of *P. subulata* as a garish cerise mat
mailbox plant, look at some of the introduced selections like 'Coral Eye',
white with a coral center; pale pink and subtle 'Laura'; the vibrant, clear
pink of 'Millstream Daphne'; and the lavender blooms of 'Millstream Jupiter'. For a small garden, seek out *P.* 'Sneewichen', a tiny white gem. *Phlox
adsurgens* is a western native that produces its pink flowers happily here in
the South—'Wagonwheel' is a choice form. The Alabama native, *P. amoena*,
is one of my favorites, both for its furry stems and for its profusion of pink
flowers. However, if I could have but one phlox, that one would be *P. bifida
alba*. In the scree, this plant forms a compact mound completely covered
with snowflake flowers for several weeks.

Rhodohypoxis baurii produces starry flowers in clear pink, white, or red,

Arenaria montana is one of the easiest and most decorative of all rock plants

low to the ground and relatively large for the foliage. This South African native is perfectly hardy but demands a dry winter. Pamela Harper finds rhodohypoxis do well planted out in her Tidewater Virginia garden. However, the first year I experimented and left the white one in the garden and put the pink and red varieties in pots at the back of my cold frame where they would get no rainfall. In April, I sank those pots back into the garden with the flower buds showing. There was no sign of the white one. Next winter I will try cloching one rhodohypoxis in the scree. English gardeners use cloches routinely. We Americans have much to learn about this gardening technique.

Ulmus parvifolia 'Hokkaido' is a tiny elm tree that ought to be in every small garden or bonsai collection. It has an attractive corky trunk and minute leaves that it drops all at once, come cold weather. A gardening friend in Pennsylvania says that his fifteen-year-old plant is about 18 inches high.

Thymes were a disappointment. I expected them to thrive in this gravelly site, but several failed. *Thymus* 'Clear Gold' is one with interesting coloration, and it has formed a nice mat.

Mossy saxifrages, on the other hand, were not expected to do well. They didn't. Of the eight or more that I planted, tiny bits of three remain. One, *S.* 'Gaiety', was kind enough to seed itself into the garden the first spring, and the seedling bloomed the next year. If it continues to maintain itself as a self-seeding annual, I will be delighted. *Saxifraga x arendsii* 'Floral Carpet' lived, made an attractive mat, and bloomed the second year. The encrusted saxifrages seem to tolerate our summers much more easily. I have not lost any of those I have, but they have not yet flowered.

Sedums all do well. One evergreen mat, *S. monregalense*, is too vigorous. In just one year, it has spread more than 24 inches. (I didn't let rampant *Sedum acre* anywhere near this garden.) The deciduous *S. cauticola* and *S. Sieboldii* form neat clumps and produce their pink flowers in the late summertime when few plants are in flower in a rock garden. I also like the smaller, deciduous *S. kamtschaticum* 'Takahira Dake'. It stays in a neat, low, round clump, and is covered with yellow flowers in early summer. In my garden, the variegated form of this sedum is more straggly in appearance.

I expected sempervivums to settle in as enthusiastically, but *S. Hookeri* has almost died off and *S. arachnoideum* 'Stansfieldii' is marginal. *Sempervivun a.* 'Tomentosum', on the other hand, has formed an attractive colony. *Sedum degadianum* and *S.* 'The Oddity' thrive.

Candytufts are perfect for the edge of this bed. The standard candytuft, *Ibiris sempervirens*, would be acceptable, but *I.s.* 'Kingwood Compact', a tighter form, was even better for the original planting. It has flowers the size of a half-dollar and blooms at 6 inches in height. At Holbrook Farm, Allen Bush offers an even more compact candytuft called *I. s.* 'Pygmaea'. It has flower clusters the size of a quarter and blooms when it is just 3 inches high. Colorado Alpines sells a yet more miniature iberis, *I. sayana*.

Aubretias, arabis, and arenarias are standard "easy" plants for a rock garden and any species or cultivars I have tried are thriving. They are all reliable, floriferous mat plants.

Aquilegias are also reliable. The tiniest and most charming is *A. saximontana*, a blue and white species from the Rocky Mountains. Must admit, I find most columbines beautiful, from this minute one to the large McKana hybrids. For this garden, however, I stick to the smaller varieties. Another that is low and compact and has blue flowers is *A. discolor*. (Taxonomists are arguing about this name. One says it may be a form of *A. flabellata*.) While *A.* 'Nora Barlow' is considered a choice plant, offered by such discriminating sources as Wayside Gardens, it is a huge plant, and I find double flowers on columbines to be very unattractive. It was eliminated.

For rock gardeners, the ultimate columbine challenge is *A. Jonesii*, with rich blue flowers above 3-inch foliage. It is hard to obtain seed of this Rocky Mount native. If you do obtain the seed, it is reluctant to germinate and if

Pulsatilla cernua, from eastern Asia, thrives in southern conditions—a luscious small perennial for the rock garden or perennial bed

you do germinate the seed, you will probably lose the plant. It is a difficult plant for rock gardeners everywhere, not just in the South.

Pulsatillas are lovely, both for flowers and for airy seed heads. The Pasque flower (*Pulsatilla vulgaris*) is the most commonly available. This plant from the mountains of Europe grows well in Piedmont gardens. Its large, starry flowers are carried above finely cut foliage. The species flower color is purple, but it is also available in *P. v.* 'Rubra', a rich wine-red form, *P. v.* 'Alba', and several other forms. You may find this plant marketed under *Pulsatilla vulgaris* or under its newer name of *Anemone Pulsatilla*. It and other pulsatilla species, like *P. patens* and *P. vernalis*, are choice plants for our gardens. (If you gather the seed, plant it immediately.)

Small bulbs enrich the flowering springtime in this garden. Species crocus, species tulips, *Ipheion uniflorem* (formerly *Tritelia uniflora*)—particularly nice in its selected form 'Wisley Blue'—pushkinias, *Scilla bifolia*, chionodoxas, and the smallest daffodils and alliums all grow well in these conditions. I intend to add more each year. John D. Lyon and McClure and Zimmerman are excellent sources of small and unusual bulbs.

Campanulas come in all sizes, as I mentioned earlier. The number of low-growing, mat types suitable for a small rock garden is large. At the Denver Botanic Garden, I was completely charmed by a small cluster of tiny blue bells nodding in the wind, as *C. cochlearifolia* peeked out of a waist-high niche in a large boulder. I'm sure rock garden curator Panayoti Kelaidis artfully tucked that small plant into a created crevice, but it looked as if the seed had blown there, and it was lovely. *Campanula portenschlagiana* (formerly *C. muralis*) was my first mat campanula, and it is still high on my list of favorites. It tumbles over a rock or down the face of a wall with a cascade of light blue-purple flowers. *Campanula garganica, C. poscharskyana, C. raineri*, and *C. rupicola* are a few of the other mat-type campanulas. *Campanula carpatica*, slightly larger, is attractive in a large rock garden, and it is widely available. Many of the others you will have to purchase from a specialist or raise yourself from seed. Above all, avoid *C. rapunculoides* should you see the seed or plant offered. It is a tall weed that resists even Roundup.

A few of the campanulas that are truly tiny and charming, are also monocarpic. It may take them several years to flower, but then they bloom and die. You must save some seed, if you want *C. orphanidea* to continue in your garden.

Two seedlings from the same batch of *Campanula carpatica* 'Alba' seed. Note the genetic diversity.

The birdsfoot violet is one of our tough, charming, and reliable wild flowers for hot, dry situations

The floriferous campanulas have another desirable characteristic: they come into bloom just after that first springtime burst of enthusiasm. *Campanula garganica* is the earliest campanula to flower in my garden and its first buds open just as the last phlox flowers drop from the stems.

Gentiana is a large genus that contains many gems for the rock garden. Every rock gardener wants to grow *Gentiana acaulis* with its large, rich blue flowers, or *G. verna*, another, smaller springtime blue beauty from the Alps. Because these are plants of the high mountain snow melt areas, rock gardeners try to keep them moist and well fed in the springtime. I have known gardeners to put perforated pipe under their gentian beds, in order to create moist, moraine conditions. Gentians generally have the reputation of being heavy feeders, unlike most of our rock plants, so I do routinely give them some plant food. Doretta Klaber's *Gentians for Your Garden* is my frequent reference for this genus. I'm a relative newcomer to gentian culture. As I'm writing this book, I'm raising about twenty-five different species from seed. Most germinated in three weeks, but in the past, I have had *G. acaulis* take up to two years to produce that first seedling. I've raised and killed *G. acaulis* twice here, so far. New seedlings are coming along in my cold frame. Maybe next year. . .

In my scree, my favorite to date is *G. scabra saxatilis*, a reliable, fall-blooming gentian with large, beautiful blue flowers on a neat, compact, low mat. I raised it from seed, and it also propagates readily from cuttings.

Iris, too, is a delightful genus for a rock garden. The small, bulbous types like *I. reticulata* and its color forms and *I. Danfordiae* flower in late February or early March here in the Piedmont. The end of March, *I. attica*, a low-growing iris with a disproportionately large flower, blooms in the scree. In mid-May, the dainty flowers of *I. gracilipes* are held above the fine foliage. *Iris minutaurea* has the shortest, finest foliage in my garden but is, alas, a reluctant bloomer. It produced a few of its charming yellow flowers its third spring in the scree.

If yours is a shady rock garden, add a bit of leaf mold and plant our native blue *I. cristata* and the white form, *I. c. alba*. Add our other southeastern native, *I. verna*, and the northern native, *I. lacustris*. *Iris tectorum* does well at the edge of our woods and would be suitable for a large rock garden.

The birdsfoot violet (*Viola pedata*) is a common native of hot, dry, roadside banks in the South, but let's never scorn the common and ordinary, if they are desirable garden plants. This violet remains one of my favorite plants in the scree. It is floriferous in the springtime, it frequently reblooms in the fall, and its attractive, cut foliage remains evergreen all year.

A backbone of evergreen plants is important for any rock garden, particularly our southern ones that are not covered by snow during the winter months. For all but the largest rock gardens, dwarf conifers provide a logical and attractive scale relationship to our small rock plants. For an evergreen vertical accent, a round bun, a weeping form, or a ground cover, there is some suitable dwarf conifer. While these choice evergreens used to be rare and unusual, today you are apt to find several types, like round mugo pines or the attractive, conical Alberta spruces, in every garden center. Specialists offer hundreds of dwarf conifer varieties and more are being introduced each year.

The fascination with rock gardening can last a lifetime. One can never know it all. The fun is in the search, the learning, the experimentation, the flowering of an unfamiliar gem from the Atlas Mountains of Morocco, the Rockies or the Bighorns, the peaks of Russia, or the high Himalayas.

For Sun

Aethionemas, particularly *A.* 'Warley Rose'
Anemone pulsatilla, including red and white forms
Aquilegias like *A. flabellata, A. saximontana,* and *A. discolor*
Arabis alpina and many other members of this genus
Aurinia saxatilis (basket of gold)
Armerias
Aubretia deltoides and cultivars
Bulbs—an extensive list of small species tulips, crocus, daffodils, alliums, colchicums, scillas, ipheions, and many others
Campanulas—many mat species, like *C. Elatines* var. garganica, *C. carpatica, C. Portenschlagiana,* and *C. Poscharskyana*
Dianthus—a huge group, many of which are suitable for the rock garden
Geranium sanguineanum var. lancastriense, both pink and white forms
Iris reticulata and cultivars
Iris attica, I. minutaurea, I. gracilipes, and many others
Phloxes—*P. subulata* selections, *P. bifida* alba, *P. amoena,* other species and hybrids
Potentilla verna nana
Sedums—again, a large assortment that are fine in a rock garden. The low-growing, clump types, like *S. kamtschaticum* (yellow), *S. Sieboldii* (pink), and *S. cauticola* (pink) are particularly useful, as is the tiny, slow-spreading *S. dasyphyllum.* For a large garden, the holly-leafed sedum, *S. populifolium,* is very attractive as are the tall-growing clumps of *S. Sieboldii* and its cultivars.
Violas, particularly *V. pedata* and *V. corsica*

For Shade

Asarums—choice ones like *A. europaeum* and *A. shuttleworthii*
Campanulas, as above. They are more lax in shade, but they do flower and are rewarding.
Chrysogonum virginianum, our native green-and-gold
Cyclamens, particularly *C. hederifolium* and *C. coum,* beautiful in flower and then as a lovely, variegated ground cover
Epimediums—several species and cultivars
Hostas—a huge group. Plant tiny species like *H. venusta* and *H. tardiflora,* or larger ones, depending on the scale of the garden.
Iris cristata—the native blue, the white, and some selected forms
Mazus repens, blue or white, a rampant grower
Phloxes—the woodland types like *P. divericata, P. stolonifera,* and *P. adsurgens*
Primroses—a large number, including *P. polyanthus, P. veris, P. vulgaris, P. cortusoides, P. Sieboldii, P. denticulata, P. Vialii, P. japonica,* and others
Sanguinaria canadensis
Scillas, *S. campanulatus, S. bifolia,* and *S. autumnalis*
Trilliums—begin with *T. grandiflorum* (its double form, 'Flore Pleno', is particularly choice) and then add any species you can obtain.

14

Vegetables, Fruits, and Nuts

"Do you have a garden?" my southern gardening friends inquire. When they ask this question, they are not asking if I grow roses, irises, or day lilies. They want to know if I have a vegetable garden. Most of us grow a few vegetables, whether we edge the perennial bed with some leaf lettuce, add a couple of tomato vines to the rose garden, plant some miniature carrots, radishes, and corn in patio containers, or harvest cherry tomatoes from a hanging basket. Some of us are moderately active vegetable gardeners, raising a fair portion of our family's peas and beans. Others, the most avid growers, raise almost every vegetable their families eat throughout the year.

Wherever we have lived, my family has always raised tomatoes. We're not alone, I learned. The number one vegetable in America is the tomato, or love apple. A 1982–83 Gallup survey found that tomatoes are grown by 94 percent of the nation's 38 million households with vegetable gardens.

Because of the commercial importance of tomatoes, universities and seed companies are putting a great deal of research into developing better, hardier, more disease-resistant, and higher-yielding tomato varieties. Many new ones are introduced each year. Homeowners would like thin-skinned, flavorful, disease-resistant varieties that produce their delicious fruits over a long period of time: commercial growers want varieties that ripen all at once for easy harvest and are tough enough for shipping, sturdy, and preferably square.

For Southerners who garden in a warm climate, it is important to select varieties labeled VFN—for example 'Red Chief' VFN. Those initials after the plant name on a label or in the seed catalogs indicate that the variety is resistant to verticillium (V) and fusarium (F) wilts, which can be devastating to tomatoes grown in the South. The (N) indicates resistance to nematodes, destructive soil-borne pests that can severely stunt plant growth.

Every gardener has a favorite variety. 'Better Boy' and 'Big Girl' are popular here. One name I hear repeatedly in our area is the 'German Johnson', a delicious, large, pink-skinned variety. The 'German Johnson' tomato is an old, open-pollinated variety that has none of the desirable disease resistance built in. The firm that supplies the seed of this attractive tomato that is so low in acid is working with a tomato breeder, attempting to produce a 'German Johnson' with VFN genes in the next few years.

For a "bragging" tomato, one gardening friend recommends Burpee's 'Supersteak'. Each fruit he raised approached 2 pounds. If you want cherry tomatoes, to date the 'Sweet 100' is the best on the market. This vine, developed by Goldsmith Seed Company, produces prolific bunches of succulent, bite-sized tomatoes on tall vines.

Bedding plant growers will offer some of the most common and popular varieties in their regions. For other tomatoes, you will have to raise your plants from seed. Each seed company has its offerings, but in response to the American passion for flavorful, juicy ripe tomatoes just picked from the garden, in 1985 Vince and Linda Sapp started a new firm, the Tomato Growers Supply Company, devoted exclusively to tomato seeds and tomato-related products. From the pages of this company's catalog, you can order more than 100 different varieties of tomato seeds, plus books about tomatoes and products for raising tomatoes.

Tomatoes come in determinate and indeterminate types. Determinate ones are usually shorter, slowing their growth as they reach their mature height. They seldom need staking. The indeterminate ones will continue to grow until frost. They need stakes, cages, or some other method of support. Every summer I receive several readers' questions about blossom-end rot, a round, black spot on the bottom of the tomato that causes the tomato to spoil. It seems to be our most annoying problem. It is important to mulch and to water tomatoes regularly, since an uneven water supply may be a culprit. However, blossom-end rot is usually a symptom of a calcium deficiency. It can be prevented by adding dolomitic limestone to your tomato garden in both spring and fall, as indicated by a soil test. Too much is worse than too little!

Do your tomato leaves curl? There are a number of possible reasons. If your curled leaf is brown in the center, with a pattern of concentric circles, it is suffering from a foliar disease called leaf blight and needs to be treated with a fungicide. However, if you turn over your leaf and see insects, they are probably aphids. You will need to get rid of those sap-sucking pests to have a healthy plant. Aphids inject toxins into the plant to digest the plant, so control is vital.

Also, tomato leaves may curl because of moisture stress—either too much or too little. Gardeners with tomatoes in containers will probably have more watering problems than those whose plants are in the garden.

Occasionally you may encounter an unusual reason for your leaf curl. For example, if your neighbor sprays his lawn with an herbicide, the drift of spray onto your tomatoes may cause a particular type of leaf curl. With this type of damage, all the branching veins tend to come together and make the leaf very slim.

Since tomatoes, unlike frost-tolerant brassicas like broccoli, brussels sprouts, and cauliflower, are tender vegetables that should not be planted out in the garden until all chance of frost has passed, you will not be buying your starter plants until late spring. If, however, you prefer to raise your own vegetables from seed, start to germinate the tomato, pepper, and egg-plant seeds early in the year. Judge when to start your plants in your area by first learning the average last date of frost. Then study the seed packet and follow its recommendations. For example, on one package of hybrid pepper seeds, directions suggest starting the seed six to eight weeks before trans-planting outside.

Here in my part of the Piedmont, the average date of the last frost is April 15. Because I like to push my garden, I usually put out my starter plants a week or two earlier. However, I listen to the weather reports closely during these weeks. I'm ready to rush out and cover the vegetable garden or the annual bed if we have a frost warning.

And do remember that an average last date of frost is just that—an average. Some years, the last frost will attack your garden days or even weeks later.

Many gardeners prefer to raise their annuals and vegetables from seed for two reasons. They can obtain varieties of plants not offered by the bedding plant industry and save money at the same time.

While interviewing several experienced, successful vegetable gardeners, I noticed that they had three things in common. They all started seeds under lights, they all put a great deal of emphasis on improving the soil, and they all viewed vegetable gardening as a year-round avocation, not simply as a pursuit for the spring and summer.

Whether you are dealing with Piedmont red clay or a porous sand as your basic soil, regularly improving it with organic matter will work wonders. Chapel Hill gardener Bob Hardison, who was one of six national finalists in the 1982 Victory Garden competition, began thirty years ago with heavy clay in his 50-by-100-foot backyard garden. After routine applications of com-post and sand all those years, today he has a rich, dark soil that is about a foot deep and wonderfully friable—soil you can poke your fingers into or crumble easily in your hand.

Hardison makes his compost by grinding several truckloads of leaves each fall, leaves that the city is happy to dump in his yard. Another gardener creates a rich compost by mixing 6 tons of old sawdust, 2 tons of chicken manure, and 300 pounds of lime. A third successful vegetable hobbyist prepares his beds each fall by layering several inches of leaves, grass clippings, and horse manure on the garden, adding a soil inoculant like Ringer's Garden Soil Builder/Winterize, and then tilling thoroughly. Whatever you can do to enrich your soil throughout the year will help you to produce better, tastier vegetables. Also, making the ground loose and friable will encourage root crops like carrots and long Japanese radishes, which cannot easily penetrate a tightly packed clay.

The virtue of fall preparation (amending, tilling, or plowing) is that the beds are ready for planting in early spring when it is still too wet to work the soil. Of course, if you have used a winter cover crop you will have to wait until it is dry enough to plow that crop under before you plant.

With good scheduling, you can be harvesting some fresh vegetables twelve months of the year. I was reminded of this fact when on January 6, a neighbor brought us a bag of crisp, flavorful leaf lettuce she had just picked in her garden, where she is growing it under a plastic tunnel. Two other friends use cold frames to produce lettuce for their winter salads, and that lettuce is so much more delicious than the tasteless, usually tired-looking iceberg lettuce that is shipped to us from California.

Kale and carrots are vegetables that will continue to produce all winter while growing in open beds without any protection. They can be left in the ground until you want them.

Beginning vegetable gardeners typically make the mistake of planting their gardens in one great burst of effort. Plants grow, everything needs harvesting at the same time, and then the garden remains empty until the following year. The secret of year-long vegetable gardening is to have seedlings or fresh seed ready to plant in the same ground from which you harvest a crop. For example, Hardison plants his favorite 'Premium Crop' broccoli early enough so that he is harvesting in May. As he harvests the heads, he pulls the plants and gives that ground over to the nearby cantaloupe plants that are just beginning to sprawl.

Most experienced gardeners also purchase or start new seedlings of the cold-hardy vegetables like broccoli, cabbage, and chard during the late summer so that they are ready to go into the garden when the days cool off in the fall. They also root tomato suckers to plant for a late crop in the fall. Almost all vegetables adapt to this late summer planting.

Those same experienced gardeners plant some lettuce seed every two or three weeks throughout the year except for our hottest summertime weeks.

Although lettuce is known to be a cool-weather crop, the variety 'Oak Leaf' will continue to produce well into the summer without bolting. In fact, unless you want a huge crop of beans or peas for canning or freezing, this principle of planting small amounts of seed every two weeks applies to many of our garden crops, including carrots, radishes, peas, and corn. This way your family will be provided with small amounts of freshly harvested vegetables over a long period of time.

Double-planting is another technique that most experienced vegetable gardeners use. They plant radishes between the slower growing seedlings of lettuce, spinach, or Swiss chard. The crop of radishes is harvested before the larger plants fill up the space. Double-planting such crops makes efficient use of the space and also helps keep the weeds to a minimum. As you pull the radishes, you also cultivate the soil in a small way.

Harvesting early and frequently is one of Dick Raymond's rules. Raymond, author of *Joy of Gardening*, says that you can harvest all the little cucumbers you want, but if you let one get 10 inches long or longer, the plant will put out no more female blossoms—and no more cucumbers. It has gone to seed. Just as we dead-head flowering plants in the garden to keep them in flower production, we should harvest our vegetables regularly so that those plants do not go to seed.

Anyone who has ever raised zucchini knows the importance of harvesting early. Miss a day of checking the garden as that crop roars into production and *Kaboom*, those dainty five-inch squash have turned into cavemen's clubs overnight.

Ardent vegetable gardening is really a daily activity—watering, mulching, weeding, feeding, and harvesting. A modest garden need not take a lot of time on any one day, but it does need that daily attention to produce the best crops, and year-round harvests of fresh vegetables will make your dinner table a gourmet's delight.

How to begin? Select a site that receives at least six hours of sunlight each day. If your yard does not offer enough sunlight, perhaps you can participate in a community garden and grow your vegetables there. We did that happily for a couple of years in Michigan. Be sure that the program provides water on site—important for vegetable gardening anywhere and essential here in the South where we have our weeks of drought.

We all adapt to our sites. You can terrace beds down a slope, build raised beds, garden in patio containers, or simply make low mounds by shoveling 2 inches of soil from the paths onto the beds. Many gardeners, particularly those with limited space, have adopted wide row gardening as the most convenient, space-saving method of vegetable gardening.

In a garden with typical individual row plantings, much of the square footage is taken up by walkways. If you plant in 3-foot-wide rows, you can reach the center of the row from each side of the bed, yet you give much less space to the walkways. Raymond is one of the proponents of this method of vegetable gardening, as is Peter Chan, author of *Better Vegetable Gardens the Chinese Way—Peter Chan's Raised Bed System.*

Both of these gentlemen make low mounds for their wide beds and do all the work while standing on the paths, never compressing the soil in the garden by walking on it. They both recommend adding a lot of organic matter to the beds and digging it in, after you remove the rocks, grass, and other debris.

"All you need to do is feed it (soil) and it will feed you," Raymond says. For example, one pound of peas or beans and one pound of 10-10-10 fertilizer sprinkled over 10 square feet of garden space will provide more than 50 pounds of peas or beans. Unlike most gardeners who build frames or wire supports for their peas and beans, Raymond believes that these vegetables should be planted and picked. He swears he does nothing else. As the plants grow, they shade the soil, thereby providing a living mulch that keeps the weeds down and helps keep the soil moist.

Both vegetables will hold themselves up in a mass planting until they are heavy with pickable vegetables. Then they lean over, but Raymond says few vegetables touch the ground. To harvest his peas, he takes a stool into the garden, pulls up the plant, picks the peas, and discards the plant.

Raymond says he is a wide-row gardener because he's lazy. I don't believe that for a moment, but he certainly is practical. Row planting originated in an era when seeds were precious and expensive. His method of sprinkling seeds over a broad bed uses today's inexpensive seeds liberally. He says his method produces 25 percent less per seed but three times as much crop for the ground space used.

When planting his seeds, he makes sure the seeds are in good contact with the soil. He covers most seeds with moist soil to a depth four times the seeds' diameter. He firms the soil with a hoe, rakes across, and then smooths the seed bed with the back of the rake.

His weeding technique is interesting. For vegetables other than peas, beans, corn, or vines, when the seedlings are just up, he drags a rake once through the garden. He says this raking looks awful but eliminates all the weeds that are just germinating and thereby cuts out 50 percent of the weeding.

Corn is the only vegetable Raymond grows in the traditional row method, hills 10 inches apart.

More gardeners are apt to follow Chan's method and plant their crops in rows, even if they have constructed wide beds of raised mounds. The gardener with lots of space lets cucumbers, melons, squash, and sometimes even tomatoes sprawl. Those with limited space encourage these vines to climb and produce while growing vertically.

After you have your basic garden construction completed, you follow the planting design you carefully worked out during the cold winter months.

Rule one—do not plant more vegetables than your family will consume. If you are interested only in fresh vegetables, then plant what you can harvest and eat. If you also want to freeze beans, prepare some pickles, and can tomato juice, then provide growing space for the necessary crops. Your garden plan will evolve from year to year. The size of your family changes—we plant much less for the two of us than we did when we were feeding six. The tastes of your family also change. Perhaps you discover the 'Sugar Snap' pea, plant a short row the first year and decide to double production the next year because it is so delicious. Our first crop of these delectable peas never saw the dining table. We ate them in the garden as we worked.

Rule two—plant only those vegetables that your family likes to eat. Just because a neat garden chart in a book you have been studying indicates rows of leeks, kale and turnips, if nobody at your home enjoys leeks, kale, or turnips, why bother to raise any? My husband hates carrots, so I plant only enough for my own enjoyment. If your children love sweet corn and you have a large enough garden, then plant several small patches of corn two weeks apart, for a succession of wonderful dinners highlighted by a platter of steaming hot corn, fresh from the garden.

Rule three—study catalogs and extension information. Learn just how much produce one plant or a 20-foot row will produce. The first year we ever attempted vegetable gardening, in my naiveté I planted twelve hills of zucchini and produced enough squash to feed a village. The next year, we planted three zucchini plants and produced enough for a neighborhood. Now, I plant one and only one zucchini plant. That's enough for the two of us. Besides, if you exhaust your supply and crave more zucchini, certainly in August most of the gardeners in the neighborhood have an enormous surplus to share.

Rule four—continue to experiment. While we all do develop old favorites, each year catalogs have pages and pages of new and interesting vegetable seed from around the world. If you like salads, raise your standard lettuce and then try some of the newer varieties. For southern gardeners, Robert Johnson of Johnny's Selected Seeds suggests 'Winter Density', a lettuce tolerant of light frosts. He says it will probably do well until Christmas in the South. Catalog companies are seeking new varieties in Europe, Japan, and other places. Breeders like Johnson are working here to improve existing varieties. He worked for a number of years to cross a red leaf lettuce with romaine types, in order to produce a red leaf on a plant with romaine habit. In recent years, we have seen an explosion of interest in oriental vegetables. You can raise your own Bok Choy, add edible chrysanthemums to your garden, or produce water chestnuts in a child's discarded plastic pool.

So, let's assume that you are ready to plant those vegetables your family craves in amounts suitable for your household, and that you have given a small percentage of space to experimentation with new and interesting vegetables.

If you are using the wide row method, mix a balanced fertilizer like 10-10-10 into the bed. Follow the recommendations of your soil test as to amount. If you are planting in rows, then make a deep furrow twice as deep as you will plant the seeds. Sprinkle fertilizer or rich compost in that small trench and fill it in half way. Then place your seeds and finish filling in the dirt.

In a few days, ferny carrot foliage, reddish beet tops, and tiny lettuce leaves begin to appear. As they become slightly crowded, *thin your seedlings*. Most beginners make the mistake of assuming that more is better. Not so. Give the plants you want to grow enough space to grow to their full potential. Repeated thinnings of carrots, basil, dill, beets, chard, spinach—every vegetable you raise from seed sown directly into the garden—will improve your final crop. You don't have to waste your thinnings. Fingerling carrots make tender two-bite nibbles for lunch or they can be pickled for attractive cocktail snacks next winter. Small lettuce plants provide the most tender salads, and it's hard to find a more delicious green for cooking than small beet leaves. Onions, too, benefit from thinning. The young, green onions are wonderful in salads or stir-fried vegetable dishes.

We are fond of Greek salads, combining our vine-ripened tomatoes with fresh cucumbers, red onion, oregano, feta cheese, and olive oil, so, along with tomatoes, cucumbers are high on our list of favorite vegetables. During the next decades, we may be eating more flavorful cucumbers in our salads, growing more productive, disease-resistant cucumbers in our gardens, and enjoying a better pickle relish on our hamburgers because of the research being done by Dr. Todd Wehner, associate professor in the Department of Horticultural Science at North Carolina State University. He heads up one of three active cucumber breeding and development programs in the United States, the other two being at the University of Wisconsin and Texas A&M.

This vegetable we take for granted has been developed from the wild

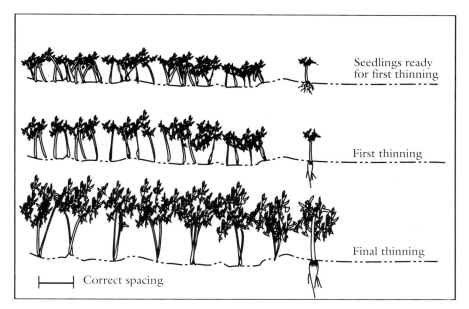

Seedlings ready
for first thinning

First thinning

Final thinning

Correct spacing

Thinning carrots

species, *Cucumis sativus*, which comes from South Asia, primarily India. Wehner exchanges seed with scientists in many other countries in order to broaden the genetic diversity. One reason to broaden the present germ plasm collection is the hope that some different cucumber will carry desirable genes that can then be used in future breeding programs. For example, at present, no cucumber carries a genetic resistance to nematodes, a major cucumber production problem. Perhaps some cucumber Wehner will obtain from some far distant country will carry a nematode-resistant gene that will be incorporated in all future cucumbers.

There is one other hope for development of nematode resistance in cucumbers. African horned melons carry a genetic nematode resistance. These close relatives will not hybridize with cukes, but Wehner guesses that within twenty years, the desirable genetic trait will have been passed to cucumbers through tissue culture procedures.

He noted that we home gardeners should grow the pickling cucumbers rather than the slicing types in our own gardens. While the thin-skinned pickling cukes will not ship well and therefore are not generally available in the grocery store, they are delicious and can be eaten peel and all. 'Sumpter' is one variety he recommends for southern gardens. Another new variety he suggests is 'County Fair 83', which should not be planted near other cucumbers. This cucumber is resistant to bacterial wilt, a significant problem carried from one vine to another by the cucumber beetles. 'Calypso' is the leading pickling cucumber in North Carolina.

Lettuce, of course, is a basic salad ingredient, and we can raise a long list of varieties. By extending the fall season with plastic tunnels or growing in a cold frame, we can produce fresh lettuce all year, except for the middle of our hot summers. The 1985 All-American Selections winner 'Red Sails' leaf lettuce performs well in southern gardens, as does 'Green Ice'. Perhaps you prefer tender butterhead varieties that don't ship well but are fine for the home gardener. When you select seed, choose varieties that are described as "heat-resistant" or "slow to bolt." My neighbor is particularly fond of a European variety that does well in our coolest months, 'Imperial' winter lettuce.

There are really only two tricks to raising lettuce. Don't cover the seed. Lettuce is one of the few seeds that demand light to germinate. Just press the seed into the surface of the soil. Water lightly. Once the seedlings have appeared, water generously and regularly. Lettuce is a greedy consumer of water. If I grow a plant indoors in my light stand, it needs to be watered twice a day or kept on a wick for a continuous supply of water.

The brassicas, which include a number of garden favorites like cauliflower, broccoli, cabbage, brussels sprouts, or Bok Choy, are cool weather crops. We can grow two cycles of these vegetables, in spring and fall. Either raise seedlings yourself, or buy transplants at your garden center. They are available in early spring and again in August. Like lettuce, broccoli demands a lot of water for a quality crop. Find a different spot in your garden each year for these vegetables. While crop rotation is desirable for all vegetables, it is mandatory for brassicas.

I have a marked aversion to having a host of small green worms fall out of my heads of broccoli when I bring them into the kitchen. I've learned that it is desirable to time the planting of that crop so that it will be harvested in May, before the cabbage moths are causing a problem. A number of vegetable gardeners are enthusiastic about the relatively new floating row covers that keep moths and beetles away from the crops. These lightweight fabrics breathe, water goes through them, and they are so light that they move up with the plants' growth. Several brands are in catalogs and available at garden centers. These products can also be used to provide a little frost protection at the beginning of winter and early in the spring.

Carrots, beets, and radishes are the most popular root crops. Your soil will determine which carrot varieties you select. The long, pointed carrots like the 8-inch ones we buy in the grocery store will grow best in light, sandy soils. Those of us with heavy soils should choose cylindrical 'Nantes', or the blunt 'Chantenay'. If you planted the long, thin 'Danvers' carrot last year and produced a crop of roots that were twisted or split, try planting one of the shorter varieties next time.

Perhaps you have had carrots heave out of the soil slightly, and you have noticed that the exposed part of the root turns green and has a slightly bitter taste. To eliminate this problem of "green shoulders" just put a little soil or mulch over the exposed part of the root. Mulching all the vegetable garden is desirable. It helps keep the moisture in the ground and also minimizes weeding. However, it does promote insect problems, particularly around the base of plants, so keep any mulch pulled away from the plants.

Beets just need to be thinned adequately and watered regularly so growth is not interrupted. Harvest before the root is more than 3 inches in diameter. The roots should be young and sweet, and the tops cook up nicely as greens. In fact, I learned recently that one of my favorite greens, Swiss chard, is an improved form of an early beet.

Swiss chard (I like 'Ruby Red') and spinach are both cool weather crops in the South. Grow them early in the spring and again in the fall. Some gardeners seeking a summertime alternative have been pleased with the flavor of the young leaves of summer spinach from the Orient, *Basella malabar*. These greens grow on long vines that need to be staked or grown on a trellis. And of course collards are traditional southern greens, and the newest hybrids are very heat tolerant. A fall crop is suggested by most growers, be-

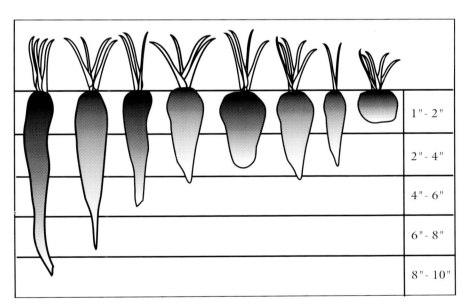

Types of carrots

cause a light frost sweetens the greens and makes them even better than those harvested the rest of the growing season.

Pea seeds should be planted in the garden at the same time you start your spinach and put out your onion sets. Here in zone 7, our time is mid-February. Zone 8 gardeners can start a couple of weeks earlier. 'Sugar Snap' peas are the one exception to the fall gardening idea. Most gardeners agree that they do not make a good fall crop.

Peppers, sweet potatoes, okra, and eggplant are vegetables that need warmth to flourish. Wait even a week or two after you plant tomatoes for these heat lovers.

If you like white Irish potatoes, they should go in the ground just after your last average day of frost. A number of gardeners don't even put them in the ground. They plant their seed potatoes in a large mound of compost, peat moss, or straw atop the ground. If you choose to grow them this way, remember that they need a lot more fertilizer and water. Harvesting is simple—just push aside the mulch. Collect a few of the small new potatoes to go with your first peas and then let the rest mature to full-sized potatoes.

Two weeks later, plant the seeds of snap beans, corn, squash, and cucumbers in the garden. Beans are one of the largest, most diverse groups of vegetables you can grow. You can grow green bush beans and yellow wax pods for your dinner table or for winter enjoyment after canning or freezing. You can raise historic beans, lima beans, foot-long beans, and a vast collection of beans for drying for winter use in soups and casseroles. Of course you will find a number of beans offered in every seed catalog, but for readability, history, and information, order the catalog of the Vermont Bean Seed Company. Like the catalog from Johnny's Selected Seeds, it makes fascinating reading for a gardener on a cold winter evening.

If you haven't tried the super sweet corn varieties that came on the market in this decade, add one to your garden this year. I have never tasted such delicious corn! And when you plant your corn, try planting in small blocks of plants, rather than in long rows. This concentration of plants helps with pollination. Plant your blocks of corn about two weeks apart and in each block, grow three to four times as many plants as you have members in your family. Check to see if the kernels are filled out as the tassels begin to turn brown, and harvest as soon as mature.

Some gardeners are enthusiastic about Jerusalem artichokes, a perennial sunflower (*Helianthus tuberosus*) that is raised for its tubers with crisp texture and nutty flavor. Having spent considerable effort in trying to eliminate these plants from a small garden, I say *beware*. Even if you think you have dug up all the tubers, the smallest pieces will regenerate the next year. If you have plenty of room and want to grow these plants at the far end of the back forty, fine. Do not add them to a small garden. I'd rather buy an occasional tuber at the grocery store.

If we had the space, one vegetable we would raise is asparagus. As that horticultural sage L. H. Bailey says, "To any person who has even a little land to use for a home-garden, no better advice could be given than to plant in a corner or at one side of it fifty or one hundred asparagus roots for his family, as no other use of that spot, ordinarily, may be expected to give more real benefit, enjoyment and value." Asparagus plants are perennials, so you must put that patch in a permanent location. Prepare a deep, well-drained, rich area. Have a soil test made of this bed. You can produce your own seedlings or buy crowns. 'Mary Washington' seems to be the variety of choice in the South. 'Jersey Giant' is another variety that thrives here. Plant the crown of each plant 8 to 10 inches deep. Most experts recommend not harvesting any spikes the first year and only taking a few the second year. The third season, you will have a full crop. It pays to prepare the asparagus bed thoroughly, because it will continue to produce this delectable vegetable for up to twenty years. For a good crop, the bed needs generous watering and feeding. Allow the ferny tops to continue to grow until they are cut down by frost.

We don't have space for asparagus, but we do always raise a few herbs. Chives decorate a perennial bed and are available for any recipe. Parsley, particularly the newer, extra curly types, can be equally decorative. It has to be planted each year, because it is a biennial. Rosemaries, oregano, and thymes grow in my scree garden. They like the heat and rock of that garden, and it provides as much sun as I can offer. Rosemaries are marginal here. Farther south, they are reliable perennial landscaping shrubs or ground covers.

One annual herb I always plant is basil because it is a favorite flavor. I dry some for later use, and I make up batches of pesto sauce to freeze for winter pasta dishes. Dill is another useful annual herb, both as a flavoring and as a cut flower.

My husband likes an occasional sprig of mint in a tall, cool drink. (If you plant any perennial mint, remember that it can be a rampant pest. Either grow it in a container or plant it in a large tin can sunk into the ground.) There are many mints one can grow—*Mentha pulegium* (pennyroyal), *M. x spicata* (spearmint), and *M. x piperita* (peppermint) are just a few of the most common.

Herbs have become more and more important since World War II. Our cooking has become more sophisticated. We like flavors of dishes from all over the world. Now our average grocery store routinely offers small packages of fresh basil, parsley, watercress, and dill. Each year, I notice that more varieties are readily available. Most perennial nurseries have an herb department, seed catalogs offer a section of herb seeds, and we also have a number of specialist herb nurseries. Many of us have been inspired by the extensive, educational, and beautiful herb garden at the National Arboretum in Washington, D.C. There are literally hundreds of different herbs we can grow, if herb gardening becomes a hobby.

If you are just beginning and would like some additional help in planning and maintaining your vegetable garden there are a number of useful books on the market. I've already mentioned books by Dick Raymond and Peter Chan. I also particularly like *Growing Vegetables and Herbs*, published by Southern Living. It is full of excellent photographs, planting charts, practical information, and even some recipes, and, unlike most gardening books, it is written about southern gardening for southern gardeners.

As I have talked with vegetable gardeners, I find that most of them also are raising some of their own fruits. Their involvement in fruit may be as simple as planting a grapevine for an arbor or using the tiny European strawberry 'Baron Solemacher' as an edging for a perennial bed, but a number of home gardeners plant small orchards, have the space and sun for a raspberry patch, and routinely grow strawberries for their families' enjoyment.

Strawberries are at the top of the list for home fruit growers. They grow well in the vegetable garden, for their requirements are generally the same— sunshine and rich, well-drained, slightly acid soil. Gardeners can choose from two types. If you want a large crop at one time for freezing, then select a June-bearing variety, like 'Tennessee Beauty' or 'Atlas'. If you are gardening in zone 7 and want some fruit sporadically throughout the growing season, select an everbearing strawberry, like 'Ozark Beauty'. For zone 8 gardeners, one expert recommends 'Brighton'.

These four are some of the strawberries that are suitable for zones 7 and 8. What I like about growing one's own strawberries is that we can raise tender varieties that do not ship well but are wonderfully flavorful—often tastier than the sturdier ones that come to us from California or other distant growing areas.

There are several different ways to grow these berries: as individual plants in hills, in matted rows, or spaced out in beds. The important thing about strawberry culture is to remove the flowers the first year, so that the plant does not bear when it is very small. Also, allow only the number of runners you need for your next crop to remain on the plant. That first year, you want to grow the biggest, healthiest rosette possible. Your fruit crop the second year will be abundant. A bed will produce for several years. You can either leave your bed alone and enjoy the crop until it becomes too sparse, or you can use the technique of one expert. Each year, he takes small runner plants and establishes them in a bed adjacent to the producing bed. Year by year, the strawberry bed rolls down his 100-foot garden. This gardener is always harvesting a premium crop. His method also automatically provides for crop rotation, which is desirable in any vegetable garden.

Just now, edible landscaping is in vogue. There is nothing new about edible landscaping. Homeowners have been espaliering pear trees on walls, planting daffodils beneath apple trees, or growing some herbs and ornamentals beside the kitchen door for centuries. Too many articles illustrate edible landscaping with slick photographs that show a flower bed edged with lettuce or feathery carrot foliage. It's easy to stage that sort of picture and it looks good. But what happens when you begin to harvest the lettuce or carrots? Any edging only looks good when it is uniform and complete. In *The Beautiful Food Garden*, now in paperback, Kate Rogers Gessert offers a number of practical ways to incorporate food plants into a decorative garden, and she suggests what to interplant to avoid holes when you harvest.

"The ideal attractive food plant would be beautiful in leaf, in flower and in fruit. It would taste delicious and have a long season of harvest. It would be perennial and effective all winter. Few food plants meet all these conditions, but some of them satisfy many," says Gessert.

The rabbiteye blueberries come close to meeting all of her requirements. The succulent berries grow on relatively tall shrubs that are attractive when they sparkle with small white flowers in the spring, are decorative and delicious when in fruit, and have richly colored foliage in the fall. What more can you ask from a deciduous shrub? These blueberries can fit attractively into almost any landscape design. Plant two or more varieties for cross-pollination. The rabbiteyes are more heat and drought tolerant than the commercial highbush varieties, so they are ideal for southern home gardens.

Each gardener has his or her favorite bramble berry. These plants have perennial roots and biennial canes. Each year, the canes that have borne fruit should be pruned out and new canes should be thinned, leaving only four to six per plant to produce the next crop. One gardener near me has eliminated all of his other brambles to grow only the tayberry, a hybrid developed in England. He finds it the most delicious berry. If we had an appropriate location in our yard and could choose from all the bramble berries grown in our area, I would plant 'Fallgold', a golden raspberry that melts in your mouth. It is the most succulent, flavorful, scrumptious berry I have ever tasted. Most summers, we are fortunate. Neighbors who are growing 'Fallgold' go on vacation and give us picking rights while they are gone. Seventh heaven!

Of course you can also grow boysenberries, blackberries, gooseberries, and red raspberries. Each is delicious in its own way. For the most successful berries for your garden, consult with your county agent. He knows which varieties grow best in his area. Also, study catalogs. Nurseries like Stark Bro's and Hastings list the appropriate zones for each variety of fruit they offer.

A number of gardeners raise grapes and kiwi vines for their decorative value as well as for their fruits. One extension agent said flatly that the native muscadine grapes are the only ones we should grow in the South. They are extremely long-lived, tolerate heat and humidity, and have considerable disease resistance. However, there are a number of other grapes that are listed for southern zones. 'Daytona' is supposed to do well even in the deep South, in zones 8–10, and 'Villard Blanc', a French hybrid wine grape, is listed for zones 6–9. Don't try to grow favorites that thrive in the north like 'Concord' or 'Thompson Seedless'. Concord grapes are marginal here in zone 7 and will not do well at all in zone 8 gardens. With the help of your local nurseryman, county agent, or catalogs, select varieties that will thrive. (More comment about kiwi vines in the chapter on vines.)

If you are intending to install a fruit orchard, small or large, for your home garden, two choices will make your orchard much more enjoyable. Select dwarf varieties, and install a drip irrigation system. Large trees are difficult to prune, spray, or harvest. Whether you are planting apples, peaches, nectarines, pears, plums, or apricots, they are all available on dwarf root stock. Watering by drip system is an efficient, economical method of water usage, and it also keeps water off the foliage, thereby minimizing foliar fungal problems. Even if you don't have garden space for an orchard, you can have a lot of fun growing a few dwarf varieties in containers—a portable, potted orchard.

Like a rose garden, a fruit orchard requires regular spraying and attention. A dormant spray is desirable before the buds break, and after they break, you will probably need to spray with a combined fungicide-insecticide every two weeks from early spring until June. Destructive diseases and several insects, like aphids and Japanese beetles, may bother your fruit trees. Since the recommended or available chemicals change from year to year, do check with your garden center or county agent to see what products are best for your home orchard. If you prefer not to spray, then you must be willing to accept some damage. Good sanitation will help to minimize problems. Purchasing resistant varieties also helps.

Pruning your trees to allow free circulation of air and to provide sunlight to all the foliage for good photosynthesis is another way to keep them at their healthiest. Along with sensible pruning, one grower strongly recommends training the young branches to shape the tree into the form you desire. He uses small bracing boards to gently force branch placement, and he also ties his branches to a protective fence he has around each tree. Some other growers use plastic bags filled with sand to weigh down the branches. The plastic disintegrates in about a year, by which time the growth pattern is established.

While we don't think of apples as fruits for zones 7 and 8, many of the old varieties will thrive here, and some of them are particularly delicious. Approximately twenty specialist nurseries are offering old varieties of apples for sale. For example, Southmeadow Fruit Gardens lists more than 150 different varieties. Also, breeders are developing modern hybrids that are suitable for the South. Southern varieties are being offered in most fruit nursery catalogs.

A number of southern gardeners enjoy figs as a delicacy. They do well in sheltered sites in zone 7 and are totally hardy in zone 8. 'Brown Turkey' and 'Celeste' seem to be the favorite varieties here. Both are self-pollinating varieties. Figs occasionally have the problem of setting fruit that drops before it is mature. That happens with some figs. It is not a varietal problem. It can occur with a cultivar purchased from a nursery. If the problem continues for several years, discard the tree and get a sucker from one that bears fruit reliably.

Persimmons are other fruits that are uncommon but treasured by the gardeners who produce them. The American persimmon is small and astringent unless completely ripe. The Japanese persimmon produces a larger fruit that is tastier to many people's way of thinking. The oriental species and its cultivars are much more tender than the American. Like the figs, these persimmons need a little protection in zone 7.

The list of possible fruits for our gardens is quite extensive. We can add mulberry trees, orchard quince, crabapples, or native pawpaw trees. I've heard friends rave about the sweet apple-pear flavor of a medlar, but I have yet to taste one. If you get seriously interested in fruiting plants, you might like to join the North American Fruit Explorers. The members of this organization are actively expanding the variety of fruits grown in our country.

While there are several nut trees we can grow successfully in the South, certainly the dominant one is the pecan. Pecan trees not only provide us with a bountiful crop of delicious nuts, but they are handsome, large shade trees for the southern landscape. Every time I drive to the coast, I admire an old farmhouse, its lane sheltered by a long row of tall pecan trees.

Select varieties that thrive in your area. Grafted, named cultivars will produce nuts for you years ahead of seedling trees, and the crop will be much better in quality. The smaller "Indian" varieties, like 'Kiowa', 'Shoshoni', and 'Pawnee' are excellent pecan cultivars for zones 7 and 8. Plant them carefully, as you would any fine shade tree, mulch heavily, and water well. Do not feed the first year. Pecans seem to need more water than other trees. If you are growing them in a nursery, use a drip irrigation system. If you are planting a few as landscape trees, be sure that they get a generous supply of water, particularly during the first two years, while their root systems are getting well established.

Several pests may bother your trees. If you find the ground littered with branch tips that are almost uniformly 18 inches in length and appear to have been sawn off, the twig girdler beetle is at work. This insect lays eggs in those tips and then cuts the branch tips off so that they will fall to the ground. I find these small branches all over our oak and hickory woods. Homeowners will usually ignore this damage unless they are trying to produce good nuts. The best control is to pick up all these branches and burn them, thus destroying the eggs.

One reader wrote that he was getting no crop on his twenty-year-old pecan trees because of small holes in each nut. Those holes are caused by the pecan weevil, another frequent pest in pecan trees. Spraying weekly between mid-August and mid-September with Sevin is the recommended treatment. Be sure to spray the ground beneath the trees as well. Cleanliness also helps. Rake up any debris before you spray, and keep the area neat.

Black walnuts are native to the cooler parts of our region and can be planted as far south as zone 9. They provide a distinctive flavor to baked goods. If you harvest some of these nuts, it is desirable to remove the hulls as soon as the nuts are ripe, to prevent the stain in the round green and black hulls from penetrating the nut shells, causing an unpleasantly strong taste in the nut meats. You can remove the hulls manually, but your fingers will carry the stains for at least two weeks. One friend suggests scrunching the hulls by dumping them on the driveway and running over them with the car—a practical solution.

Once hulled, scrub the nuts and spread them on a screen or tray to dry. Then crack and store the nut meats in the refrigerator or freezer.

Almonds, filberts, butternuts, and chestnuts are other nut trees that are fine trees for the South. Most nut trees need a cross-pollinator, so check with your nurseryman or study the Hastings or Starks Bro's catalogs for precise information. Almond trees not only produce the nuts but are covered with pink flowers in the springtime. Like all the plants I most treasure, nut trees give us double value for the garden space they inhabit.

15

Propagation

Perhaps you don't think of yourself as a propagator, but if you have ever planted a marigold seed, stuck a stem cutting of an impatiens in a glass of water, or divided some day lilies to share with your neighbor, you have indeed been propagating plants.

While I enjoy all aspects of gardening—except the inevitable weeding—propagating is the most fun of all. After years of gardening, it continues to seem like a miracle when I scatter some dust-like seeds of a saintpaulia hybrid over the medium in a pot and nine months later produce a flowering African violet, or come home from visiting a friend's garden with a small twig of a shrub in my pocket, root it, and soon have a flourishing copy of that shrub growing in our yard.

Old plants need to be renewed; new plants demand a chance. Through seeds, cuttings, and divisions, we amateur gardeners can delight in the old and experiment with the new. The most avid amateurs are even working with hybridization and propagation by tissue culture.

Supplies

It doesn't take fancy equipment to be a propagator. Check your local garden centers or garden supply catalogs and you will find everything you might need—pots of all sizes, flats, miniature greenhouses, plug propagation kits, peat pots, compressed peat pellets, labels, and a number of potting mixes, seed starter mixes, and soil components like perlite and vermiculite. You can purchase sophisticated equipment or begin in a very simple way.

In our early, frugal days of marriage, I was the ultimate scrounger. During spring clean-up days in my community, I often leaped out of my car and rescued flats and pots my neighbors had discarded at curbside. I cut labels out of Clorox bottles and used discarded plastic coffee cups, egg cartons, coffee cans and cut down milk cartons for plant donations to the garden club sales. I had great fun gardening on a very limited budget. In 1985, Carol Boston wrote a book about gardening on a tight budget. *The Pennypincher's Guide to Landscaping* is full of economical ideas I could have used when I was twenty-five.

Today time is more precious than money. I am content to buy my pots by the case and my labels by the thousand. You will find that many wholesalers will allow a retail customer to purchase at wholesale prices if the volume of the sale is large enough. Frequently friends, neighbors, or garden clubs arrange group purchases of supplies.

While I still have a considerable collection of sturdy plastic pots that I have used and reused over the years, I am slowly phasing out the odd sizes by potting contributions to plant sales and gifts for friends in them. In my nursery area, I've learned it is easier to water correctly and to move flats about if the flats and pots are of uniform size. To store used pots, I first soak them in a pail of water which contains 10 percent bleach. Then I rinse them off with the hose, let them dry, and stack them.

For indoor gardening, I use tiny 1½-inch pots for gesneriad, rhododendron, and begonia seedlings. Other, larger seedlings go directly into 3-inch pots. From there, a few are potted on into 6-inch pots, but most of the seedlings go outdoors into the nursery area in light-weight, inexpensive 3-inch plastic pots, twenty-four to a flat.

Outdoors, I intend to get most of the plants into the ground from these 3-inch pots. Some trees and shrubs are moved on into quart, gallon, and a few even into 5-gallon containers before they find their permanent homes.

Every plant, or flat of plants, is correctly labeled. If you are growing five different plants, it's easy to remember their names. If you are growing 500, it's impossible. Once a plant collection is of any size, labels are a must.

Seeds

We have a number of reasons for raising plants from seed. Some vegetables, like radishes and carrots, are never sold as transplants but are always started in situ in the vegetable garden. We may choose to raise our broccoli, salad greens, marigolds, and impatiens from seed because it is cost efficient to produce our own seedlings, or because we want to grow varieties that are not otherwise available.

Bedding plant growers produce millions of plants each year and we have some superb wholesale bedding plant nurseries in the South. While some of the growers are experimental and innovative and introduce some new plants each year, generally they all tend to raise large numbers of a limited selection of varieties—the standard petunias, geraniums, marigolds, cabbages, tomatoes, peppers, and other plants. If you are looking for lettuce 'Green Ice', you may not find it among the lettuce seedlings at your garden center. If you find 'Green Ice', you may not find 'Red Sails', and you certainly will not find celtuce, Japanese Swiss chard, or perilla for your salads.

In the typical bedding plant display, you probably will find one or two varieties each of a large tomato, a patio-type tomato and an Italian. If you prefer to try 'Celebrity' or 'Bragger' for your slicing tomato or want to raise the succulent, small patio tomatoes of 'Bitsy', it is likely that you will have to start those plants from seed.

The same is true of annuals and perennials. If you simply want some impatiens for a shady nook, or red geraniums for pots on the sunny patio, plants will be available. If, however, you want 'Super Elfin White' dwarf impatiens or Geranium 'Jolly Red Wink', with its lovely, large red flowers with white centers, again, probably you will have to raise them from seed.

One gardening acquaintance of mine takes a sensible approach, I think. She gardens extensively, and each year she raises from seed all those plants that she cannot purchase. She does not give growing space or gardening time to any seedling she can purchase as a bedding plant. If you want to adopt this policy, early in the year you can check with your garden center manager as to which varieties of vegetables, annuals, and perennials he will be carrying in the spring, and then you can order your seed accordingly.

If I remember correctly, the first seeds I planted in my own garden were some nasturtium seeds—nice, large, round, easy-to-handle seeds. We all begin with something simple, whether it is nasturtiums, marigolds, or tomatoes. Novice gardeners should first grow easy varieties of plants and then move on to more challenging propagation.

Gardens and gardeners tend to evolve. Brian Halliwell, assistant curator of the alpine house at Kew Gardens in England, when asked why he specializes in alpines, said he started with roses, then progressed to trees and shrubs, and finally reached alpines. "Like classical music," he said. "You start with Strauss and eventually finish with Mozart's string quartets."

So as we raise plants, experiment with soils and fertilizers, read about plants, and visit other gardens, we continue to mature as gardeners. While most experienced gardeners still enjoy marigolds, roses, and geraniums, we also want to raise alpines, or exotic primroses, difficult orchids, or rare gesneriads or rhododendrons. We haunt the pages of specialist catalogs and order rare plants from these growers. But for many unusual plants, the only possible way to obtain them is to raise them from seeds offered by general seed catalogs, specialist catalogs, or the seed exchanges of plant societies.

So you've ordered from several seed catalogs and plant society seed lists. The first small stack of seed packets is waiting on your desk. Now what?

As in so many other aspects of gardening, there are a number of different ways to produce seedlings. One way or another, you need to provide moisture, a well-drained medium, food, and light. The seeds will do the rest. You can plant many seeds directly in the vegetable garden or flower bed. For many others, however, it is helpful to get a head start by growing the seedlings indoors for a while. I start my plants indoors under lights, because it gives me more control over conditions than I have in the open garden, where tiny seedlings have to cope with animals, leaf-drop, insects, the washing of excessive rainfall, temperature swings, and other vicissitudes.

If you have ever tested the viability of old seed by putting some on a wet paper towel and keeping them in a warm place for a few days, you know that moisture can be enough to break the seeds' dormancy and start them into growth. A few, like *Thermopsis caroliniana* (Carolina lupine) or *Calonyction aculeatum* (Moon Vine) need to be scratched with a file, rubbed between two pieces of sandpaper (scarification), or soaked in warm water; seeds from many evergreens and from perennials like *Kirengeshoma palmata* need to be mixed with a moistened medium and put into the refrigerator for a period of time (stratification); but most annual, perennial, and vegetable seeds just need moisture.

As soon as a seed germinates, it begins to put forth first a root and then a tiny leaf or leaves. Media like perlite, vermiculite, peat moss, sterilized soil, or milled sphagnum moss can serve as anchors for the new roots of germinating seedlings and as conduits for water and food to the new plants. You can mix your own blend of peat moss, perlite, and vermiculite or buy sterile, soilless seed-starting mixes at your garden center.

When talking about various media, the important word is "sterile," You don't want weed seeds or fungal and insect problems bothering your newly germinated seedlings.

At Bellingrath Gardens in Mobile, Alabama, Pat Ryan uses Jiffy Mix as a seed medium and then blends his own potting soil of compost, pine bark, perlite, and peat moss, which he sterilizes. He then adds Osmocote, a slow-release fertilizer.

Bob McCartney, propagator at Woodlanders, a South Carolina nursery specializing in southeastern native plants, mixes his own blend of sand, perlite, and bark, which he uses for both seed propagation and potting. He amends that mix with peat moss for ericaceous plants.

Food becomes important as soon as the seedlings appear. Each seed you plant is a fascinating little package of stored energy. It contains enough of its own food to support that initial spurt of growth. To keep the young seedling developing vigorously, begin feeding regularly with a dilute solution of a balanced fertilizer. It's easy to use any water-soluble plant food like Rapid-Gro or Peters at one-fourth the recommended amount.

To utilize that food through the complicated process of photosynthesis, light is required. As soon as the seedlings germinate, give them as much light as possible, whether you are growing on a sunny windowsill, in a greenhouse, in a cold frame, or under fluorescent lights. The light requirement for seedlings is very high. If your seedlings are leggy and weak in appearance, they are not getting enough light.

Because I have neither a greenhouse nor sunny windowsills (our home has 4-foot roof overhangs), I raise my seedlings under fluorescent lights. My light garden happens to be in the laundry room of this house, but you can have an indoor light garden anywhere you have room for a table and a 4-foot fluorescent light fixture. I know gardeners who have light setups in attics, basements, spare bedrooms, kitchens, bathrooms—even garages.

Each of those gardeners has a favorite way of starting seeds. If you are having good results with seeds, don't change your way of doing things. I'm of the "if it ain't broke, don't fix it" school of thought. But if you've had problems and want to try a new method, here is the system I've developed as I've been raising seedlings under lights the past twenty-five years.

For almost all seeds, from easy tomatoes and marigolds to challenging alpines, I take a 3-inch shallow pot of plain #3 vermiculite, scatter the seeds on top of the vermiculite, sprinkle a little more vermiculite over the seeds (except for tiny seeds which I don't cover at all), label with the plant name, the seed source, and the date, and stand the pot in a pan of water to soak.

When the pot is thoroughly wet, I put it in a plastic bag, seal it tightly and put it under lights. The bag is not opened until seedlings appear. Most annual, perennial, and vegetable seeds germinate quickly, but some, like the alstroemeria seed I planted in March that didn't germinate until November, take a long time. One advantage of using a sealed bag is that the container needs no watering until after the seeds germinate and the bag is opened.

I make one exception to that rule of not opening the bag until I see germination. If, on inspection, I notice any sign of a fungus on the surface of the vermiculite, I open the bag and dust on a light layer of a fungicide. Minute fungus spores are in the air around us, and even when I use just plain vermiculite, often one pot in a batch will become contaminated.

After trying all the media mentioned earlier—which all work—I prefer plain vermiculite. The only medium I don't like to use is milled sphagnum moss, which many experts recommend because of its reputed antifungal properties. It tends to cake, however, and a tough layer on the top of the pot or flat makes it difficult for small seedlings to struggle through. If you want to use it, milled sphagnum works better in a mixture than alone.

The technique for sowing seeds varies according to the size of the seeds and their requirements for germination. With a packet of large seeds, like beans or marigolds, you can open the package, pour the seeds into the palm of one hand, and then place them evenly around the pot or flat or poke them in individual holes you have made with a pencil or a dibble.

When you pick up a packet of smaller seeds, like campanulas, hold it by the top and flick it several times with a snap of your fingers so that all the seed falls to the bottom of the envelope. Then rip off or cut off the top of the packet, squeeze the packet slightly open in one hand, and sow the seeds by gently tapping that hand with the other hand. With each tap, a few seeds will roll down the channel created by the envelope's edge. After a little practice, you will be able to tap out very small seeds one at a time.

For the powdery fine seeds of begonias or gesneriads, I dump the seed into the palm of one hand, pick them up between the thumb and forefinger of the other hand and scatter them over the pot with a gentle circular rubbing motion. Some gardeners like to mix these tiny seeds with sand and then spread the sand mix on the medium.

Just because you have a packet full of seeds, don't feel you have to plant them all at once. Seeds purchased from professional seed companies are usually of fine quality, with excellent germination percentages. If you want just ten tomato plants, plant ten seeds, plus three or four more as insurance. Seal the rest of the seeds in their packet and store all packets of surplus seeds in a closed container in your refrigerator or freezer. Most stored seed will be viable even after several years of freezer storage.

Many seeds germinate best with bottom heat, so I line my bagged pots up on a 70–75° heating cable. (Cables are inexpensive and available at most garden centers, but if you are just beginning to raise your plants from seed and don't want to invest in a cable, you can warm a few pots or flats by putting them on top of your refrigerator.)

For the few plants, like cyclamen and violas, that require darkness for germination, I put the pots of seed under the bench, covered with cardboard. I'm careful not to cover lettuce or aquilegia seeds, because these need light for good germination.

From then on, I enjoy the game of seeing what has germinated each day. Large seedlings are obvious, but I look through a 10-power stamp collector's lens to see if minute seedlings like ramondas have germinated. Some seedlings, such as rudbeckia, will pop up in two days. Impatiens and tomato seeds germinate in seven days. Other seeds, including difficult alpines, bulbs, and trees, may take a year or more. I've had *Gentiana acaulis* and *Mahonia repens* come up as long as two years after seeding. (Bagged pots that do not germinate the first spring are moved outdoors to a shaded area where I hold them for about two years, checking every month or two for germination. Plastic bags seem to hold up for approximately two years. Nurserymen who start their seedlings in open pots have to spray their seedling pots daily. The bag method is much easier for an amateur gardener.)

As soon as seedlings appear in a pot, I take that pot off the heating cable, and move it, still bagged, to another shelf where I place it as close to the lights as possible. When I feel that the pot of seedlings has completely germinated, I gradually begin to wean the seedlings away from their high-humidity environment by slowly opening the bag.

I emphasize "slowly" because when I began raising plants from seed, it was at this stage that I lost a number of seedlings. While truly tough plants like marigolds will never notice that they have been whisked from 100 percent humidity to your room's humidity of 40 to 60 percent or less, most seedlings need a little hardening off during this transition.

The first day, I undo the twist tie and crack the bag open. The next day I open the bag a bit more, and by the third day, it's half open. Then I unbag the pot and return it to its position under the lights.

At this point, I begin fertilizing the small plants. Since the vermiculite contains no nutrients, the newly germinated seedlings will grow until they have used all the food in their seed embryos, and then they will just sit there, neither growing nor dying.

In my hobby, of course, my aim is to produce the healthiest, largest plants in the shortest period of time, so I push the plants with constant feed, using a 25 percent solution of water-soluble fertilizer in every watering.

Controlling the food supply is a technique some professional nurserymen use to manipulate their crops. One can hold plants for months, if necessary, by not providing fertilizer.

For example, I observed Mike Kartuz, a gesneriad specialist, manage his plant supply using this method. He kept pots full of small seedlings in a holding condition under lights—watered but not fed. Whenever he needed more saintpaulias or gloxinias for the greenhouse, he potted up some of these unnourished plants and began to feed them, and they immediately took off.

While most instructions say, "Transplant seedlings after the second set of permanent leaves," I don't follow that advice. Most plants are potted up as soon as I can grasp the seedlings. With impatiens, marigolds, and tomatoes, for example, I often transplant when the first true leaves are beginning to show in the center of the cotyledon leaves.

There are exceptions. I found I was losing saxifrage seedlings after transplanting, so I consulted Linc Foster, author of *Rock Gardening*, an expert grower of many alpines and a specialist in saxifrages. He urged me to leave saxes in the same pot for more than a year. They move most successfully after the seedlings have begun to form clumps of their rosettes. Dick Weaver, propagator at We-Du Nurseries, says that he uses the same technique with gentians—moves clumps rather than individual seedlings.

As a potting medium, I use 50 percent Baccto potting soil, 25 percent vermiculite, and 25 percent perlite. There are a number of potting soils and soilless mixes on the market, many of which can be perfectly satisfactory. These mixes vary widely, so you may have to experiment to find one you like. Many commercial growers in this area recommend Pro-Mix. Because the soilless mixes drain so quickly, frequent watering is necessary. I found that I prefer some soil in the mix to minimize waterings.

Jim Borland, former propagator at the Denver Botanical Garden, raised all of his plants, from alpines to cacti, bog plants, and impatiens, in a peat-perlite mixture. He grew more than 3000 different varieties of plants in this mix, varying it only slightly for two groups. He added a bit more perlite for the cacti and succulents, and he used slightly more peat moss for the ericaceous plants like azaleas and kalmias.

Cuttings

Depending on the plant you wish to propagate, a cutting can be a leaf, a section of a leaf, a piece of the root, a section of the stem, or the tip of the newest growth. Softwood cuttings are those taken during the growing season; hardwood cuttings, during dormancy. Use a sharp knife or a razor blade to take your cuttings—I prefer the latter. Sharp pruners are satisfactory for woody plants and stout perennials. If I am making cuttings of any linear material, like columneas, phloxes, or azaleas, I remove about 4 inches from the tip of the new growth, using a diagonal cut. I then strip off the lowest set of leaves, pinch out the tip of the cutting, and insert the cutting into the medium so that the node from which the leaves were stripped is covered. Roots will appear at that node. The pinching encourages side buds to grow, thus producing the beginnings of an attractive, bushy plant.

Most gardeners are generous people, delighted to share a piece of a shrub or a perennial with an interested visitor. I often come home from a garden visit with a small handful of cuttings to root. I also usually send my visitors away with some small seedlings or cuttings of plants they have admired in my yard. For cuttings, I just pop the cutting, along with a label, into a plastic bag. Ask, and 99 percent of the time, the gift of a cutting is gladly given.

Collectors are a curious breed, however. Like cooks who will not share a recipe—or give it to you but omit the essential ingredient that gives the dish its pizzazz—there are some gardeners who will never share something rare and wonderful. I knew an orchid grower in Michigan who would discard divisions of a unique orchid rather than give them to friends or donate them to his orchid society. It was important to him to be the only one possessing that rare plant. I have another friend, in Hillsborough, North Carolina, whose mother will not give her a cutting of an unusual old rose. That

Calendar

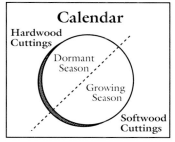

Hardwood Cuttings

Dormant Season

Growing Season

Softwood Cuttings

Tools for Taking Cuttings

Single-Edge Razor Blade

Sharp Knife

Pruning Shears

Types of Cuttings

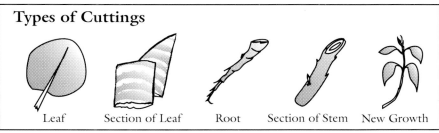

Leaf   Section of Leaf   Root   Section of Stem   New Growth

Propagation of Tip Cuttings

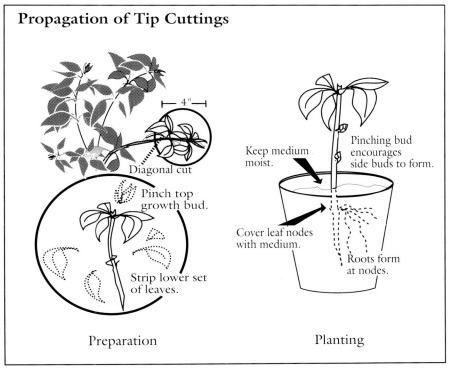

4″

Diagonal cut

Pinch top growth bud.

Strip lower set of leaves.

Keep medium moist.

Pinching bud encourages side buds to form.

Cover leaf nodes with medium.

Roots form at nodes.

Preparation

Planting

Plant propagation by means of cuttings

mother would probably walk through fire for her daughter, but share a unique plant, *never*!

Plant collecting is an addiction, of course—one of the healthier ones, I think. I often laugh at myself. Unmoved, I can see and admire 100 plants in a garden. Then I spy *the one*, and a wave of unadulterated greed sweeps over me. It's ridiculous, but it happens. Got to have that plant!

If you share this addiction and find yourself overwhelmed by the urge for a particular plant, beg, purchase, or propagate the plant, but please do not steal it. One affluent and aristocratic gardener I know has been banned from several private gardens. His reputation precedes him. He could afford to buy any plant in the world, but for years he has snipped and pinched his way through gardens or lagged behind the group in national parks and quickly whisked out his trowel and popped a rare wild flower out of its site and into a plastic bag. His lovely garden is full of rare plants, but he is not a popular gentleman!

But let's assume you have a bag full of cuttings honestly acquired. What do you do with them? For most cuttings, it is desirable to get them into the propagating medium as quickly as possible. Exceptions are plants like geraniums and cacti, where the cuttings need to be left exposed to the air and neglected on a dry shelf for a day or two until the end of the cutting has callused. Then and only then should one put those cuttings into a propagating medium. They tend to rot, otherwise.

Sometimes it is not possible to handle cuttings quickly. If you are far from home and offered valuable cuttings, buy an inexpensive foam picnic cooler and carry the cuttings home in cool comfort. Throw a little ice in the bottom of the cooler, cover the ice with a thick layer of newspaper, and then add the cuttings in their plastic bags, each correctly labeled, of course.

At home, if you are too busy to work immediately or if you have too many cuttings to handle at one time, put the sealed bags of cuttings into the refrigerator for a day or so. Most plants tolerate this type of storage.

A good cutting is always firm and turgid, its cells full of moisture. If your cuttings look droopy, try soaking them in a pan of water to revive them before you stick them. If you are taking cuttings from your own garden, plan ahead. Give the mother plants a good soaking the day before and then try to do your work early in the morning, particularly if you are taking azalea, rhododendron, or other cuttings in the heat of mid-July.

When my husband and I were in England in 1981 for an international rock gardening conference, we listened to professional nurserymen and propagators Phillip Brouse (now director of Wisley) and Peter Hutchinson describe their techniques. While propagators at most American nurseries, like Monrovia, rely heavily on hormones, these English growers have moved away from hormone use. They give particular attention to the health of their stock plants. They believe that the material a gardener starts with must have a high ability to regenerate. Their research indicated that cuttings with high regenerative capacity are juvenile, with young, vigorous growth.

Mature plants flower and set seeds. Brouse says this ability to flower depresses the ability to regenerate missing parts, so he takes the plant out of flowering by pruning hard. With severe pruning, food, and heat, he promotes new, healthy, juvenile growth on stock plants and then takes his cuttings from this new growth.

Hutchinson thinks it makes no difference what material you put your cuttings into. He has placed rhododendron cuttings (*without* removing the bottom leaves) in fast-draining mixes of peat and grit, peat and perlite, bark and grit, and bark and perlite, with equally good results.

For your propagation of cuttings, you need a container, a medium, a method of providing considerable humidity, and, for some woody plants, a rooting hormone.

The container can be a pot, a flat, a section of a cold frame, or greenhouse bench. Most cuttings do not require much light for rooting. The medium can be peat and perlite, peat and sand, vermiculite and perlite, or simply plain vermiculite, perlite, sand, or fine gravel, or a commercial mix. Successful amateur and professional propagators have used all of the above, with good results.

I have tried a number of media and find that I have the best results with plain coarse perlite for most cuttings, a mixture of peat and sand for azaleas and other ericaceous plants, plain sand for succulents like sedums and sempervivums, and gravel for cuttings rooting under constant mist. Like most aspects of gardening, there is not one right way to do things. Many different methods work, and you just have to find those that you like.

The humidity is very important. You want to offer close to 100-percent humidity to your cuttings. If you have a greenhouse, you can take a section of bench and enclose it in plastic or you can install an intermittent mist system over an open bench.

Most of us do not have a greenhouse, and we simply want to root a few African violet leaves, phlox and dianthus cuttings, or azalea and rhododendron cuttings to share with friends, offer to the community plant sale, or add to our gardens. We are not propagating on a commercial scale.

If you have just a few cuttings to root, Dorothy Bonitz of Hampstead, North Carolina, showed me a simple method. She takes a plastic foam coffee cup and pokes several holes through the side, about ½ inch above the base. She fills the cup with perlite, adds her cuttings, covers the cup with a clear plastic cup which creates the greenhouse effect, and then stands the cup in a container of dilute fertilizer mix. She keeps the level of the liquid always above the holes in the cup.

I'm using the same technique this year, on a slightly larger scale. Jiffy Products has introduced a Gro-Cell Greenhouse, which is simply an 11-by-11-inch tray, a clear plastic dome and a plastic form with sixteen 2¼-by-2¼-inch perforated cells. I have filled fifteen cells with perlite and use the empty cell as a monitor for the liquid level. Each cell comfortably holds nine cuttings of phlox, thyme, armeria, and other plants I am propagating.

Marie Tietjens is known as the lady with the crystal garden to her Pennsylvania gardening friends. Shady parts of her yard are dotted with glass jars, under which she roots cuttings of all sorts of outdoor plants, including evergreens, roses, woody shrubs, and perennials. Perhaps your grandmother brought home rose cuttings from a neighbor's yard and started them underneath a discarded mayonnaise jar. This homey, old-fashioned method works well for a hobbyist. If you try propagating under a glass jar, put the jar on the north side of a fence or in some other shady location. Also, keep that part of the garden evenly moist. Never let it dry out completely.

For house plants like African violets, hibiscus, and columneas, I keep a translucent plastic sweater box filled with moist vermiculite. Whenever I take a cutting, I pop it into the box. In three or four weeks, I give the cutting a gentle tug. If it resists, it is rooted and I pot it. If leaves drop and the cutting looks as if it is dying, I remove it and dust the box with a fungicide. Periodically, I wash out the box with a bleach solution and start afresh.

For an occasional cutting, you can simply use a pot of your favorite medium, stick the cutting in, water it well, and enclose it in a plastic bag until rooting occurs. I know some African violet growers who have limited space. They put a leaf in a bag with some moistened medium, seal it, and hang it at the side of their light garden until it roots and produces offspring. Orchid growers do much the same thing with cymbidium back bulbs. Dick Weaver says that we can use the back-bulb technique with many of the terrestrial orchids, like *Bletilla striata*.

Be careful not to put a closed container in sunlight. You will cook the cuttings. Use fluorescent lights or a windowsill that gets no direct sunlight.

When visiting large wholesale nurseries during recent years, I have noticed that more and more, they are direct-sticking a number of their cuttings. They put geraniums, succulents, and many other easy-to-root cuttings directly into pots of soil. For a commercial operation, direct-sticking is cost effective; it eliminates one whole step in the propagation process.

For home gardeners, too, this technique can be useful for some plants. I have used it successfully for miniature geraniums growing under lights in a high humidity indoor garden.

As in all propagation of cuttings, humidity and fast-draining media are the keys to success. A dried-out or soggy cutting is a dead cutting. Of course nurserymen have extensive mist or fog systems to ensure that the cuttings are kept uniformly moist.

Fungi and bacteria can cause problems in such wet conditions. Some professionals routinely include a fungicide in their misting program. Here at home, I observe my seedlings and cuttings daily and use a fungicide only when I see a problem.

It's not difficult for the enthusiastic amateur to set up a simple mist or fog system. Mist nozzles are available from any greenhouse supply center and a number of garden catalogs. One amateur rose grower here propagates his rose cuttings on an outdoor bench in full sun, using an intermittent mist system. In California, I used a continuous mist system. My mister was in full sun, surrounded by pots with large cuttings inserted in gravel. I was able to put roots on almost any plant or shrub I tried, and because one can use large cuttings with this method, I produced larger-than-typical rooted cuttings to pot on.

Just as I wean seedlings away from the 100 percent humidity of the closed plastic bags, it is important to reduce the misting gradually after the cuttings root. You cannot snatch a rooted rose from under a mist system, plant it in a rose bed, and expect it to survive under normal rose care.

In 1986, the propagator at Cypress Gardens in Florida was having a problem with transition in his nursery area. Plants rooted easily in the new fog house, but he was losing material when he potted the plants and moved them into ordinary greenhouse conditions. He needed a transition house with intermittent mist so that he could give the plants a gradual period of adaptation to normal growing conditions.

Whether you are a commercial grower propagating thousands of plants for your market or a home gardener who wants to share a few plants with friends, if you give the plants the appropriate tender, loving care you will be rewarded with healthy, thriving seedlings and rooted cuttings.

There is one other method of making cuttings that home gardeners often overlook. Root cuttings are a simple way of producing a number of plants of a choice variety of astilbe, viola, cardinal flower, butterfly weed, and some other plants. The one thing to remember is apical dominance. This phrase simply means that the top of each root cutting must go up, not down, in your pot or flat.

Fall and winter are the best time to take root cuttings. There are several ways to take this type of cutting. You can dig up the entire plant, wash off the soil, cut off some of the long roots (to be further cut into short cuttings), and replant the plant. Or you can unearth one side of the plant's root system, take a few cuttings and fill the dirt back into the hole. At a 1987 winter study weekend sponsored by the American Rock Garden Society, Bill

Brumback, propagator at Garden in the Woods in Massachusetts, suggested one rather peculiar method that would be possible in a propagation area but not in your display garden. To use his method, you have to be reasonably familiar with the plant. You need to know the diameter of the root ball. If the astilbe or butterfly weed has a 20-inch root ball, then you would cut a considerably smaller circle around the plant and lift the plant out of the hole. You then leave the hole unfilled, undisturbed. Eventually, small plantlets will appear all around the side of the hole, where the roots were cut—more plants to enjoy and to share.

Division

Many of our garden perennials can be easily propagated by dividing the plants. Some plants, like irises and day lilies, need to be refreshed by division every three years to keep them at their peak and others, like phlox and columbine, should be divided when the center of the plant peters out and all of the healthy new growth is in a circle around that nonproductive center. If we want a rapid increase in the number of some plants, like hostas and primroses, we can divide the clump each year.

Dividing can be as simple as uprooting a foam flower, washing soil off the roots and gently teasing apart individual rosettes, each with its own root system, or it can be hard work, cutting apart viable plantlets with a hatchet or butcher knife. Even for plants within the same genus, like primulas and hostas, some varieties come apart easily and others need to be cut apart.

In his book *Plant Propagation in Pictures*, Montague Free demonstrates a sensible, old-fashioned method of separating tough clumps. Rather than cutting them apart, he prefers to take two spading forks in the center of the clump, back to back, and pry the sections apart. Although there are several newer books on propagation for the home gardener, I am fond of Free's book because of its generous number of illustrations. Whether taking cuttings, air-layering, or dividing perennials, he demonstrates the technique quickly and clearly in his photographs.

As a general rule, plants should be divided right after flowering. However, we adapt to our southern heat and frequent drought in propagating as well as growing. I find that I have the greatest success dividing my plants in very early spring or in the fall after the rains have started. For example, most books, written for the British or for gardeners in northern climates, recommend dividing polyanthus primroses after flowering, but I have had better luck here dividing them in the period between November and March. It certainly is possible to divide them after flowering, *if* you will keep them generously watered during the summer.

On one of our mild winter days, I am often out unearthing a clump of astilbe or epimedium. If you divide perennials like these in winter, just be sure that you have a bud and some roots in each division. Replant the divisions immediately, water them in, and they will flourish.

Layering

The one other propagation technique many home gardeners often use is layering. Perhaps you have had a rosemary or forsythia branch that was resting on the ground root itself with no assistance from you. Such layering is a method that you can use deliberately to root azaleas, rhododendrons, and many other shrubs.

Select a branch that will easily reach the ground. Cut into the outer layer of the branch at an angle, prop the small slice open with a toothpick, dust the cut surface with a rooting hormone, and bury the cut area of the branch in the top inch or two of soil. Hold it down with a rock or pin it down with wire. In a year, that layered branch should be well rooted and can then be separated from the mother plant and transplanted.

Other Techniques

There are numerous other propagating techniques for the avid gardener. One rose hybridizer whipped out his grafting knife and showed me how to bud a rose. He quickly cut a T-shaped graft site in the outer layer of the rootstock. (He raises a number of seedlings for rootstock.) Then he took a small, canoe-shaped bud from a desirable rose and slipped that bud into his T slit. He then bound the graft with grafting tape. He finds that his grafts take in about three weeks.

An amateur collector of old apples grafts scions (tip cuttings from vigorously growing trees) from old varieties he has located onto dwarf understock he purchases. This understock is called an interstem. To create an interstem, the supplier has already made one graft, putting a dwarf rootstock like M 27 onto a variety with a large root system, like 'Northern Spy'. These interstem rootstocks anchor better in our clay soils and also hold up better in periods of drought. This gardener uses a cleft graft, one of several possible grafts. Grafting may sound difficult, but he says anyone can learn to do it in ten minutes. I've only tried it once, putting a columnea onto a compatible tall, woody gesneriad to make a standard. It worked.

A hosta fancier told me how to multiply the reluctant hostas, like *H. tokudama*, by scraping soil away from the stem and stabbing the stem several times with a paring knife. Sure enough, the following year, that plant developed rooted shoots at each of those wounds.

In California I learned that some of the native plants there would germinate only after fire, so growers would start those seeds in clay pots, cover the top of the soil with pine needles, and set the needles afire.

Keen lily growers peel bulbs apart and root each individual scale. You just stick each scale about halfway into a flat of moist medium. This technique works well for alliums and Atamasco lilies too. Lily hobbyists also collect and grow the bulbils that form along the lily stems. Sempervivum specialists also tear their plants' rosettes apart and root each tiny leaf.

Fern hobbyists start their plants from spores. Jane Welshmer, a local grower, began growing ferns when she lived in Birmingham, Alabama, and continues her enthusiasm here. She has more than sixty species in her Chapel Hill garden, most of which she has raised from spores.

She begins with a transparent plastic shoe or sweater box. Any similar airtight container will work. First, she places a 1-inch layer of perlite or vermiculite to provide drainage. She then sprinkles a thin layer of charcoal topped with an inch-thick layer of commercial potting soil.

It is important to moisten the container thoroughly before introducing the spores. This is a matter of judgment. As Jane says, "The mix should be thoroughly moist, but the top of the soil should not be squushy."

With the box prepared, she then sprinkles spores over the surface, dates and labels the box, and puts the lid on. Germination rates vary considerably. Some ferns begin in two or three weeks; others take eight to ten months. The first thing she sees is a greenish bloom on the soil. The cells are dividing until they reach the prothallia stage. A prothallium is a tiny, kidney-shaped plate. When Jane sees these little plates scattered over the soil's surface, she gives the box an additional spray of water. Soon she sees the first little fronds coming out of each little plate.

When the baby ferns are large enough, she transplants them to a nursery box, still completely closed. When they are then large enough to go into the garden, she hardens them off by opening the box gradually and misting frequently.

Like Jane Welshmer, a number of gardeners are raising their own ferns from spores. And some amateurs have even built or purchased laminar airflow units and are growing orchids from seed or tissue culture, using sophisticated media and sterile conditions.

While most of us will be content raising easy plants from seed or cuttings, or by division, I'd urge anyone who is interested in learning more about difficult plants or more sophisticated techniques to seek out a library or a professional propagator who has a collection of the publications of the International Association of Plant Propagators. This lively group is doing work on the frontier of propagation. Every three years, each member must present a program on his work to remain a member of the group. The bulletins of this association are packed with propagation information and well indexed.

16

Pests, Diseases, and Chemicals

Garden pests come in a wide variety of shapes and sizes. They range from microscopic, worm-like soil pests like nematodes, which can cause stunting and dieback in many plants, to large, four-footed animals that munch their way through our flower, fruit, and vegetable crops. We live with some pests, we try to minimize others, and certain ones we attempt to destroy. Not only do crops flourish and plants grow more quickly in the South, but, as a counterbalance, our bugs and diseases are also more vigorous and prolific. We don't have the helpful control that rigorous winter weather and frozen ground provide gardeners in states farther north.

How you deal with pests and diseases in your garden depends on your philosophy and your needs. If you must produce insect-free lettuce for the commercial market or a perfect, unblemished rose for competition, you will undoubtedly use some garden chemicals. If you prefer to garden without chemicals, you will accept some damage. In some cases, you may get good results with biological pest controls. For example, amateur and professional gardeners are using BT, the bacteria *Bacillus thuringiensis*, as a weapon against leaf-eating caterpillars and *Bacillus popillae* (Milky Spore Disease) against grubs in the ground.

Today we have quite a list of desirable predators available from firms specializing in biological controls, and I am sure that considerable research will continue in this field. Also, in the future, genetic engineering may offer some interesting and valuable solutions to garden pests. Understandably, today most of that research is being directed toward agricultural crops that are so important economically. However, I suspect that over the years, much of this space-age research will filter down and be of considerable benefit to the home gardener.

"Organic gardening" is a term that some garden writers hesitate to use today. It has developed a pejorative ring to it. Ten or fifteen years ago, some

truly kooky garden practices were recommended by organic gardeners—
practices that had no basis in fact. Before I suggest that vegetable gardeners
interplant their crops with marigolds to discourage nematodes, I want to
see a scientific study done by a specialist at a reputable university. Well,
marigolds have been studied. It turns out that that simple remedy, touted by
organic gardeners for a number of years, is effective. Studies done in the
Netherlands, Brazil, Israel, and here in the States at the University of Georgia and the Connecticut Agricultural Experiment Station all have proved
that marigolds do suppress nematode populations. As a garden writer, I can
enthuse about any gardening idea that is based on solid, scientific research.

A number of other ideas propounded by organic gardeners are sensible
and practical. Any gardener would be wise to select resistant plant varieties,
occasionally use physical barriers, and learn about the life cycles of pests that
may affect his crops. If the concept is new to you, and you want to read a
lengthy book on the subject, seek out *Organic Plant Protection*, published by
Rodale Press, publisher of the magazine *Organic Gardening*.

Many of us who use garden chemicals are using an integrated pest management system without even realizing it. IPM, a horticultural buzz phrase
of the 1980s, simply means that the gardener does not use chemicals as a
preventative measure, or spray or dust on a schedule, but rather, monitors
the trees, shrubs, lawn, and garden regularly, catches any problems early,
and treats them appropriately. The garden displays in The Land at Epcot
Center at Walt Disney World near Orlando, Florida, have introduced thousands of gardeners to IPM, as well as to hydroponic gardening. There the
scientists use cultural, mechanical, physical, biological, and chemical controls and educate visitors about all their techniques.

Professionals have devised a number of ways of judging what is an acceptable level of infestation. For example, to decide whether you have a grub
problem in your lawn, dig up a foot square section of sod and examine soil
and roots for grubs. One expert says that you should treat the lawn if you
find more than five grubs per foot. For each pest or disease, each gardener
has to decide what is an acceptable level of damage in his garden.

If you have been bothered by too many mole tunnels running under the
surface of your lawn, eliminating the grubs will also eliminate the moles.
Grubs are one of the mainstays of mole diet. When we once sprayed our
California lawn to kill grubs, the effect on the moles was dramatic. These
pests that had previously interlaced the lawn with their tunnels would dig
into the lawn a few inches, find no food, then turn around and leave.

In most instances, I won't discuss specific chemicals and their uses in this
book, because that entire subject is complicated and is constantly evolving.
Just a few years ago, Chlordane was the chemical of choice for lawn grubs.

Today it is off the market. Pick up many older gardening books, and you will find the now-outlawed DDT recommended. It is wiser today first to identify the problem and then go to your local garden center and find out what is available to treat that particular insect or disease. We are all subject to a number of national laws, monitored by the Environmental Protection Agency, and we also must follow our state laws. What is legal for amateur application in one state may not be available in another. In North Carolina, the Agricultural Extension Service puts out an annually updated *North Carolina Agricultural Chemicals Manual*, which contains current recommendations and is available through North Carolina State University. Some of our neighboring states have similar publications. Others do not.

If you have some old containers of garden chemicals and wonder if the products are still viable, or if you are having your home treated for fleas or roaches and are apprehensive about the chemicals the exterminator plans to use, there's an information center you can call. For up-to-date information on pesticides, call 1-800-858-7378. This hotline is manned by the National Pesticide Telecommunications Network twenty-four hours a day, seven days a week. Most of their calls come from homeowners, but many are from physicians with questions about toxicity and veterinarians seeking information about pets and pesticides.

I blithely say "identify the problem." Easier said than done, sometimes. If you are a beginning gardener and don't know an aphid from a ladybug or a gall from an oak leaf blister, collect a specimen and take it to your experienced neighborhood gardener, your local garden center, or your county extension agent for identification.

Check your newspaper. Often county extension agents, assisted by master gardeners, hold clinics for plant problems during the gardening season. (By the way, if you want to learn a lot about gardening in your area in a short period of time, become a master gardener. Many extension offices nationwide offer this program. Participants receive thirty hours of instruction and then return the favor by working for the office for thirty hours, answering phone questions, lecturing, running clinics and the like. Every friend who has participated in this program has found it a rewarding experience.)

After you have identified your problem, the next step is to treat it. Whatever product you use, *read the label* and apply it properly. Follow directions precisely. It is illegal to use a pesticide in a manner other than that stated on the label.

Cleanliness is not only an attractive attribute in a garden, but it also helps to minimize or avoid problems. For example, picking up spent camellia blossoms will lessen the problem with petal blight. Take all of the residue from the vegetable garden and add it to the compost pile. Pruning off a pyracantha or cotoneaster branch that is afflicted with fire blight, indicated by dieback of growing tips, will prevent that bacterial infection from spreading. Be sure to disinfect your pruners by using alcohol or bleach. Pick galls off your azaleas and any leaves with black spot from a rose, and like any fungal or bacterial trash, burn them or put them in the garbage, do not add them to the compost heap. If fungal spores don't have the chance to blow around the garden, your efforts at cleanliness in your garden this year will minimize fungal problems next year.

Excellent drainage also helps to minimize fungal problems. The need for good drainage is a constant theme for southern gardeners. It doesn't matter whether I am interviewing a rosarian, a rhododendron hobbyist, or a perennial gardener, each will rate drainage as the most important cultural requirement.

Also, keeping plants healthy and unstressed will help them to resist infections. Not to anthropomorphize our garden plants, but I do feel they are like humans in that respect. I know that if I am healthy and vigorous, I resist picking up colds from friends and never catch the flu bug my husband brings home from the office. If I get run-down, I pick up an infection every time. I've observed that if plants are maintained in an uninterrupted pattern of healthy, vigorous growth, they too seem to resist bacterial and fungal problems. If they are stressed, particularly by a lack of water at the necessary times, then they become vulnerable to a host of problems.

Controlling weeds not only keeps the garden more attractive, but it eliminates that haven for pests, mites, and diseases.

Avoiding overhead watering by using drip systems or soaker hoses helps to lessen fungal problems. A number of gardeners are enthusiastic about the relatively new soaker hoses made out of old tires that gently leak their entire lengths. They can be buried. Don't throw your watering hose down with its nozzle in the mud, where it can pick up any infection and spray it around with your next watering. Mulches also prevent fungal spores from splashing onto foliage and causing leaf diseases. Being neat or careful in your garden in a lot of little ways will pay off. You will have fewer problems and need to use fewer chemicals.

Gardeners studying information about pests and diseases in the garden are akin to medical students reading their first medical books. The students come down with every rare disease that has ever been described. A gardener who pages through Cynthia Westcott's authoritative book, *The Gardener's Bug Book*, can become equally overwhelmed by the vast number of horticultural problems that exist in our world. Fortunately, like the medical students who never develop all the esoteric diseases, we will probably only have to deal with a relatively few garden pests and diseases. I'll mention some of the most common ones.

The first pest we see in our garden each spring is not an insect but a slimy gastropod—a slug, or its cousin, a snail. With the first warm evenings, these two creepy-crawlers appear in droves, leaving glossy slime trails on foliage and eating a vast number of leaves during the night. They can demolish a flat of *Primula veris* seedlings overnight. Probably every gardener has an indicator plant in his garden. On our woodland trails, as I've mentioned, the slugs head for the primroses and the hostas. I watch those plants for the first nibbled leaves, and then I put out the bait. Pet owners may prefer to use one of the liquid slug and snail chemicals. While the pellets do slightly resemble pet food, our eighteen- and sixteen-year-old cats have completely ignored the bait all of their lives. However, Pam Harper wrote that three of her friends had lost a puppy, a grown dog, and a cat respectively from slug pellets.

Those gardeners who do not want to use any chemicals will be out with flashlights after dark, looking under boards, flats, and leaves to catch and smash these pests. More subtle people lure slugs to their death with shallow plates of beer. A dash of salt will totally destroy a slug or snail, but since salt is not a desirable addition to the garden, you might only use it once, as a curious experiment. (I must say that salt was very effective in removing the blood-sucking leeches that attached themselves to our group of trekkers in Nepal. One dash of salt, and those slimy things dropped off my legs.)

Aphids are probably the first insects you will encounter in your garden. They are small, sucking insects that come in a wide range of sizes and colors. You will find them on the most succulent new growth. While most aphids I have seen are pale green, I was fascinated to see bright orange ones on a neighbor's orange butterfly weed and gray-blue ones on the gray-blue growing tips of Russell lupines. They reproduce rapidly and are extremely prolific, so it pays to treat the first signs of an infestation. All rosarians are familiar with aphids, because tender new rose buds are a favorite habitat for these insects.

In addition to aphids, we frequently see fluffy white insects in the axils of leaves or on the stems of some plants like clematis and day lilies. If you see what looks like tiny pieces of cotton on your plants, you have mealybugs. They cling to their posts, unlike white flies, which will zoom into the air in a small cloud should you brush against an infested branch.

White flies and a number of other pests, like scale, tend to be found underneath the leaves, so experienced gardeners learn to turn leaves over when checking indoor or outdoor plants. Scale insects look like little hard bumps on your camellias, hollies, orchids, ferns, and other plants. A dormant spray is the most effective treatment for your garden plants. Indoors, which method you choose to cope with scale depends on the size of the problem. Like mealybugs, scale can be removed from a plant by using rubbing alcohol. If you have only five scale insects on one orchid, it is easy to wipe them off with a dampened tissue. If you have 100 badly infested plants in a greenhouse, you will probably want to use an appropriate chemical.

Some of our plants, like azaleas and columbines, are particularly susceptible to leafminers, small larvae that tunnel between the layers of a leaf. Plants seldom die from this infestation, but the tracking network disfigures the foliage.

Less frequently, narrow little insects called thrips may become a problem. I've had just two annoying bouts with them over the years. Indoors, they once invaded a collection of African violets. Another time, in the garden, they were ruining the flowers on gladioli. You seldom see these insects because they hide in the blossom crevices. However, they like to pierce pollen sacs, so if you find yellow pollen drifting down the lowest petals, suspect thrips. Hold a piece of paper beneath the flower, tap gently and some of the small insects will fall out and you can then verify your suspicions.

If you see a speckling or a fine webbing on your primroses, junipers, or many other garden plants during a hot, dry period of the year, you probably have one of several mites attacking your plants. These are very tiny, almost microscopic, pests. Since they are not insects, but relatives of spiders, you cannot eliminate them with broad-spectrum insecticides but you must purchase a miticide. Indoors, cyclamen mites often bother African violets as well as cyclamen. Suspect you have an infestation if the center growth is stunted, gray, and twisted.

Other pests you may see routinely in your garden are several different types of caterpillars and hornworms. Handpick or spray, depending on your inclinations and the infestation. Check your trees in early spring for signs of tent caterpillars. You want to be sure to remove the tents before the pests are mature and ready to leave their home and munch their way through the host tree. You can simply scrape small tents out of the tree crotches and step on them. If we leave the problem too late, my husband carefully burns them out of the trees. Like many other pests, tent caterpillars have favorite hosts. We find them in one crab apple tree every year. They never bother the other variety of crab tree in the yard. The fall webworms make a similar ugly cocoon in the autumn. Bagworms may make a bag of host plant tissue in a number of trees and shrubs. Their preferred hosts are conifers. Remove by hand or spray.

June brings a wave of Japanese beetles every year. While they will skeletonize a number of plants, they are particularly fond of roses, crape myrtles, apple and plum trees, clematis, and mallows. Again, spray or pick, depending on the size of the problem. One neighbor keeps a small can of kerosene in her garden and wages daily war with the beetles by knocking them into the can. Traps that attract and capture Japanese beetles are on the market, but current research done at the University of Kentucky indicates that these lures trap only part of the infestation. Those beetles remaining on the plants attract additional beetles to your garden, and the defoliation may be *increased* by as much as 50 percent if you use the traps. Fortunately, it is a relatively brief invasion.

One nurseryman finds that lacebugs are the biggest pests on his azaleas. They cause a mottling and yellow stippling of the leaves. He uses Orthene as a control.

Most rosarians spray routinely to control aphids and other insects, mildew, and black spot. If you are enjoying a few roses in your home garden, you may be satisfied with the modern version of an old-fashioned pest control method. Today, many gardeners are using Safer Insecticidal Soap. This product was developed by Sergei Condrashoff, former research entomologist with the Canadian Forestry Service, based on research done by Dr. George Puritch during the 1970s. Puritch accidentally discovered that a fatty acid emulsifying compound, used as a control in a pesticide test, killed 100 percent of a balsam wooly aphid colony. Puritch was intrigued, researched fatty acids, and learned that some fatty acids are highly insecticidal, others are fungicidal, while hundreds of others seem to be biologically inactive.

Safer Insecticidal Soap, developed from those fatty acids which are insecticidal, is quite effective against aphids, mealybugs, whitefly, psyllids, scales, spider mites, spittle bugs, other true bugs, rose slugs, and earwigs. It is the best spray for white flies on vegetables.

For the homeowner and indoor gardener, insecticidal soaps are particularly attractive, because they can be used in one's home with complete safety, unlike traditional pesticides. And for tender plants, like ferns, which are apt to suffer as much from a pesticide applied to control scale as from the scale pests themselves, these soaps offer a very useful alternative.

The easiest way to apply insecticidal soap or any garden chemicals is with a good sprayer. Whatever the job, whether it is pruning roses, shoveling bark, or spraying fruit trees, the work is done more efficiently and effectively if you have the right tool. To apply chemicals, the appropriate sprayer may be a hand spritzer, like a Windex bottle, if you have only five pots of plants on the patio to treat. On the other hand, if you have an extensive home orchard, you probably will want an electric or gasoline-powered sprayer that can reach easily into 25-to-30-foot trees. For a small planting of fruit trees, a trombone sprayer is economical. Most homeowners, who are managing their lawns, shrubs, small trees, vegetables, and flowering plants, will find an intermediate type, a compressed-air sprayer, desirable. In fact, it is wise to have two and keep them clearly labeled *Insecticides* and *Herbicides*.

Compressed-air sprayers come in a range of sizes. We have found the ones with a tank capacity of 2½ gallons are perfect for our purposes. They are large enough that we don't have to stop every few minutes to refill the tanks and light enough that I can comfortably carry one around in the garden.

Quality tools are always a good investment, so buy a sprayer made by a reputable firm. The top-of-the-line sprayers are made of stainless steel. They are sturdy, they will not corrode, and they are expensive. It has been our experience that a galvanized tank corrodes quickly and is a bad investment. Tanks lined with plastic are satisfactory. For a reasonably priced sprayer, find one with a tank made of high quality plastic. When you shop, look for features that give you exact control over the spray. In the flower garden, you will want a fine spray; in other situations, you may need a coarse stream. Adjusting the nozzle determines the pattern of the spray, and if you are using a compression sprayer, high pressure helps produce a mist, while low pressure results in coarse droplets.

Given a choice, I prefer to spray on a still day. If there is a slight breeze, be sure that you are standing upwind. You *must* pick a calm day if you are using an herbicide. Beware of drift. You may intend to kill the weeds in your gravel driveway and wind up devastating your neighbor's flower bed.

Sometimes you may need to be highly selective when using an herbicide. In the woods, I carry an old cookie sheet to use as a barrier between the oak seedlings I want to spray and the desirable primroses, hostas, daphnes, or irises I want to protect. Sometimes professional foresters cover a new planting of trees with large tin cans before giving the area an overall herbicide treatment. The nozzle should be adjusted for a coarse spray for weed control.

If you want a beautiful lawn, control the weeds with the appropriate herbicide. You will see herbicides described as "preemergence" or "postemergence." For example, it is easier and therefore more desirable to kill crabgrass before the seedlings germinate or emerge, so use a preemergence herbicide very early in the spring. Treat weeds like dandelions with a postemergence herbicide.

One of the most useful sprays is a dormant oil spray for shrubs, trees, and other woody plants. I suspect that many homeowners think that dormant spraying is just for professional orchard growers. Not so! A dormant spray applied to our roses, camellias, azaleas, and all the other woody plants before the buds break in late winter prevents a number of pest problems from starting. It helps to control aphids, scale insects, mites, mealybugs, and a number of other pests and diseases that overwinter on our plants.

Pathogens are much more difficult for amateur gardeners to identify than visible pests. We see the symptoms of disease, not the microscopic cause.

Home gardeners tend to ignore problems like mildew on crape myrtles or leaf blisters on oaks unless the disease is serious enough to affect the life of the plant. Unsightly foliage is one thing—dead trees or shrubs are quite another.

Careful selection of plants will help to minimize our disease problems. We can and should select disease-resistant tomato varieties. New varieties of mildew-resistant crape myrtles are now available. The United States Department of Agriculture has developed fourteen disease-resistant cultivars, which it is distributing to nurseries in 1988. Many antique roses do not have the problems of finely bred, modern hybrid teas. Whether you are shopping for trees, shrubs, flowers, or vegetables, read the descriptions carefully and seek out the improved, disease-resistant forms.

Our plants can be afflicted by a number of rots. The one I hear the most complaints about is Phytophthora root rot, a devastating rot that affects rhododendrons, azaleas, boxwoods, and many other woody plants. Good cultural practices, particularly providing excellent drainage, will minimize this problem. Relatively new and expensive fungicides, Subdue and Aliette, prevent the growth and development of this pathogen.

In the South, the fungus, which can be killed farther north if the soil freezes, survives and lives in the soil. If we introduce an infected plant into our site, we will always have the pathogen.

Ciba Geigy, producer of Subdue, is now marketing this product in small amounts for the home market. Rhône Poulenc produces Aliette. It will be several years before it is available for the home gardener. Both products will be used mainly by our commercial nurserymen, although I know some dedicated rhododendron and azalea hobbyists who routinely apply Subdue. Using such a fungicide takes regular applications from April until October. It is a lot of work, and only the most keen amateur gardeners will get into such extensive management.

Since identifying pests and diseases can be difficult, I would urge each serious gardener to invest in one or more of the excellent publications offered by the North Carolina Agricultural Extension Service. The information is valid for southeastern states. It is thorough and well illustrated. *Diseases of Woody Ornamental Plants and Their Control in Nurseries* ($5.00), *Insect and Related Pests of Vegetables* ($7.00), *Insect and Related Pests of Flowers and Foliage Plants* ($3.50), and *Insect and Related Pests of Shrubs* ($6.00) are available to any interested gardener from any state. Send a check to Publications, North Carolina State University, Box 7603, Raleigh, NC 27695-7603. I like these publications because the information is based on regional experience and research. For a recent general book on disease, to accompany the Westcott general book on pests, *Diseases of Trees and Shrubs*, by Wayne A. Sinclair, Howard H. Lyon, and Warren T. Johnson was published in 1987 by Cornell University Press. Another excellent book is *Pests of Ornamental Plants*, by Pascal P. Pirone.

In addition to insect pests and diseases, gardeners have to contend with a number of four-footed pests in our gardens. The more rural the garden, the more animals we are apt to encounter. I probably get more questions about voles than about any other animal. You think a mouse is a mouse? Not necessarily. Pine mice and meadow mice are actually voles. Voles are ubiquitous throughout America; seventeen species exist in our country. There's even one small vole content to munch in the arctic tundra. In the South, we have four different species.

If your cat presents you with a corpse on the front doorstep or you have trapped a small animal, first identify it. It may be a mouse, a vole, a mole, or a shrew. Moles are about the same size as the voles, but they do not harm your vegetation, other than disturbing roots with their tunnels. Both moles and shrews are insect eating. A mole can be recognized by his broad, spade-like front paws, which dig so efficiently, a pointed nose, and the lack of external ears. Shrews are smaller—only 1½–2 inches long—and have extremely pointed noses.

Voles are about the same size as mice, but they have smaller eyes and ears. They are not terribly selective. They will eat rhododendrons, dogwoods, apple trees, bulbs, garden plants and other greenery. Perhaps you have seen a hole approximately the size of a quarter in your garden. That is probably the entrance to a vole's run. Depending on the species, voles make runs either just above ground or below.

While several rodenticides are on the market, labeled for use in orchards, none is available to the home gardener. Trapping is the most effective method we have. To trap a vole, use a common mousetrap and bait it with a sunflower seed, a piece of apple, or peanut butter. Place the trap near a hole or down in the run, located so that the voles will run across the baited end. Cover the trap with a large pot or basket. Continue to set traps in the same location until you catch no more. My neighbor across our country road caught thirty-two voles one summer—twenty of them from one runway.

Another neighbor asked, "What can I do about these damn rabbits?" with a twinge of desperation in his voice. "They're eating everything in sight, including my iris."

If you have ever gone out to harvest your leaf lettuce at its crisp peak of perfection and found it nibbled to the ground, you too were probably ready to turn into an ogreish Mr. McGregor chasing Peter Rabbit out of your lettuce patch. Beatrix Potter may have found bunnies adorable, but many gardeners *hate* rabbits.

Erecting a barrier is the best method of rabbit management. To be fully effective, it should be 36 inches high, but a 24-inch one will stop all but the most aggressive rabbits. Three products will serve as good barrier materials: bird netting, chicken wire, or decorative rabbit fencing. Bird netting is the least expensive and the easiest to handle. The gardener can flip it up on the support line, mow, and replace. A better-looking, more costly fence can be constructed out of chicken wire. The decorative fence is the most expensive and most attractive barrier.

Whichever barrier is used, be sure to choose a mesh no larger than ½ inch. Most of the garden damage is caused by tiny bunnies just big enough to leave their mothers, and they can wiggle through 1-inch mesh. The other secret of success with rabbit barriers is to hang the netting or wire in an L shape, running the base of the L outside the garden. The rabbit will run up to the garden, hit the fence, and be standing on the fencing, so it cannot tunnel underneath.

An electric fence of two wires, 4 and 6 inches high, is also very effective.

Chemical repellents are on the market. They have to be used with care and reapplied after rain. Old-fashioned repellents like hair, blood meal, and nicotine are of limited efficacy. One extension agent said, "They are partially to largely effective if applied diligently, repeatedly—and if the rabbits have another source of food." The same is true of twirlers, pie pans, and inflated owl or snake balloons. A current fad seems to be hanging bars of deodorant soap throughout the garden. Whatever tricks gardeners try, animals quickly learn to ignore them.

You can attempt to control the population, but if you understand that one female rabbit may produce up to forty bunnies in a good year, you know it's like trying to hold back the tides. I like the story about the male and female rabbits that were chased into a hedge by a fox. They kept peering out. The fox was still there. Finally, the male rabbit turned to the female and said, "Let's just stay here and outnumber him."

Of course rabbits and voles are not the only four-legged pests that bother gardeners. Deer have become a major problem in many parts of the country. How aggressive they are depends on the size of the herd and the food available. When we lived in California, deer were just charming wild animals occasionally bounding through the large ranches nearby, until we experienced a season of extreme drought. That summer, they browsed on my front lawn, selected primroses out of the garden beside the house, and ate all the new growth on the roses.

Judging from a 1987 article in *Pacific Horticulture*, the deer problem has worsened in California. Many Connecticut rock gardening friends are resorting to desperate measures. After deer came into her garden and ate more than 150 rare gentians in one night, Ellie Spingarn singlehandedly erected a fence around 2 entire acres. At first, she installed one level of 3½-foot estate fencing topped by several strands of barbed wire. That was not enough for the ravenous Connecticut herd. The hungry deer were going right through the strands of barbed wire, so she installed a second tier of estate fencing (to 7 feet) and topped that with 3½ feet of barbed wire. This 10½-foot barricade almost completely controls the deer problem in her yard.

If food is plentiful, then a little fence, a piece of fishing line, or an electric wire will serve to turn deer away from your garden. If they are truly hungry, you will have to go to extremes—sturdy fences up to 12 feet high. One recent study suggests that while deer can jump up to 12 feet if they have a good run at the fence, two low fences several feet apart will deter them because they cannot jump a broad space. There is no easy solution to the deer problem. Of course you may be luckier than one gardening friend of ours. He built a large pond, primarily to supply water for his extensive vegetable garden. Next door, his nongardening neighbor thought that deer were "cute" and put out a salt lick to attract them. What paradise for the animals—salt, water, and food, all within yards of each other.

Pets can help. Our friend's barking, bounding Labrador retriever somewhat discourages the deer. We have found that hunting cats are a great asset. Ours have killed moles, shrews, mice, voles, and occasionally small squirrels and rabbits. Other than the cats' unattractive proclivity for leaving entrails at the front door just as company is arriving, I do treasure their hunting talents.

In one nearby town, squirrels are the worst animal pest. Kind gardeners trap them in a Hav-A-Hart cage and then release them in the next county. Of course, if many gardeners are running around the country transporting squirrels, possums, and raccoons in this fashion, they are just redistributing the pest population. Southern tradition has it that squirrels are the basic ingredient in Brunswick Stew, so some gardeners have no hesitation about shooting squirrels in season.

Do check your state laws. We have some peculiar ones. For example, it is perfectly legal to shoot a mole here in North Carolina, but to trap a mole legally requires a depredation permit from the state.

I mentioned raccoons. We have seen none in our yard, but neighbors with a tempting crop of corn are infuriated. They would be perfectly happy to provide an ear or two for a hungry coon. But that's not the way raccoons operate. They come in the garden and nibble a little from each and every ear of corn in the garden. Some gardeners trap raccoons alive and transport them. One swears he keeps these pests out of his corn by putting a radio blasting rock music in a metal garbage can in the middle of the corn patch. There is no easy solution to some of our pest problems.

Even birds can be a nuisance, if you are growing a tasty fruit or berry crop. Some gardeners construct a screened area around their fruits. Other find that a cover of bird netting protects the crop satisfactorily.

With each pest, whether it is a small insect or sizable mammal, we have to decide just how far we will go to protect our vegetables, fruits, flowers, and trees and shrubs—and sometimes, ourselves.

Two pests that attack gardeners, not the garden, are chiggers and ticks, both new to me when we moved to North Carolina. Chiggers are infuriating because one cannot see them. I much prefer to take a satisfying slap at a blood-sucking mosquito than to wake up with a row of maddeningly itchy bites around my waist, where some invisible chiggers have crept up my legs and lodged beneath the waistband of my jeans. The drugstore remedies I have tried have been ineffectual. I just scratch and endure. To prevent these bites, you can dust your feet and legs with Flowers of Sulphur or spray with one of the insect repellents before you go outdoors. I can't be bothered, because I am in and out so often. For an article that tells you more than you ever wanted to know about chiggers, read the July 1981 *Smithsonian*.

While a chigger bite is annoying, a bite from a tick can be dangerous. It is important for us all to be aware that a certain percentage of our ticks carry Rocky Mountain spotted fever, an illness that is fatal if left untreated, or Lyme disease, which is severely debilitating. Both are totally curable with the proper antibiotic. Since 1970, North Carolina has led the nation in the number of cases of spotted fever, and each year a few people die unnecessarily. The symptoms of this illness resemble flu—headaches, high fever, aching joints and muscles, and sometimes a rash. If you have flu symptoms and have had a tick bite within fourteen days, see your doctor.

We usually carry the first tick into the house on our gardening clothes sometime in April. Gardeners farther south will see them even earlier. I recommend giving yourself, your children, and your pets routine tick checks during the warm months. It is desirable to remove a tick quickly from a person or animal. Gently pull this pest off the skin with tweezers or a tissue. Since they have hard bodies and are difficult to kill, I've found that flushing them down the toilet is the easiest method of disposal. Wash the bite and apply an antiseptic.

It is particularly important to alert guests from other parts of the world that they have a slight chance of developing this infection. In 1984, I led a group of gardeners from Japan, England, Norway, France, and from twenty-three other American states on a June tour of the Green Swamp, other wild coastal sites of orchids and carnivorous plants, brushy areas in the Sandhills, and a number of gardens. I warned them of the possibility of Rocky Mountain spotted fever so that no one would go home and have his doctor shrug off the flu symptoms in some part of the world where this problem does not exist. A number of us had tick bites, particularly after the day mucking through the Green Swamp, but ironically, only I was fortunate enough to meet an infected tick.

Two poisonous arachnids I have not encountered are the black widow spider and the brown recluse. They exist in our area, but they tend to be in secluded, out-of-the-way spots. Common sense suggests wearing gloves if you are reaching into shrubbery to weed or remove dead leaves. Bring your gloves into the house, don't leave them in a gardening shed or on your outside steps, where they might provide a tempting shelter for any spider, poisonous or not.

Poisonous snakes are another reality of southern living. I know that copperheads are on our hill, but I have yet to see one. The first summer I was paranoid. I wore boots, took a walking stick every time I went into the woods, and scanned the ground carefully every time I stepped over a fallen log or pile of rocks. Now I go up the woodland trails in my sandals, carrying a flat of plants, never seeing the ground or thinking about snakes. I understand that they are not aggressive but will retreat from noise and movement. Copperheads will take offence if you step on them, however. A year or so ago, a Duke student put her foot down on a copperhead on a paved campus street and, understandably, it bit her. A gardening acquaintance who lives on the busy main street of Chapel Hill gathered an armload of honeysuckle with which to decorate her home. She dumped the honeysuckle in the sink and went to the other side of the kitchen to make a phone call. When she turned around, a copperhead was draped over her soap dish. (I learned from her that, at least in our town, the fire department is the place to call if you have a snake problem.) Good friends lost a dog to snakebites. The dog was small, and it was bitten several times. The veterinarian surmised that the dog interrupted mating snakes, so exercise a little additional caution in the springtime. Learn to identify the dangerous snakes of your county and state. If you are bitten and then kill the snake, try not to ruin its head when hitting it with a hoe or some other implement. (I realize this suggestion demands an inordinate amount of self-control in a panicky situation.) The hospital staff can identify the variety by its head. And even if you are a true ophidiophobe, try to leave the black snakes alone. They are the neighborhood "good guys" of the snake world. They eliminate many rodent pests. (Of course if one is raiding your bluebird house, you may be tempted to take drastic measures.)

Bees, hornets, and wasps are one other group of pests that bother the gardener, not the garden. Occasionally, a swarm of bees will leave its hive and wander. Should you discover a misplaced swarm in one of your trees during the spring, don't try to deal with it yourself. Call your county extension agent. He should be able to put you in touch with a local beekeeper who will come and remove the swarm. In other seasons, call an exterminator.

Remove the beginnings of wasps' or hornets' nests as the insects start construction around your home. The mud dauber wasp builds tunnels on the wall in neat parallel rows of mud huts. Potter wasps build geometrically perfect round nests on tiny stems that adhere to the side of the house. Yet others live underground or in trees. It is useful to have a can of wasp and hornet spray on hand. Should you find one of the large paper nests in a tree, wait until after the first freeze. The bold-faced hornet that builds those interesting abodes lives there for only one generation, so it is safe to destroy the nest during the winter. If you have small children, you may want to save that nest for a school project.

If, after reading all of these pages about pests and diseases, you are beginning to feel like one of those medical students I mentioned at the beginning of the chapter, take heart. You probably will encounter most of these problems rarely, if ever, and if you deal quickly with those that do visit your garden, your problems will be minimal.

17

Conclusion

Despite chomping bugs and moldering fungi, despite the depredations of voles, deer, cats, dogs, possums, and other wildlife, despite droughts, hail damage, ice storms, punishing winter drops in temperature, miserable summer muggs, and occasional tornados that knock the tops out of trees, southern gardeners persevere. What's more, we call it fun.

The most casual of us put in a little work to develop a low-maintenance landscape that presents an attractive face to the world while we spend leisure time on the golf course or at the beach.

The most ardent of us find no time for golf. We are addicts. An addiction to plants and the art/science of growing them is the most healthy addiction I know, but it is definitely an addiction. In his charming book from the 1920s, *The Gardener's Year*, Karel Čapek puts it well. "Let no one think that real gardening is a bucolic and meditative occupation. It is an insatiable passion, like everything else to which a man gives his heart."

We begin each new gardening year with the perusal of an ever-growing stack of wish books—the seed, bulb, perennial, and nursery catalogs for the new season. It's easy to get carried away when ordering the new seeds and plants while curled up in my favorite chair before a fire on a blustery January evening. I do, every year.

Then come the specialty seed lists from the plant societies. Experienced gardeners seeking the most rare seeds know that these orders must be returned by the next mail, so they stay up late into the night, weeding through the list from the Alpine Garden Society, or the American Rock Garden Society, the Royal Horticultural Society, the American Rhododendron Society, the New England Wild Flower Society, or any number of other plant societies. The keenest gardeners are seed donors to their favorite societies—altruistically, because they want to share their wealth by disseminating rare and lovely plants; selfishly, because they want first crack at the seed lists.

With the first species crocus bloom in the garden, the first seeds arrive in the mailbox. From then on, the gardener is in full production, sowing seeds indoors; removing leaves from the perennial beds; dividing primroses, yarrows, boltonias, and a host of other perennials; throwing fertilizer on all garden beds, under all the shrubbery, and at the green tips of every bulb leaf that appears; heeling in recently arrived shipments of plants from faraway nurseries; pruning trees and shrubs; planting perennials, trees, and shrubs from the home nursery area; watering the plants in the cold frame as needed; starting the earliest vegetables for the spring garden. I make a list. As I cross one job off that list, I seem to add two more.

More small bulbs bloom. The first daffodils appear in the woods, and indoors, the first seeds germinate. I begin to feed the seedlings and start on the propagation production line, transplanting the most vigorous seedlings daily, always pushing them with fertilizer in order to develop the largest, sturdiest small plants as quickly as possible.

Each day brings more flowers, from the subtle beauty of a small aconite to the showy, splashy, large blooms of a tree peony. Our southern spring is at its peak when the woods are sparkling with the understory bloom of thousands of white dogwoods, every azalea is covered with flowers and the ground is carpeted with our native blue phlox.

Gardeners are torn, this time of year. We want to be in our own gardens twelve hours a day, and yet we want to visit every other nearby garden at its peak of bloom, and we also want to travel—travel to England to be inspired by the great gardens like Sissinghurst and Hidcote or to Japan where we might begin to develop an appreciation of that serene, philosophical type of gardening; fly to Crete to hike the mountain passes in search of rare wild flowers; or drive through Colorado and Wyoming to botanize in our own American mountains.

As the weather warms up and all danger of frost is past, we plant out our tomatoes, peppers, and okra, put pots of begonias and impatiens on the patio, plant the dahlias and other summer bulbs, and luxuriate in the first glorious explosion of rose bloom.

With a sudden blast of summer heat, gardening becomes more of an endurance test, a survival challenge, here in the South. The air conditioning is turned on. The house windows are all closed, and we can no longer enjoy the bird songs and the music of the crickets and tree frogs.

I try to beat the heat by going out at dawn to divide the day lilies and move the hoses from one part of the yard to another. Watering becomes a major effort, particularly during those summers when we have eight, ten, even twelve weeks without rain. City gardeners are sometimes restricted in water usage. Country gardeners worry about their wells running dry. We all pray for rain and curse the thunderclouds that tease and tantalize us but then pass overhead without releasing a drop of moisture on our gardens.

While each primrose in the garden retreats to a scorched bud, the summer perennials reward us with vibrant color. Many gardeners are enhancing their perennial gardens with the subtle charms of unusual grasses that have become available in recent years, and more and more of us are growing drought-tolerant native plants that perform well with little or no watering.

To my husband, picking the first luscious, ripe tomato from his vines is his summer treat. He eats tomatoes out of hand, as if they were peaches or apples. We both look forward to the first, juicy, succulent ears of super sweet corn on the dinner table.

With the first rains, the first cool nights, the garden begins to come alive again. The primroses put out healthy green rosettes, and a number of plants, like roses and dahlias, produce another burst of bloom. Smart vegetable gardeners install their fall and winter gardens, which may be even more rewarding than the springtime ones here in the South.

The long and glorious fall delights gardener and nongardener alike. We don't need to go to New England for vibrant color. Our maples, dogwoods, gingkos, liquidambars, and all the other colorful deciduous trees paint our roadsides and bedizen the edges of the lakes.

The garden winds down, but slowly, slowly. I often have a last rose in the garden in early November. But one still night in late fall, the first frost nips the impatiens, and we know winter is on its way.

Wise gardeners have brought their house plants in early, so that they adjust to indoor conditions before the furnace is turned on. Outdoors, we all rush around to do those few chores that must be done before a severe freeze—mulch the perennials, spread pinestraw over the nursery pots, rescue the tender caladiums or tuberous begonias we have planted, and prepare the vegetable garden for the following year's crops. Late in the fall, we plant bulbs for the following spring.

December and January are the slowest months for southern gardeners. However, those who choose to develop a twelve-month garden enjoy the sparkle of *Prunus mume* trees in bloom before Christmas; the perfume of the fragrant honeysuckle, *Lonicera fragrantissima*, from December until March; witch hazels and early bulbs in January. Even a lovely iris, *Iris unguicularis*, decorates the winter garden. And the vegetable gardeners harvest kale and all their root crops, while dreaming of summertime corn, cucumbers, beans, and tomatoes.

The cycle never ends. Our gardening world ever expands as we read more books, new and old; as we meet other gardeners and exchange experiences and information; as we study catalogs and visit growers; as we experiment with unfamiliar plants and new growing techniques. One never can know it all, and that's what keeps most of us fascinated with this art/science of gardening. We look ahead to next season, next year, and the most patient of us look ahead five to ten years to see the first flowers on a rhododendron, orchid, or frittilary seedling. Gardeners are optimists, and that optimism is rewarded when the flowers bloom, the fruits and vegetables are harvested, and the landscape is lovely.

Recommended Nurseries

General Seed Catalogs: Flowers and Vegetables

W. Atlee Burpee Company, 300 Park Avenue, Warminster, PA 18991
The Country Garden, Route 2, Crivitz, WI 54114. Seeds of flowering plants desirable
    in a cutting garden.
Gurney's Seed and Nursery Co., 2d and Capitol, Yankton, SD 57079
Harris Seeds, 3670 Buffalo Road, Rochester, NY 14624
J. L. Hudson Seedsman, Box 1058, Redwood City, CA 94064
Earl May Seed and Nursery, Shenandoah, IA 51603
Park Seed Co., Cokesbury Road, Greenwood, SC 29647
Stokes Seeds Inc., Box 548, Buffalo, NY 14240
Thompson and Morgan Inc., PO Box 1308, Jackson, NJ 08527
Otis Twilley Seed Co., Inc., PO Box 65, Trevose, PA 19047
Wyatt-Quarles Seed Co., Box 739, Garner, NC 27529

Specialist Catalogs: Fruits, Nuts, Shrubs, and Trees

Bear Creek Nursery, PO Box 411, Bear Creek Road, Northport, WA 99157
Camellia Forest Nursery, 125 Carolina Forest, Chapel Hill, NC 27516. Cold-hardy
    camellias and rare shrubs. $.50
Chestnut Hill Nursery, Inc., Route 1, Box 341, Alachua, FL 32615. Specialist in
    chestnuts.
Tom Dodd's Rare Plants, Drawer 95, Semmes, AL 36575. $.50
Henry Field's Seed and Nursery Co., 407 Sycamore, Shenandoah, IA 51602
Forestfarm, 990 Tetherow Rd., Williams, OR 97544. Small starts of woody plants; an
    extraordinary list. $2.00
Gossler Farms Nursery, 1200 Weaver Road, Springfield, OR 97477
Hastings, Seedsman to the South, 434 Marietta St., NW, PO Box 4274, Atlanta, GA
    30302
Henry Leuthardt Nurseries, Eash Moriches, NY 11940. Espalier specialist.
Miller Nurseries, Canandaigua, NY 14424
Musser Forests, Indiana, PA 15701
Nuccio's Nurseries, Box 6160, Altadena, CA 91001. Camellias.
Salter Tree Farm, Route 2, Box 1332, Madison, FL 32340

Siskiyou Rare Plant Nursery, 2825 Cummings Road, Medford, OR 97501. Emphasis on alpines. $1.50

Southmeadow Fruit Gardens, 15310 Red Arrow Highway, Lakeside, MI. 49116. Antique varieties.

Stark Bro's Nurseries and Orchards Co., Louisiana, MO 63353

Transplant Nursery, Parkertown Rd., Lavonia, GA 30553. Native and evergreen azaleas.

Bulb Catalogs

Blackthorne Gardens, 48 Quincy St., Holbrook, MA 02343

W. Atlee Burpee Co., 300 Park Ave., Warminster, PA 18991

P. J. & J. W. Christian, Pentre Cottages, Minera, Wrexham, Clwyd, N. Wales, U.K.

Daffodil Mart, Route 3, Box 794, Gloucester, VA 23061

International Growers Exchange, Inc., 16785 Harrison, Livonia, MI 48154

John D. Lyon, 143 Alewife Brook Parkway, Cambridge, MA 02140

McClure & Zimmerman, 1422 West Thorndale, Chicago, IL 60660

Mitsch Daffodils, Box 218, Hubbard, OR 97032

Park Seed Co., Cokesbury Road, Greenwood, SC 29647

Clive Postles Daffodils, The Old Cottage, Purshull Green, Droitwich, Worcestershire, WR9 0NL, England

Rex Bulb Farms, Box 774, Port Townsend, WA 98368. Lilies.

Anthony J. Skittone, 2271 Thirty-first Avenue, San Francisco, CA 94116

Van Bourgondien, 245 Farmingdale Road, Babylon, NY 11702

Herbs

Caprilands Herb Farm, Silver St., Coventry, CT 06238

Sandy Mush Herb Nursery, Route 2, Leicester, NC 28748

Vegetable Specialists

The Cook's Garden, PO Box 65, Londonderry, VT 05148

Johnny's Selected Seeds, 305 Foss Hill Road, Albion, ME 04910

Le Jardin du Gourmet, West Danville, VT 05873. $1.00

Le Marche-Seeds International, PO Box 190, Dixon, CA 95620

Piedmont Plant Co., PO Box 424, Albany, GA 31703. They sell starter vegetable plants by mail order.

Shepherd's Garden Seeds, 7389 West Zayante Road, Felton, CA 95018

Tomato Growers Supply Company, PO Box 2237, Fort Myers, FL 33902

Vermont Bean Seed Company, Garden Lane, Fair Haven, VT 05743

Perennials

American Daylily and Perennials, PO Box 7008, The Woodlands, TX 77387

Kurt Bluemel, 2543 Hess Rd., Fallston, MD 21047. Ornamental grasses.

Bluestone Perennials, 7211 Middle Ridge, Madison, OH 44057. They ship small starter plants.

Crownsville Nursery, PO Box 797, Crownsville, MD 21032. $2.00
Fancy Fronds, 1911 Fourth Ave. West, Seattle, WA 98119. Fern specialist.
Far North Gardens, 16785 Harrison Rd., Livonia, MI 48154. Primroses. $2.00
Holbrook Farm and Nursery, Rt. 2, Box 223 B, Fletcher, NC 28732
Iron Gate Gardens, Route 3, Box 250, Kings Mountain, NC 28086. Hostas and day
    lilies.
Montrose Nursery, Box 957, Hillsborough, NC 27278. Cyclamen and unusual
    perennials. $1.00
Powell's Gardens, Route 3, Box 21, Princeton, NC 27569. $1.50
Rice Creek Gardens, 1315 Sixty-sixth Ave. NE, Minneapolis, MN 55432
Surry Gardens, Box 145, Surry, ME 04684. $2.00
Andre Viette Farm and Nursery, Route 1, Box 16, Fishersville, VA 22939. $1.00
Wayside Gardens, Hodges, SC 29695. $1.00
We-Du Nurseries, Route 5, Box 724, Marion, NC 28752
White Flower Farm, Litchfield, CT 06759. $5.00, refundable

Roses

Antique Rose Emporium, Route 5, Box 143, Brenham, TX 77833. $2.00
Donovan's Roses, Box 37800, Shreveport, LA 71133
Historical Roses, 1657 West Jackson St., Painesville, OH 44077
Hortico, 723 Robson Road, RR 1, Waterdown, Ontario, Canada L0R 2H0
Jackson and Perkins, 1 Rose Lane, Medford, OR 97501
Mini-Roses, Box 4255, Dallas, TX 75208
Nor'east Miniature Roses, 58 Hammond, Rowley, MA 01969
Roses of Yesterday and Today, Brown's Valley Road, Watsonville, CA 95076. $2.00

Southeastern Native Plants (nursery-propagated)

Niche Gardens, Rt. 1, Box 290, Chapel Hill, NC 27514
We-Du Nurseries, Route 5, Box 724, Marion, NC 28752. Also offer a number of rare
    plants, including Oriental counterparts of our natives.
Woodlanders, Inc., 1128 Colleton Ave., Aiken, SC 29801

House Plants

Glasshouse Works, 10 Church St., Box 97, Stewart, OH 45778
Kartuz Greenhouses, 1408 Sunset Dr., Vista, CA 92083. Gesneriad and begonia spe-
    cialist; many other rare plants.
Logee's Greenhouses, 55 North St., Danielson, CT 06239

Rare Seed

Chiltern Seed Company, Bortree Stile, Ulverston, Cumbria, LA127PB, England
Maver Nursery, Rt. 2, Box 265 B, Asheville, NC 28805. Extraordinary offerings of
    seeds from around the world.
Plants of the Southwest, 1812 Second St., Santa Fe, NM 87501

Geranium Specialist

Shady Hill Gardens, 821 Walnut St., Batavia, IL 60510

Garden Supplies

Clapper's, PO Box A, 1121 Washington St., West Newton, MA 02165
Gardener's Eden, PO Box 7307, San Francisco, CA 94120
Gardener's Supply, 128 Intervale Rd., Burlington, VT 05401
David Kay, 4509 Taylor Lane, Cleveland, OH 44128
Ringer Corp., 9959 Valleyview Rd., Minneapolis, MN 55344
Smith & Hawken, 25 Corte Madera, Mill Valley, CA 94941

Antique Varieties

If you are interested in old varieties of vegetables, fruits, nuts, herbs and native plants, order the *Seed and Nursery Directory* from the Rural Advancement Fund, PO Box 1029, Pittsboro, NC 27312. It lists many firms that are actively saving and promoting antique varieties, important for the genetic diversity they provide. $2.00

Plant Societies

Alabama Wildflower Society
George Wood
Route 2, Box 115
Northport, AL 35478

Alpine Garden Society
E. Michael Upward
Lye End Link, St John's
Woking, Surrey GUV21 1SW
England

American Boxwood Society
Katherine D. Ward
PO Box 85
Boyce, VA 22620

American Camellia Society
Ann Blair Brown
PO Box 1217
Fort Valley, GA 31030

American Conifer Society
William Schwartz
1825 N. 72d St.
Philadelphia, PA 19151

American Daffodil Society
Ms. Leslie Anderson
Rt. 3, 2302 Byhalia Rd.
Hernando, MS 38632

American Dahlia Society
Mark Alger
2044 Great Falls St.
Falls Church, VA 22043

American Fern Society
Dr. L. Hickok
University of Tennessee
Knoxville, TN 37996

American Gourd Society
John Stevens
PO Box 274
Mt. Gilead, OH 43338

American Hemerocallis Society
Sandy Goembel
Rt. 5, Box 6874
Palatka, FL 32077

American Horticultural Society
PO Box 0105
Mount Vernon, VA 22121

American Hosta Society
Jack Freedman
3103 Heatherhill Dr.
Huntsville, AL 35802

American Iris Society
Jeana Stayer
7414 East 60th St.
Tulsa, OK 74145

American Ivy Society
Elizabeth Carrick
PO Box 520
West Carrollton, OH 45449

American Magnolia Society
Phelan A. Bright
907 South Chestnut St.
Hammond, LA 70403

American Orchid Society
6000 South Olive Ave.
West Palm Beach, FL 33405

American Peony Society
Greta Kessenich
250 Interlaken Rd.
Hopkins, MN 55343

American Plant Life Society
Dr. Thomas Whitaker
PO Box 150
La Jolla, CA 92038

American Pomological Society
Dr. L. D. Tukey
103 Tyson Bld.
University Park, PA 16602

American Primrose Society
Brian Skidmore
6730 West Mercer Way
Mercer Island, WA 98040

American Rhododendron Society
14885 S.W. Sunrise Lane
Tigard, OR 97224

American Rock Garden Society
Buffy Parker
15 Fairmead Rd.
Darien, CT 06820

American Rose Society
PO Box 30,000
Shreveport, LA 71130

Aril Society International
Donna Downey
5500 Constitution NE
Albuquerque, NM 87110

Azalea Society of America
PO Box 6244
Silver Springs, MD 20906

Cyclamen Society
Dr. D. V. Bent
9 Tudor Dr.
Otford, Seven Oaks
Kent TN17 4LB
England

Friends of the Fig
Jack Thomas
PO Box 636
Rockmart, GA 30153

Gardenia Society of America
Box 879
Atwater, CA 95301

Georgia Botanical Society
Dr. Frank McCamey
4876 Andover Ct.
Doraville, GA 30360

Hardy Plant Society
Kathleen Emmerson
1205 S.W. Harbor
Lincoln City, OR 97367

Herb Society of America
300 Massachusetts Ave.
Boston, MA 02115

Heritage Roses Group
Charles Walker, coordinator for
southeastern states
1512 Gorman
Raleigh, NC 27606

Mitzi VanSant, coordinator for
TX, OK, AR, MS, LA
810 E. 30th St.
Austin, TX 78705

Holly Society of America, Inc.
Mrs. C. F. Richardson
304 North Wind Road
Baltimore, MD 21204

Indoor Gardening Society of America
R. D. Morrison
128 West 58th St.
New York, NY 10019

Louisiana Native Plant Society
  Richard Johnson
  Route 1, Box 151
  Saline, LA 71070

Marigold Society of America
  Mirebelli
  PO Box 112
  New Britain, PA 18901

Mississippi Native Plant Society
  Travis Salley
  202 N. Andrews Ave.
  Cleveland, MS 38732

Missouri Native Plant Society
  John Darel
  PO Box 176
  Jefferson City, MO 65102

National Chrysanthemum Society, Inc.
  Galen Goss
  5012 Kingston Dr.
  Annandale, VA 22003

National Gardening Association
  180 Flynn Ave.
  Burlington, VT 05401

North American Fruit Explorers
  Robert Kurie
  10 South 055 Madison St.
  Hinsdale, IL 60521

North American Lily Society
  Mrs. Dorothy Schaefer
  Box 476
  Waukee, IA 50263

North American Vegetable Explorers
  Gregory Williams
  Route 1, Box 302
  Gravel Switch, KY 40328

North Carolina Wild Flower
Preservation Society
  Mrs. S. M. Cozert
  900 West Nash
  Wilson, NC 27893

Perennial Plant Association
  217 Howlett Hall
  2001 Fyffe Court
  Columbus, OH 43210

Southern Garden History Society
  Old Salem, Inc.
  Drawer F, Salem Station
  Winston-Salem, NC 27108

Tennessee Native Plant Society
  Dept. of Botany
  University of Tennessee
  Knoxville, TN 37996

Texas Horticultural Society
  PO Box 10025
  College Station, TX 77840

Virginia Wildflower Preservation Society
  PO Box 844
  Annandale, VA 22033

Suggested Reading List

Bailey, L. H. *Standard Cyclopedia of Horticulture*. 6 vols. New York: Macmillan Co., 1914.

Boston, Carol. *The Pennypincher's Guide to Landscaping*. Englewood Cliffs, N.J.: Prentice-Hall, 1985.

Brown, Emily. *Landscaping with Perennials*. Portland, Oreg.: Timber Press, 1986.

Bruce, Hal. *How to Grow Wildflowers & Wild Shrubs & Trees in Your Own Garden*. New York: Van Nostrand Reinhold Co., 1982.

Chan, Peter. *Better Vegetable Gardens the Chinese Way*. Pownal, Vt.: Garden Way Publishing, 1985.

Clarke, J. Harold. *Getting Started with Rhododendrons and Azaleas*. Portland, Ore.: Timber Press, 1982.

Cox, Peter A. *Dwarf Rhododendrons*. New York: Macmillan, 1973.

Darden, Jim. *Great American Azaleas*. Clinton, N.C.: Greenhouse Press, 1985.

Elbert, George A. *The Indoor Light Gardening Book*. New York: Crown Publishers, 1973.

Evans, Ronald L. *Handbook of Cultivated Sedums*. Northwood: Science Reviews Ltd., 1983.

Everett, Thomas H. *The New York Botanical Garden Illustrated Encyclopedia of Horticulture*. 10 vols. New York: Garland, 1980.

Foley, Daniel J. *Ground Covers for Easier Gardening*. New York: Dover Publications, 1972.

Foster, F. Gordon. *Ferns to Know and Grow*. Portland, Ore.: Timber Press, 1984.

Foster, H. Lincoln. *Rock Gardening*. Boston: Houghton Mifflin Co., 1968.

Free, Montague. *Plant Propagation in Pictures*. Garden City, N.Y.: Doubleday & Co., 1957.

Galle, Fred C. *Azaleas*. Portland, Ore.: Timber Press, 1985.

Genders, Roy. *Bulbs*. Indianapolis: Bobbs-Merrill Co., 1973.

Halfacre, R. Gordon, and Anne R. Shawcroft. *Landscape Plants of the Southeast*. Raleigh, N.C.: Sparks Press, 1986.

Haring, Elda. *The Complete Book of Growing Plants from Seed*. New York: Hawthorn Books, 1967.

Harper, Pamela, and Frederick McGourty. *Perennials*. Tucson, Ariz.: HPBooks, 1985.

Hill, Lewis. *Pruning Simplified*. Pownal, Vt.: Storey Communications, 1986.

Hunt, William Lanier, *Southern Gardens, Southern Gardening*. Durham, N.C.: Duke University Press, 1982.

Jaynes, Richard, ed. *Handbook of North American Nut Trees*. Knoxville, Tenn.: Northern Nut Growers Association, 1969.

Jekyll, Gertrude. *Colour Schemes for the Flower Garden*. Salem, N.H.: Ayer Co., 1983.

———. *Wall and Water Gardens*. Salem, N.H.: Ayer Co., 1983.

———. *Wood and Garden*. Salem, N.H.: Ayer Co., 1983.

Justice, William S., and C. Ritchie Bell. *Wild Flowers of North Carolina*. Chapel Hill: University of North Carolina Press, 1979.

Klaber, Doretta. *Gentians for Your Garden*. New York: M. Barrows & Co., 1964.

———. *Primroses and Spring*. New York: M. Barrows & Co., 1966.

Lawrence, Elizabeth. *A Southern Garden*. Chapel Hill: University of North Carolina Press, 1967.

———. *Gardens in Winter*. New York: Harper, 1961.

———. *The Little Bulbs*. Durham, N.C.: Duke University Press, 1986.

Lee, Frederic P. *The Azalea Book*. Princeton, N.J.: D. Van Nostrand Co., 1965.

Lloyd, Christopher. *Clematis*. London: Collins, 1977.

Martin, Laura C. *The Wildflower Meadow Book*. Charlotte, N.C.: Fast & McMillan Publishers, 1986.

Nightingale, Gay. *Growing Cyclamen*. Portland, Ore.: Timber Press, 1982.

Phillips, Harry R. *Growing and Propagating Wild Flowers*. Chapel Hill: University of North Carolina Press, 1985.

Pirone, Pascal Pompey. *Diseases and Pests of Ornamental Plants*. New York: Ronald Press Co., 1970.

Reilly, Ann. *Park's Success with Seeds*. Greenwood, S.C.: Geo. W. Park Seed Co., 1978.

Simonds, John Ormsbee. *Landscape Architecture*. New York: McGraw-Hill Book Co., 1983.

Sinclair, Wayne A.; Howard H. Lyon; and Warren T. Johnson. *Diseases of Trees and Shrubs*. Ithaca, N.Y.: Cornell University Press, 1987.

Stone, Doris. *The Great Public Gardens of the Eastern United States*. New York: Pantheon Books, 1982.

Synge, Patrick M. *Flowers & Colour in Winter*. London: Michael Joseph, 1974.

Terres, John K. *Songbirds in Your Garden*. New York: Hawthorn Books, 1977.

Vertrees, J. D. *Japanese Maples*. Forest Grove, Ore.: Timber Press, 1978.

Welch, Humphrey J. *Manual of Dwarf Conifers*. New York: Theophrastus, 1979.

Westcott, Cynthia. *The Gardener's Bug Book*. Garden City, N.Y.: Doubleday, 1973.

Whitcomb, Carl E. *Know It & Grow It*. Tulsa: privately published, 1978.

Wyman, Donald, *Shrubs and Vines for American Gardens*. New York: Macmillan Co., 1949.

———. *Trees for American Gardens*. New York: Macmillan Co., 1965.

Yepsen, Roger B., Jr., ed. *Organic Plant Protection*. Emmaus, Pa.: Rodale Press, 1976.

Index